"Hector Bolitho is of the fortunate of this earth, knows it and,
with becoming modesty, says as much."
The New York Times

HECTOR BOLITHO & DEREK PEEL

Henry Hector Bolitho was born in New Zealand in 1897. He was educated at Seddon Memorial College in Aukland, and served in the Royal Air Force during the Second World War.

He published his first book, *The Island of Kawau*, in 1919. Mr. Bolitho's globetrotting travels were recounted in many of his subsequent books, such as *Thistledown and Thunder, a Higgledy-Piggledy Diary of New Zealand, the South Seas, Australia, Port Said, Italy, Paris, England, Madeira, Africa, Canada, and New York* (1928); *Haywire: An American Travel Diary* (1940); and *The Angry Neighbours: A Diary of Palestine and Transjordan* (1957). *My Restless Years* was published in 1962.

Among his other books were novels, stories, poetry, biographies (perhaps the best-known of which was *Albert the Good and the Victorian Reign* [1932]), and collections of letters. *A Biographer's Notebook* appeared in 1950.

Hector Bolitho died in England in 1974.

Derek Peel contributed research and accompanied the author on the walks described in *Without the City Wall*. Other than what is found in the Introduction (see page xi), no other biographical information about him has come to light. The editor of the present volume would welcome hearing from anyone who knows the details of Mr. Peel's life and career, for use in later editions.

A COMMON READER'S LONDON LIBRARY

WITHOUT THE CITY WALL

An Adventure in London Street Names

HECTOR BOLITHO

AND

DEREK PEEL

A COMMON READER EDITION
THE AKADINE PRESS
2002

Without the City Wall

A COMMON READER EDITION published 2002 by
The Akadine Press, Inc., by arrangement with
John Murray Publishers Ltd.

Cover design by Jerry Kelly.
Cover photograph: St. Paul's Cathedral.

A COMMON READER'S LONDON LIBRARY,
A COMMON READER EDITION, and fountain colophon
are trademarks of The Akadine Press, Inc.

ISBN 1-58579-042-7

10 9 8 7 6 5 4 3 2 1

SERIES EDITOR'S NOTE

We know about the naming of cats; but what about the naming of streets? Is it also "a difficult matter" to unriddle *their* meanings?

Absolutely — as you discover in the beguiling and endlessly informative pages of Hector Bolitho's and Derek Peel's *Without the City Wall: An Adventure in London Street Names*. Age-old carelessness and confusion account for so many of the wonderfully unexpected derivations uncovered by Bolitho and Peel. Consider, for example, the sources of "Eel Brook Common" and "Paddington," as summarized in a review of the book's original 1952 edition:

"[The book's] chief pleasure is in the search itself, in the confident anticipations which were not fulfilled, the obvious guesses which were proved wrong — a tantalizing, often irritating, search, haunted by two things: the careless genius of Londoners for corrupting names, and what Mr. Bolitho calls 'the discord of scholars.' When he found an Eel Brook Common, and imagined boys fishing in one of the now buried streams of London, only to discover that 'Eel' was 'Hell' in an earlier map, and as soon as he had changed his mental picture of the place to a haunt of robbers and bawds, to find again that 'hell' was a corruption of 'hill,' he must have felt ready to abjure all romance. And when he found Paddington derived first from *Padre ing tun*, the father's town meadow, and then from *Pad ing tun*, the village at the pack (or pad) horse meadows, he must have been tempted to throw the book across the railway station. What he says is, 'one must be cautious of scholars.'"

Which is not to say that the names of streets can't in general have a more far-reaching and subtler significance. When George Steiner asks in an essay "Why are American streets so silent to the remembrance of thought?" his point is that the differences between European and American cultural achievements and outlooks are suggested by even something as typically unregarded as their respective street-naming inclinations:

"My own childhood," Steiner notes, "transpired between the Rue Descartes and Rue Auguste Comte, between a square dedicated to Pascal and a statue of Diderot. The most voluptuous of central European chocolates is named after Mozart, the most seductive of steak-dishes after Chateaubriand and Rossini. Such kitsch pays tribute to a formidable recognition."

Steiner's observations have stuck with me through the years because a similar, if less formidable, sort of recognition played a small part in my own upbringing. My childhood home was located on the steeply sloping Lindbergh Place. As a result, the aviator must have been the first historical figure whose achievements I learned about, on my own, outside the grammar school classroom; and when, eventually, my classmates caught up, and came to know something about Charles Lindbergh's solo flight across the Atlantic, I tried to retain my street-wise edge by claiming to have discovered that the Place was named for Lucky Lindy because he'd actually once landed a small plane on it. (I was never a very convincing liar, however.)

Obviously there are many London streets devoted to "remembrance of thought"; there's an "Addison Crescent," a "Beethoven Street," a "Carlyle Square," and so on through the alphabet. But to borrow again from that earlier reviewer, the English have their own unique perspective on even such commemorative naming:

"[Hector Bolitho] quotes Leigh Hunt prophesying that London would follow the Parisian fashion of naming streets after men of letters, and gives the literary list, from the 19 Byron streets to one named after Leigh Hunt. But it is not a way to satisfy the English. Our way is to prefer the names (as 'Bromley' from 'bramble') which contain, however darkly, a picture of the past, and if names of people are used, to prefer those, however humble, which belong to the place. Of this cold-blooded literary renaming Mr. Bolitho found what must be one of the most absurd — the changing of Cut Throat Lane to Wordsworth Road."

Thus, whatever their origins, London's street names on the north side of the Thames are a rich jumble of history lessons. Those of us who love the city are fortunate that Hector Bolitho and Derek Peel became fascinated with learning what they could of those lessons, and that they then shared their discoveries with us.

Thomas Meagher
Editorial Director, COMMON READER EDITIONS

WITHOUT THE CITY WALL

CONTENTS

LIST OF ILLUSTRATIONS

A map for each borough appears in its relevant chapter

ACKNOWLEDGMENTS

The authors are particularly indebted to the librarians and surveyors of the seventeen Metropolitan boroughs who have contributed ideas and information that is new and authentic. The final manuscript of each chapter has been read and corrected by the librarian concerned. The authors may thus claim that they have done their best to discontinue old errors and avoid making new ones.

The authors also thank those who have kindly given permission for the use of the illustrations which are listed below :

Brighton Art Gallery and Museum : Drawing on page 91 and Pl. No. 73.

British Transport Historical Records : No. 55.

Cornelia, Countess of Craven : Nos. 18 and 53.

Joseph Coghlan-Briscoe, Esq. : No. 62.

Fitzwilliam Museum, Cambridge : No. 40.

Foundling Hospital : No. 39.

Keystone Press Agency Ltd. : No. 28.

National Portrait Gallery : Nos. 1, 2, 5, 11, 15, 23, 25, 41, 44–47, 50–52, 54, 56–58, 63, 65, 66, 69 and 74.

Messrs. Novello and Co. Ltd. : No. 71.

Public Libraries Committee :

    Bermondsey : Nos. 30, 34 and 35

    Bethnal Green : Nos. 24, 26, 27 and the engraving on page 72.

    Chelsea : Drawing on page 180.

    Finsbury : Nos. 6–9.

    Fulham : No. 70.

    Hackney : No. 17.

    Hammersmith : Nos. 72, 75 and the engraving on page 208.

    Hampstead : Nos. 42 and 43.

    Holborn : Nos. 12 and 13.

    Islington : Nos. 3 and 4.

    Kensington : Nos. 59–61.

    Poplar : Nos. 32, 33, 36 and 37.

    St. Marylebone : No. 49 (Ashridge Collection).

    Shoreditch : Nos. 19–22.

    Stepney : 17th-century map, page 85, and Pl. No. 31.

    Stoke Newington : No. 16.

Public Record Office : Entry in *Domesday Book*, page 161.

Victoria and Albert Museum : No. 64.

The authors wish to acknowledge the kindness of Messrs. John Bartholomew & Son, Ltd., of Edinburgh, who have permitted the use of their copyright Plan of London as the basis for the seventeen small maps reproduced in this book.

INTRODUCTION

I first met my collaborator in 1949, after he had been drudging in the City for fifteen months. In 1945 he had been wounded while fighting as a Commando in Italy ; and during 1947 he had served with the army in Palestine. We agreed that a business man's desk was cramping and dull after the careless hazards of war. He was working with a firm in Smithfield market, and the only mental escape from the match-box of his office life came when the overseas telephone bell rang : when voices from a bigger world ordered 4,000 cases of Australian rabbits for Antwerp, 25 tons of meat extract for Paris, or 100 tons of livers for the Genoese.

When I met him some weeks later he told me that he had found a cure for his boredom, in lunchtime expeditions to the second-hand bookstalls in the Farringdon Road, and among the streets of the old City. His first discovery was that the name, SMITHFIELD, was not so dull after all. On a Saturday afternoon in the autumn of 1949 he took me there, and I walked under the almost ecclesiastical arches of the meat market, silent and deserted, with pools of blood-soaked sawdust, and porters' caps and aprons foul with dry gore, mocking the Victorian correctness of the architecture above. We walked out, past the tall, pretentious iron gates that shut the market in for its week-end nap ; we turned our backs on the red brick façade—red as the butchers' trade within—crossed the square, and then entered the beautiful Priory Church of ST. BARTHOLOMEW THE GREAT. We stood in the shadows of the Choir : the reluctant October light came through the high windows and touched the clasped marble hands and forehead of a recumbent monk. It was the tomb of Rahere, a " pleasant-witted gentleman " who had been one of King Henry I's minstrels, before he spurned the frivolities of the Court and took holy orders.

As we stood there, Derek Peel told me the story of Smithfield ; the first chapter of London's history he had learned, from his lunch-hour wandering in the City streets.

In Norman times, the land on which the church of St. Bartholomew stands was a big open meadow, called *Smoothfield* ; and here, almost one thousand years ago, the people of London traded in woven stuffs and livestock. The market belonged to the King, but he lost its revenues to the Church, through the cleverness of Rahere, who had kept his cunning when he renounced the world. The monk had been stricken with a fever whilst on a pilgrimage to Rome, and when he returned to England, he told King Henry of a dream in which St. Bartholomew had appeared, commanding him to build a hospital, and a church, as thanks to God for his recovery. The King was persuaded to part with his market as the site for both the Priory Church and St. Bartholomew's Hospital, which have survived into our time, as monuments to King Henry's benevolence and the monk's enterprise. And Rahere's *Smoothfield* has become Smithfield, through the centuries.

That evening, after dinner, we spread reference books on a table, and we found out a little more about the story of Rahere. He had obtained another concession from his King : a charter authorising the annual Bartholomew Fair, which was held on *Smoothfield* until as late as the 1850's. The Fairs inspired Ben Jonson's famous play, which was revived during the Edinburgh Festival of 1950. We found several records of jousts, wrestling-matches, side-shows and wild beasts at *Smoothfield* ; perhaps the most vivid of which was written by Dr. King, early in the 18th century.

> I was at Bartholomew-fair : coming out, I met a man who would have taken off my hat ; but I secured it, and was going to draw my sword, crying out—" Begar ! " " Damned Rogue ! " " Morbleu ! " &c., when on a sudden I had a hundred people about me crying—" Here, Monsieur, see Jepthah's Rash Vow."—"Here, Monsieur, see the tall Dutchwoman."— " see the Tiger ! " says another.—" See the Horse and no Horse, whose tail stands where his head should do."—" See the German Artist, Monsieur. . . ."

The first search into the history of a London place-name awakened my curiosity, and I began to study my map of the City with a stirring sense of adventure. The following Saturday, I went with Derek Peel to other markets in the City—LEADENHALL and BILLINGSGATE, after reading some of their history during the week. Leadenhall's name has not changed during more than six hundred and fifty years. At the beginning of the 14th century, " *La Ledenhalle in Garscherche* [Gracechurch] *Street* " was a mansion with a great hall roofed entirely with lead. The owner, Sir Hugh Neville, allowed the surrounding ground to be used as a local market, until "Dick" Whittington bought the manor for the City Corporation. In 1445, more than twenty years after his death, Leadenhall was opened as a City market. Among the books we read for our history was Stow's *Survey of London*. The 16th-century chronicler wrote of the famine of 1512, when Leadenhall market was used to succour the people in time of need, as well as for the profit of the merchants. " . . . when the Carts of Stratford came laden with bread to the Citie . . . one man was readie to destroy an other, in striuing to bee serued for their money : but this scarcitie lasted not long ; for the Maior in short time made such prouision for Wheate . . . and stored it vp in Leaden hall, and other garners of the Citie."[1]

During the Restoration, Leadenhall became a flourishing shopping centre, and the Spanish Ambassador was so impressed by its abundance that he remarked to King Charles II, " There is more meat sold in your market than in all the Kingdom of Spain."

Billingsgate, the oldest of all London's markets, has what must also be one of the oldest names that survive in London—if we are indulgent with legend and treat it as fact. In the 5th century B.C., the British King, Belinus Magnus, father of King Lud, erected a water-gate through which goods from ships on the Thames could be transported to the walled city.

Little more of the early history of Belinus's Gate has been recorded ; but it must have been a blessing to the rugged traders of two thousand four hundred years ago. We know that customs dues were being paid at *Blynesgate* in the year 979, by order of King Æthelred the Unready ; and that, by the time of Edward III, the wharf had become the principal fish market in England. Here you could buy mackerel for a half-penny each, or a whole gallon of oysters for tuppence. Much of the fish, including salmon, came from the Thames—until the water was polluted by the noisome factories and gasworks built along the banks in the last century.

The building we found at Billingsgate, dated 1877, did not help to clarify or enhance the picture of old Belinus Magnus. But we did our best to believe in the antiquity of the market, as we walked down Fish Street Hill—where the early fish-mongers had their houses and shops ; and as we passed into the smelly market, to read the names of the traders over the stalls—Lascelles, Allengame, Jocylene, and

[1] Stow, vol. I, pp. 156–7.

Lefebvre. We were told that there is an aristocracy of fish-sellers—
some descended from merchants who came from Denmark, Holland
or Belgium, in the 1770's ; that the good names of Forge, Goldham,
Grove and Lynn, which we saw, are the Percys, Cecils and Cavendishes
of this ancient trade.

After a third expedition into the City, we had accumulated such
a library of reference books about London street and place-names—
Stow, Cunningham, Thornbury and Walford, Lysons, Leigh Hunt,
and so on—and we had become so zealous in our amateur researches,
that we decided to pause for breath and make a plan.

We found so many books about London and Westminster (shelf
upon shelf of them intimidated me when I went to the London
Library), that we agreed to ignore the two Cities and to make our
excursions farther afield ; to the seventeen Metropolitan boroughs
that lie " Without the City Wall ", on the north side of the Thames.

The fastidious Londoner, who seldom ventures beyond the
Mansion House in the east and the porticoes of Belgravia in the west,
might imagine that the outlying boroughs are no more than what
they seem : Islington, with its dingy, close-packed houses, each with
its scrubbed doorstep and looped lace curtains, revealing a geranium
plant within ; Kensington, with its villas, pledged to a spiky code of
respectability ; or Bethnal Green, with its long streets of dusty little
shops—meek, poor, and depressing.

My collaborator and I shared this view, before our adventure
began ; before we saw the pre-Reformation tower and Georgian
houses of Islington, or the streets, now given over to smutty-faced
cottages, in which Daniel Defoe wrote Robinson Crusoe, where
Charles Lamb enjoyed his own house and garden, beside the New
River, or where Milton dozed in the sun. All of them are
remembered in the names of thoroughfares in the boroughs where
they worked and lived.

The history of outer London—of the many, once tranquil, villages
that have been absorbed into the capital city during the centuries—
is revealed in the correct little metal street-signs, screwed on to the
expressionless side-walls of shops and houses. If we seek out these
street-signs, we are able to trace what lies beneath the harsh asphalt and
squalid gutters, or beyond the closed doors with their garish ruby
and sapphire-glass fanlights—the stories of the men and women who
have created the biggest city in the world. The span of this history

is immense : behind King's Cross Station is Boadicea Street, built near the field of the Queen's last battle—in Bethnal Green is the Rogers Estate, named after a younger warrior, Maurice Rogers V.C., who was killed in Italy in 1944.

We do not pretend that we have been pure scholars in our circumnavigation of London, proving every claim we make—although, in this matter, we boast a better conscience than many historians and cartographers before us. The published records of the Metropolis have given us some rude surprises—none ruder than during our first search in the streets of Finsbury. The index of one of our atlases gave us a tantalising clue—*Bunyan Station*. Neither of us had ever heard of such a place, and when we telephoned the underground railway office we were assured that it was not on any of their lines. We turned from the index to the map and read, again, *Bunyan Stat.* Only after we had asked postmen and bus-drivers in the City Road to help us, did we realise that cartographers and index makers sometimes fall out. A postman looked at the map and told us that the reference was to the *statue* of John Bunyan, in the cemetery of Bunhill Fields.

This incident made us cautious of scholars, with their imposing footnotes and lists of references. We realized that we would have to call on the help of Common Sense in our progress. My collaborator, younger than I am, and, after the Bunyan experience, suspicious of printed authority, gave me a fine example of the use of Common Sense when we were still exploring Finsbury. We walked along a business thoroughfare named CHISWELL STREET, opening out of Finsbury Square. One could imagine an Alderman Chiswell, or a prosperous builder whose enterprise was celebrated in the naming of the street. We first searched the *Dictionary of National Biography* and found Richard Chiswell, " publisher at the ' Rose and Crown ', Paul's Churchyard " ; his son, " Richard the younger ", a " Turkey merchant " who " travelled in the East " ; and Trench Chiswell, an antiquary and Member of Parliament in Yorkshire. But there was no Chiswell likely to have given his name to a street in Finsbury. We then turned to *The Place-Names of Middlesex* and found that Chiswell is derived from the Saxon word, *ceosol*, meaning flint, or gravel.

Derek Peel telephoned the Borough Engineer and asked him if the man who tended the sewers in this district could tell him the nature of the geological strata below Chiswell Street. Two days later the Engineer reported that there were large deposits of flint and gravels as there had no doubt been when the Saxons gave a name to the land, perhaps thirteen centuries ago.

When we decided that our researches might assume the shape of a book, we outlined the boundaries of the seventeen Metropolitan boroughs north of the river. Then we consulted local librarians and historians—an erudite and helpful company. We then waited until the Spring, to begin our organised expeditions, which are traced on the maps in this book.

Our starting-point we chose by accident. We were driving through ISLINGTON when we came on a number of streets with the name BARNSBURY—a corruption of the name of William de Berners, the first lord of the manor in these parts. While passing along BARNSBURY STREET, we realised that we were on the crest of a ridge. The point of vantage made us think of nature's hill imprisoned beneath the roadway ; a hill from which the early Britons were able to survey the woods and valleys beyond. We opened our copy of *The Place-Names of Middlesex* again, which lists the many versions of the name Islington, since pre-Norman times. The earliest form was *Gislandune* [1] which, according to the etymologists, was the hill, or dune, of Gisla.

Were we—shut in by the shabby little houses of Barnsbury Street—standing with the ghost of Gisla beside us ? And was Gisla a Saxon swine drover, who gave his name to the hill, and thus to Islington ? This image refreshed us in our enterprise.

HECTOR BOLITHO.

---

[1] In the *Domesday Book*, the form is given as *Isendone*, then *Iseldone*. There is an ISELDONE STREET in the north of the Borough of Islington.

2.   WALTER RICHARD SICKERT, BY E. KAPP

1.   JOHN QUICK, BY T. LAWRANSON

3. CANONBURY TOWER

4. THE ANGEL IN 1815

CHAPTER ONE

Islington

" Thence walked through the ducking-pond fields ; but they are so altered since my father used to carry us to Islington, to the old man's at the King's Head, to eat cakes and ale (his name was Pitts), that I did not know which was the ducking-pond nor where I was."

SAMUEL PEPYS.

" I have a cottage in . . . Islington . . . I feel like a great lord, never having had a house before."

CHARLES LAMB.

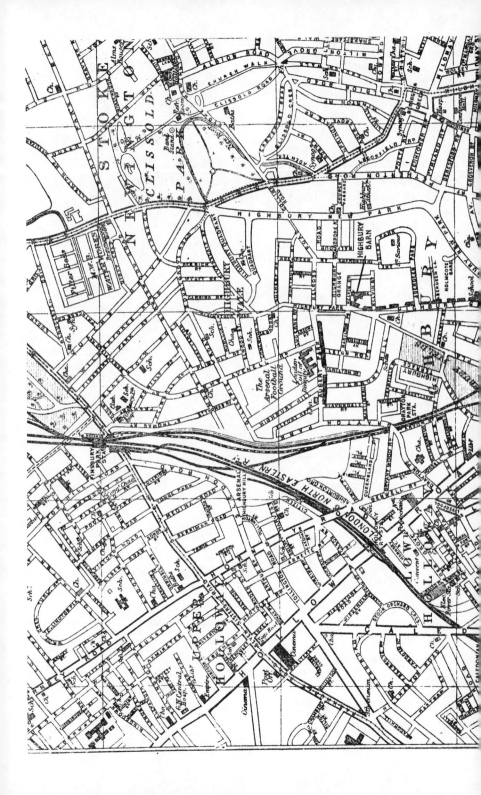

We left the ghost of Gisla, with the cool wind from Hampstead on his cheek, and travelled east along Barnsbury Street to busy Upper Street. After about a quarter of a mile we turned into CANONBURY SQUARE and PLACE, in the district of CANONBURY, called after the canons of St. Bartholomew's, who built a manor house here in the 14th century. It was an incredible shift of scene, from the traffic bedlam and brisk shops of Upper Street, into this leafy stillness where two buildings have survived from before the dissolution of the religious houses. They are CANONBURY TOWER (Pl. 3), which is the most important example of late Tudor architecture in North London, and part of Canonbury House (in Alwyne Place), which was the mansion of the early manor. It was rebuilt about 1520 by the famous Prior of St. Bartholomew's, " old Prior Bolton with his Bolt and Tun ". In what remains of the house there are some beautiful and ornate plaster ceilings dating from the 16th century. Canonbury Tower, stalwart and venerable, rises sixty-six feet against the changing London sky. According to some records the tower also was built by Prior Bolton ; and this version is displayed by the present owner, on a notice board near by. When we began to ask about the early building, we came on our first clash of historical authorities. The Secretary of the Islington Antiquarian and Historical Society,[1] upon whom we called, and who greeted us with both coffee and scholarship, suggested that as Prior Bolton's rebus does not appear on the walls of the actual tower, the credit might go to " rich Sir John Spencer ", who acquired Canonbury House and the surrounding lands in 1570. Through his daughter's marriage they came into the possession of the Comptons,[2] afterwards Marquesses of Northampton. (The estates are now controlled by the Marquess of Northampton's Trust.) Tradition has it that Elizabeth Spencer eloped with William Lord Compton, with pleasing ingenuity : she was let down from her window in a baker's basket, to join her lover who was waiting with his horse, beyond the garden wall.

Almost two hundred years later Canonbury Tower was let out to lodgers, among them Oliver Goldsmith, who lived there from 1762 to 1764. It must have been about this time—he was then

[1] Frank V. Hallam, Esq.
[2] COMPTON ROAD leads into Canonbury Square.

4

forty-four years old—that he wrote his *Elegy on the Death of a Mad Dog*.

> In Islington there was a man,
> Of whom the world might say,
> That still a godly race he ran,
> When'er he went to pray . . .

Sir John Spencer had lined some of the rooms in the tower with beautiful panelling which was carefully preserved there until war began in 1939, when the trustees moved it to Castle Ashby in Northamptonshire, for safety. It has since been replaced, and the charm and mellow character of the interior of the tower is complete again. For those who like a dash of cloak and dagger with their history, there are bullet-holes in the panelling of one of the rooms, said to be the result of a duel in the 17th century.

On either side of the tower in Canonbury Place are six or seven fine Georgian houses. We went there in April and found a touch of country elegance about this tranquil corner of London. Below the tower was a garden, with a chattering fountain, white pigeons cooing in a loft, and an arthritic old mulberry tree, of King James's time ; all set in a cool lawn, most carefully mown.

We left the Square by CANONBURY ROAD, which runs south-east, and we paused to hunt out several small side streets with stories in their sober names. Dr. William Hawes, who founded the Royal Humane Society in 1774, is remembered in HAWES STREET ; HALTON ROAD and FOWLER ROAD were named after wealthy landowners who helped to develop Islington from being a charming village into an area of close-packed prosperity.

As we travelled among the smaller by-ways of the Borough, we were cheered by the variety of the famous names celebrated in the streets. Near the south-eastern boundary, to which we came by way of Canonbury Road, New North Road and Shepperton Road, we found BAGFORD STREET, in memory of John Bagford, the antiquarian bookseller whose collection of books on the history of printing is now in the British Museum. Later we came on QUICK STREET, to recall John Quick (Pl. 1), King George III's favourite comedian. To the north of the Borough is AUBERT PARK, commemorating the gallant scientist, Colonel Aubert, who raised the Islington Loyal Volunteers at the time of the Napoleonic Wars. There is also PLAYFORD ROAD, after John Playford, the music publisher, and BALFE STREET, after Michael William Balfe (1808–70), the Irish composer of *The Bohemian Girl, The Rose of Castile* and *Il Talismano*, who lived in Islington. Only recently the Borough Council immortalised the late Walter Sickert (Pl. 2) in SICKERT COURT, a building of modern flats near where the painter lived for some years.

After travelling about three-quarters of a mile south-east from Canonbury Square, we came to the boundary where Islington merges into Shoreditch and Hackney ; where we found the remains of a windmill tower, but no appropriate street name, on the site of the white lead manufactory [1] that flourished in Islington Fields in the 18th century.

> White lead was sent us to repair,
> A lady's face and China ware.

But we were seeking for names, not ruins, so we turned north again, along Southgate Road, then west, along BALLS POND ROAD, which recalls the tavern and pond for duck-shooting kept there by John Ball during the reign of Charles II. In his *Handbook for London*, published in 1849, Peter Cunningham wrote of Islington, " This village, originally famous for its ducking-ponds, its cheesecakes and custards, is still celebrated for its cowkeepers." It was sad for us that we found no Cheesecake Lane, or Custard Alley, to remind us that these delicacies, made in Lower Holloway, were hurried on horseback to eager buyers in the London streets. The cheesecakes and custards are forgotten, but the " ducking-ponds " are remembered in Balls Pond Road ; and there is good evidence of the cowkeepers— who were finally ousted by the 18th-century industrialists—in LAYCOCK STREET, the name of a prosperous farmer, and especially in RHODES STREET. Rhodes Farm, which included land now occupied by the Angel underground station, at the extreme south of the Borough, once belonged to kinsmen of Cecil Rhodes, whose dairy herds grazed there until early in the 19th century.

Balls Pond Road leads into St. Paul's Road and to the district of HIGHBURY, from which at least fifteen places and streets take their name. At the busy junction of St. Paul's Road, Holloway Road and Upper Street, we were within a stone's throw of HIGHBURY FIELDS,

[1] An article on the subject, by Rotha Mary Clay, appeared in *Country Life*, June 23, 1950.

6

CRESCENT and PLACE—all recalling the ancient manor—so named for the obvious reason that it was high above the neighbouring districts of Canonbury and Barnsbury ; just as HOLLOWAY took its early name from the simple fact that it was a road worn between steep banks, —a " way in the hollow ". The nicest survival of Highbury's name is in the HIGHBURY BARN TAVERN, built on the site of the old manorial barn or granary—at the corner of what are now Kelvin Road and Highbury Park. Unfortunately, the name is all that does survive of this once merry house. Early in the 19th century many of the people attending the dances and band performances at the inn became so tipsy, noisy and destructive in the small hours of the morning, that the owner lost his licence. The building fell into decay and was demolished. The present tavern, built above the dust of the old, is new and shining, with not a ghost left to remind us of the days when pubs were pubs, and it was no shame for a pot-valiant man to sing and dance his way home with the dawn.

We crossed from the east to the west of the Borough, at this junction of Holloway Road and Upper Street, and, by way of High- bury Station Road and Offord Street, we came to the long CALE- DONIAN ROAD. Caledonia being the Roman name for Scotland, we first imagined this to be an ancient place-name, but it did not come to this part of London until 1815, when the Caledonian Asylum— now at Bushey—was founded " for the relief of the children of soldiers, sailors and mariners, natives of Scotland, who have died or been disabled in the service of their country ".

The Caledonian Road borders an area once known as *Copenhagen Fields*, now the Metropolitan Cattle Market. The name, which survives in COPENHAGEN STREET, crossing the Caledonian Road, has a misty origin. It recalls the presence of a Danish Prince or Ambas- sador who lived in the neighbourhood during the Great Plague of 1665. The first form was *Coopen-hagen*, and it is curious that while almost every London historian agrees that this mysterious Dane was of noble birth, none of them gives his name. It was in the middle of the last century that *Copenhagen Fields*, still an open tract of land, became the Metropolitan Cattle Market—the biggest of its kind in the country. Slowly, by accident more than design, its character and name were changed. Twice each week, when the yards were cleared and cleaned after the raucous cattle sales, antique dealers and pedlars put up stalls from which they sold old clothes, jewels, curios, meat and vegetables. In time this conglomeration of traders covered a great part of the thirty-five acres, and Londoners came to call it the Caledonian Market. It was closed during the 1939–45 war, and has not yet been reopened. But some of the 2,500 pre-war stallholders have begun a new trading centre in Bermondsey, whither they have transferred not only their stalls, but the name Caledonian as well.

It was in Copenhagen Street that we suddenly came on BOADICEA STREET, a cul-de-sac which did not suggest Tennyson's "isle of blowing woodland" as a background for the warrior-queen. It was a sad little street, with half its houses bombed and, at the end, a bleak and forbidding school ; all unworthy of the legend that Boadicea fought her last battle nearby ; on the plain south of the twin hills of Highgate and Hampstead.

We followed the Caledonian Road to its southern end, and then turned east, into Pentonville Road ; and, moving beyond the Borough boundary, we soon came upon THE ANGEL [1] (Pl. 4)—one of the most agitated traffic cross-roads in London. We might have sighed that such a romantic place can lose its charm through the unhappy passage of time. The Angel is now a tea-shop, given over to whispered gossip and the clatter of cups. But for three hundred years the name belonged to a noisy, friendly London inn, with sawdust on the floor, the thump of tankards on its beer-soaked bar, and the singing of Cockney bawdy songs. A fog forms over the story before then and we have not been able to find exactly how The Angel got its name. But it is supposed that it was originally associated with the Knights of St. John of Jerusalem, who used the picture-sign of the Annunciation upon hostelries in other parts of the country. (St. John's Gate, which we have described in our chapter on Finsbury, is less than a mile away.)

A few minutes from The Angel—having returned within the Borough boundary—we found CRUDEN STREET, named after the eccentric Alexander Cruden, author of *Concordance to the Holy Scriptures*. Cruden—born in chilly Aberdeen—was a queer mixture of scholar, Sabbatarian and crazy dreamer. Soon after the publication of his Concordance, he " relapsed into insanity " and was shut away. When he was free again, he assumed the title of Alexander the Cor-

---

[1] Although The Angel is actually in the Borough of Finsbury, topographers always include it in Islington. It was mentioned as a coaching-inn as far back as 1638.

rector and toured the country, "reproving Sabbath-breaking and profanity". This high-minded care for his fellow-men did not deter him from "crackpot courtships", dreams of knighthood, and of a seat in Parliament. Cruden died "at his prayers" in his lodgings in Camden Passage, Islington, on 1st November, 1770. Islington is an amiable Borough : Cruden's sins and craziness were forgotten ; and only his *Concordance* was remembered, when a street was appointed to bear his name.

Cruden Street hides itself, off St. Peter's Street, east of Islington Green. Almost next door is peaceful COLEBROOKE ROW, named after a prosperous local family. Part of the Row was renamed in 1890, and it was here, at what is now No. 64 Duncan Terrace, that Charles Lamb lived, and wrote, from 1823 to 1827. Lamb described the house and garden in a letter to his friend Bernard Barton, the Quaker poet :

> When you come Londonward, you will find me no longer in Covent Garden ; I have a cottage in Colebrook Row, Islington ; a cottage for it is detached ; a white house with six good rooms in it ; the New River (rather elderly by this time) runs (if a moderate walking pace can be so termed) close to the foot of the house ; and behind is a spacious garden with vines, (I assure you), pears, strawberries, parsnips, leeks, carrots, cabbages, to delight the heart of old Alcinous. You enter without passage into a cheerful dining-room, all studded over and rough with old books ; and above is a lightsome drawing-room, with three windows, full of choice prints. I feel like a great lord, never having had a house before.

Leading from Colebrooke Row we found ELIA STREET, to remind us that it was under the pseudonym of Elia—the " gay, light-hearted foreigner " who worked with him as a fellow-clerk in the old South Sea House—that Lamb published his essays in *The London Magazine*. His cottage is marked by a County Council plaque, but Lamb would not feel "like a great lord " if he lived there now, for the house has endured many changes. You no longer " enter without passage into a cheerful dining-room ", and the " spacious garden " is covered by a big galvanised-iron garage. When we saw the house, a gallant little lilac bush was doing its lonely best, in memory of the vines, the pears and the strawberries.

The NEW RIVER, mentioned by Lamb, had been " constructed " in 1613 ; a formidable enterprise, almost forty miles long, that supplied London with pure water. There is no place-name in Islington to recall this ambitious water channel, but, on Islington Green, there is a memorial to Sir Hugh Myddelton, the designer. Unfortunately, Sir Hugh had to wait until 1862 before he was sculptured, so he appears as a petrified Victorian rather than as a sturdy 17th-century knight. He is flanked by two smaller marble figures holding pitchers that spout water, when the authorities think to turn it on.

Next to its supplies of food, a city's first needs are water and drains. It is interesting to trace this importance in the names that settled on the land, hundreds of years ago. The babbling brooks and refreshing springs are now buried deep, under close-packed villas and roadways, heavy with lumbering traffic ; but their names are not lost. It is with three of these, WHITE CONDUIT STREET, *Islington Spa*, and SADLER'S WELLS, that our expedition to Islington must close.

White Conduit Street is just behind The Angel. We found a reference to *Condyte Feld* as far back as 1540, when there was doubtless a conduit or water channel running this way. By the end of the 18th century the surrounding land, covering about four acres, had become one of the chief pleasure grounds on the edge of London. In the centre of handsome gardens was White Conduit House, celebrated for its entertainments, its cakes and cream. Part of the original white stone conduit was still intact until the house was pulled down in 1849. Here also was the White Conduit Fields Cricket Club, where the groundsman was Thomas Lord, also destined to give an important name to London. When the club was dissolved in 1787, Thomas Lord made a new cricket ground in the space that is now Dorset Square, in St. Marylebone. This was the first Lord's Cricket Ground. When the square was built in 1814, Lord's moved to the present site, in St. John's Wood.

In writing of Islington Spa and Sadler's Wells, we must step cautiously. To begin with, Sadler's Wells is now within the boundaries of Finsbury, but we claim that its historical interest belongs here, as the site was part of the " village " of Islington in the 17th century. But the confusion lies deeper than this. Many books on old London mention Islington Spa and Sadler's Wells, and make them one. As recently as 1932, Mr. Harold P. Clunn wrote in *The Face of London*, " Sadler's Wells takes its name from a spring of mineral water once called Islington Spa, rediscovered by a Mr. Sadler in 1683 in the garden of a house which he had then just opened as a music room. This spring has been preserved and can be seen in the Theatre."

The Secretary of the Islington Antiquarian and Historical Society disagrees : he has assured us that, although the two " wells " were close together, there is no evidence in his archives to suggest that they were ever connected.

By the beginning of the 18th century Islington Spa was famous, and the waters were so blessed with healing minerals that the place was called " New Tunbridge Wells ". During June, 1733, the daughters of King George II, Princesses Amelia and Caroline, condescended to visit the gardens almost every day. Sarah Siddons took the waters there, and the great Beau Nash was once Master of Ceremonies.

At the close of the century, Islington Spa had become the last hope of great numbers of incurables and the death rate was soon so high that the creatures of fashion withdrew. A story used to be told by Dr. Abernethy, the famous surgeon of St. Bartholomew's, of an invalid arriving at lodgings in Islington and remarking on the broken stairrails. " Oh, it's no use repairing 'em," said the landlady. " The men always break 'em again bringing down the coffins." Thus Islington Spa lost its magic, and its reputation : but not so Sadler's Wells.

Mr. Sadler's Music House had been open some years when, in 1683, his workmen came on a holy well that had been concealed at the time of the Reformation. Mr. Sadler analysed the waters and found iron in them. From this time his patrons came not only to hear his musicians, but also to take cures at the well. Today, Mr. Sadler is known from Los Angeles to the Danube, because of the ballet company that tours the world, in his name ; but the once-famous spring bubbles in obscure darkness, deep below the theatre.

CHAPTER TWO

Finsbury

" I have heard that in a great pit in Finsbury . . . many
who were infected and near their end, and delirious also,
ran wrapped in blankets or rags and threw themselves in
and expired there, before any earth could be thrown upon
them. . . ."

A Journal of the Plague Year.
DANIEL DEFOE.

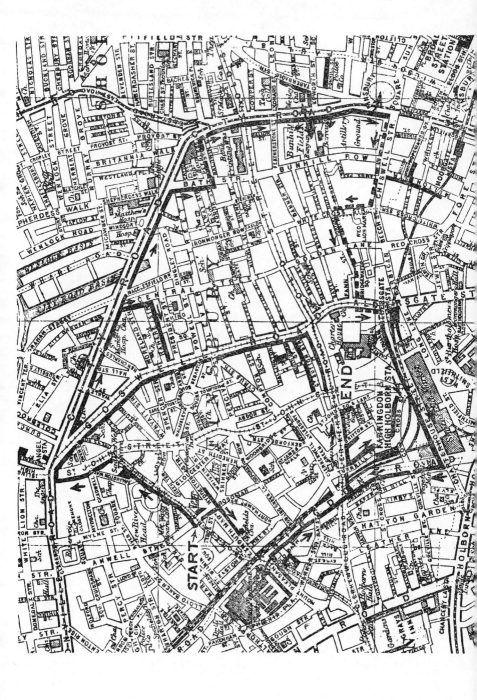

Before beginning our adventures in FINSBURY we made separate enquiries into the origin of its name. I first studied a translation of the 12th-century chronicler, William Fitzstephen, who described the " great Fen or Moor which watereth the walls of the City on the north side ". This district, first known as *Moorfields*,[1] and later as *Fensbury Fields*, lay between what are now FINSBURY SQUARE and FINSBURY CIRCUS. Until the Fen was drained in 1527, it was a recreation ground for the youth of London, whose chief fun in winter was a form of skating on a big pond. Fitzstephen wrote, ". . . some tie bones to their feete,[2] and vnder their heeles, and shouing themselues by a little picked Staffe, do slide as swiftly as a bird flieth in the ayre, or an arrow out of a Crossbow. . . ."

Here was a lively picture of boys and girls in 12th-century Finsbury, skimming over the frozen pond on their bone skates : an exciting ice-ballet, with Breughel figures against a white background. And there was the reasonable deduction, that the word Finsbury had developed from the early descriptive name given to the " great Fen ".

When my collaborator joined me next day, he spoiled my easy solution by producing the verdict of the etymologists,[3] who agree that the name Finsbury is the simple combination of an Anglo-Scandinavian personal name, *Fin*, with the termination, *bury*, implying that the land was originally the manor of a man named Fin ; a neighbour, and rival, maybe, of Gisla or his kinsmen. The etymologists trace the evolution of the name from *Finesbir'*, in 1235, to *Fynesbury* in 1347, and *Fenysbury* in 1535.

We began our journey, this time on foot, from the steps of the Finsbury Town Hall, which stands on a triangular island, surrounded by quick tides of traffic. The streets that fan out from the solid, municipal island suggest vastly different episodes in Finsbury's story. The main traffic was passing along ROSEBERY AVENUE, which was opened by the great Liberal leader in 1890. Nearby were MYDDELTON STREET, named after the designer of the New River,[4] and ROSOMAN

[1] There are MOORFIELDS, MOOR LANE and MOORGATE across the boundary, in the City.
[2] A pair of medieval skates, " fashioned from polished animal bones ", are among exhibits in the Guildhall Museum.
[3] *The Place-Names of Middlesex*, p. 93.
[4] See chapter on Islington, p. 10.

STREET, recalling the enterprising owner who took down the existing music house in 1765 and built the first Sadler's Wells Theatre
—of which one wall still stands, in Arlington Way. Another
thoroughfare we found near the Town Hall was EXMOUTH MARKET,
which has a long story to tell. Its present name celebrates the valour
of Admiral Lord Exmouth (1757–1833) who first distinguished himself at the Battle of Lake Champlain. Before this, the story of this
part of the Borough is less noble, if more exciting. Exmouth Market
is on land that was formerly *Spa Fields*; well-known in the 18th
century for its chalybeate springs, to which Londoners hobbled for
their cures. In 1816, following the failure of the harvest, 30,000
people gathered on Spa Fields to protest against the Corn Laws and to
vote an address to the Prince Regent. The meeting ended in a riot
during which citizens were maimed and houses burned to the ground.
In 1843, some of the land had been sold for use as a burial ground and
there was a fierce scandal when the proprietors were proved to be
exhuming and burning bodies, to make room for new and profitable
interments. But these villainies associated with the name of Spa
Fields ended in names of virtue and respectability. On the site of
Spa Fields Chapel stands the Church of the Holy Redeemer and the
once sordid burial ground is now an open, planted space, with a
football pitch, and gardens by which the young may play and the old
may doze in the sun.

They were a curiously mixed company of ghosts to awaken from
the dreamless dust about Finsbury Town Hall : Lord Rosebery, Sir
Hugh Myddelton, Rosoman, and the hero of Lake Champlain.

We walked along Rosebery Avenue, to the Sadler's Wells Theatre,
of which we have already written. But there is one street-name in
this connection which we must not miss, before we pass on. When
reading a history of Sadler's Wells Theatre we came on Joe Grimaldi
(Pl. 5), "the most celebrated of all English clowns", born in 1779,
and credited with having appeared at the Wells Theatre, as a monkey,
at the age of three. His fame crossed the oceans, but he never grew
too big for his Finsbury shoes. He appeared at Sadler's Wells almost
every year of his life, and he lived at many addresses in the Borough.
There is a small street in the north-eastern corner which bears his
name. To be born and to play in GRIMALDI STREET must be a double
blessing to any Finsbury child, brought into a world where laughter
is in such short measure.

16

5. JOSEPH GRIMALDI, BY J. CAWSE   6. THOMAS SUTTON

7. THE WESLEY MUSEUM

8. THE CHARTERHOUSE

9. ST. JOHN'S GATE, CLERKENWELL

We turned from Sadler's Wells and made our way to The Angel ; then along the northern boundary of the Borough, by City Road. On our right, a little way off the main road, we paused to look at RAHERE STREET, named after the monk of Henry I's time, of whom we have written in the Introduction. We soon came to BATH STREET and the neighbouring PEERLESS STREET, which have a joint history going back to the 17th century. The present Bath Street was then part of a stretch of open land, surrounding a small lake, so deep and dangerous that many people were drowned there, and it came to be known as *Perilous Pond*. With nice ingenuity, when the pond was made into a safe bathing place, the name was changed to *Peerless Pond*. Peerless has remained, long after the pond, and it is now the name of a street filled with a collection of little houses, dull as any that an architect could inflict on the land.

Parallel with Bath Street is CASLON STREET, in memory of William Caslon (1692–1766), the famous type designer, who built his first foundry in adjoining IRONMONGER ROW—the centre for type founders two hundred years ago. The name of Caslon has survived, not only in the street-name : a kinsman of the great William still rules the fortunes of the firm in another part of London.

Our next stop along City Road was BUNHILL FIELDS, where we had our curious adventure while searching for Bunyan " Station ". [1] Bunhill Fields form a cemetery, with an amiable name but a mournful history, going back to the beginning of the 16th century. The name, compounded from *bone* and *hill*, survives in an earlier form in BONHILL STREET, which lies beyond City Road. In 1549, one thousand cart-loads of bones from St. Paul's charnel were brought to Bunhill, or Bone Hill, and, during the Great Plague—according to Defoe—the old dead were covered by new corpses, and the land became a common pest-field. He wrote in his *A Journal of the Plague Year*, " I have heard that in a great pit in Finsbury . . . many who were infected and near their end, and delirious also, ran wrapped in blankets or rags and threw themselves in and expired there, before any earth could be thrown upon them . . ."

When the plague was subdued, the London Council enclosed the ghastly pit within a brick wall and leased it as the Campo Santo of the Dissenters—to those who objected to the burial service laid down in the Book of Common Prayer.

[1] See Introduction, p. xv.

John Bunyan, who died in Holborn in 1688, after his ride from Reading to London, through the rain, is buried in Bunhill Fields ; also Daniel Defoe (1660–1731),[1] who had lodgings in Moorfields nearby. Here too are the graves of Isaac Watts, author of *When I survey the Wondrous Cross*, who died in 1748 ; and of William Blake (1757–1827), who lies near the " dear and too careful and over-joyous woman " who was his wife. " How many have fallen there ! They stumble all night over bones of the dead."

Milton was also associated with Finsbury for many years, and he died in his house there, 125 Bunhill Row, on November 8, 1675, " with so little pain or emotion, that the tide of his expiring was not perceived by those in the room ". Milton was buried " the next Thursday, in the church of St. Giles, Cripplegate, beside his father ". But his name lives in MILTON STREET and MILTON COURT, in the south of Finsbury, near where he used to sit in the garden before his house.

On the other side of City Road, from Bunhill Fields, are two buildings on a plot of land which is sacred to Methodists all over the world. Here John Wesley (1703–91) built up his formidable mission, and here is the charming little house (Pl. 7)—now a museum—where he lived, and died. There is a Wesley Street in St. Marylebone, Wesley Place in Southwark and Wesleyan Place in St. Pancras, although the ardent reformer has been awarded no street-name in the district where he lived. But, near WESLEY'S CHAPEL, is EPWORTH STREET, named after the village in north Lincolnshire, where he was born. Behind the Chapel runs TABERNACLE STREET, where George Whitefield's " Tabernacle " was built by his supporters after he separated from Wesley in 1741. During the years of Whitefield's mission the street was called *Windmill Hill*. A survey of the manor in 1567 refers to the " High Field or Meadow Ground where the three windmills stand, commonly called *Finsbury Fields*". When White-field died, the memory of his mission was considered more important than the image of three old windmills against a 16th-century sky, so Tabernacle Street was named.

We continued along City Road, passing Epworth, Tabernacle and Bonhill Streets on the left. On the right lay THE ARTILLERY GROUND, headquarters of the *Honourable Artillery Company*—Britain's most ancient military body—founded in the reign of Henry VIII, in 1537. These grand flashes of history do little to brighten the drab monotony

[1] See Chapter on Stoke Newington, pp. 47–8.

of the present streets, and when we came to Finsbury Square it was not easy to imagine the apple-cheeked Londoners of the 12th century speeding on their bone skates, where now the lumbering red bus and pert taxicab shove each other for bonnet room in the crowded square. We turned west from Finsbury Square, along Chiswell Street,[1] and then made a hurried journey to CHARTERHOUSE STREET and CHARTER-HOUSE SQUARE, our next place of enquiry.

It was late in the day and the first stillness of evening was already coming to the narrow side streets. Behind us was Smithfield Market and, nearer, the poor hangers-on of the big meat business—the offal dealers who pursue their melancholy trade in dark little shops, with sulphur-yellow jets of flame illuminating the open boxes of repulsive intestines. It was from this scene that we turned, to look at Charterhouse (Pl. 8) for the first time.

The shades that moved in the April half-light formed a long procession ; beginning with the melancholy ghosts of Pardon Churchyard, in which more than fifty thousand bodies were buried, during the 1384–7 plague. All that survives from this early chapter of Finsbury's story is in the name of PARDON STREET, to the north of Charterhouse.

The history that concerns us here began in 1365 when Sir Walter de Manny founded *le Charthous next Smythfeld*, and covered the burial ground with the Carthusian monastery that survived until its dissolution by Henry VIII. The name Charterhouse, an English corruption of the French *Maison chartreuse*, occurs in other parts of England—Charterhouse-on-Mendip and Hinton Charterhouse, where Carthusians built their religious houses. After the Reformation the old Charterhouse monastery in London was twice used for great occasions : Queen Elizabeth stayed there while her coronation was being prepared, and James I held his first court there, after he entered London.

Early in the 17th century Charterhouse was owned by Thomas Sutton (Pl. 6), a rich coal owner from the north. When he died in 1611, he endowed the buildings as an alms-house for eighty " gentle-men by descent and in poverty, soldiers that have borne arms by sea or land, merchants decayed by piracy or shipwreck, or servants in the household to the King or Queen's Majesty ". He also endowed the Charterhouse school that has become so famous—originally for the education of only forty boys.

The school moved to Godalming in 1872 and the Merchant Taylors'

---

[1] Chiswell Street. See Introduction, p. xv.

School took over the site. Then they also moved to the country. But the modern equivalent of " gentlemen by descent and in poverty " remained in occupation of the alms-houses until they were obliged to scatter during the recent war.

There was an austere sadness about Charterhouse. We looked at the noble buildings, with their war wounds, from the darkening pavement nearby, and imagined the shades of Addison, Steele, Wesley and Thackeray, who were boys at Charterhouse, guarding the memorial to Thomas Sutton's benevolence, through the long night. But this early 17th-century businessman-benefactor is not forgotten in Finsbury. A hundred yards to the north of Charterhouse, parallel with Clerkenwell Road, we came on GREAT SUTTON STREET, which perpetuates his name.

We walked back into Charterhouse Street and then into long, busy FARRINGDON ROAD, a continuation of Farringdon Street in the City, named after Sir William Farnedon, or de Farndone, a sheriff in the late 13th century. When Farringdon Road in Finsbury was constructed in 1856, it gave the Victorians an opportunity to quash one or two street-names that could hardly be looked upon as genteel addresses. Many descriptive, if inelegant, names—Slaughterhouse Lane, Thieve's Alley, Savage Row and Cutthroat Lane—disappeared during the great, respectable century. In naming Farringdon Road it was possible to do away with many minor courts and alleys, and their names—including Coppice Row (a modification of Codpeece Roe, and earlier, Codpiss Row), a notorious brothel area, and Hockley-in-the-Hole, once famous for bear-baiting and boxing bouts, in which women tried their muscles as valiantly as the men. In a public print of 1722 we read : [1]

> I, Elizabeth Wilkinson, of Clerkenwell, having had some words with Hannah Hyfield, and requiring satisfaction, do invite her to meet me on the stage, and box with me for three guineas, each woman holding half-a-crown in each hand [this was to prevent scratching] and the first woman that drops her money to lose the battle !

The challenge was accepted with equal gusto :

> I, Hannah Hyfield, of Newgate Market, hearing of the resoluteness of Elizabeth Wilkinson, will not fail, God willing, to give her more blows than words, desiring home blows, and from her no favour.

[1] Cunningham's *Handbook for London*, vol. I, p. 383.

The Victorians left their mark on the street-names of the city that spread so richly during the last century. The Queen's name was given to no less than 77 streets and places, and 69 terraces, mansions, arcades, mews and squares were dedicated to Prince Albert. But, as we have seen, the Victorians also used their blue pencils on the old maps, so that many full-blooded and descriptive place-names have been lost for ever. We found only one with bawdy associations, opening off the Farringdon Road, which has been allowed to stay.

In the second part of *Henry IV*, Act III, Falstaff speaks of the moral trespasses of Shallow, " This same starved justice hath done nothing but prate to me of the wildness of his youth, and the feats he hath done about Turnbull-street."

Shakespeare's Turnbull-street was the present TURNMILL STREET, " a noted haunt of harlots between Clerkenwell Green and Cow Cross ", in his time. There was *Trimullstrete* in Edward III's day, with three water-mills in a graceful river-side setting. And COW CROSS STREET no doubt began as part of the same rural scene. Today the two streets half encircle Farringdon station, with no hint of water-mills or harlotry to remind us of their early history.

When we made our last search among the streets off the Farringdon Road it was already too dark to read the name-plates at the corners. But we found two more places, at the northern end of Farringdon Road, that must be mentioned. The first, MOUNT PLEASANT, reveals a note of sarcasm. This is now the biggest postal sorting office in the world, but when it was named it was the local dump for refuse and cinders. We also walked through COLD BATH SQUARE, to the south-east of the post office. Cunningham's *Handbook for London* informed us that this was once *Cold Bath Fields*, " so called from a well of cold water, formerly situated in fields, but now built over ". In 1794 a House of Correction was opened in these fields and it apparently vied for horror with its neighbour in Bridewell, which had been opened in 1553 as a reformatory " for the strumpet and idle person, for the rioter that consumeth all, and for the vagabond that will abide in no place ". The sadistic beating of whores in both these prisons compelled Southey and Coleridge to write in *The Devil's Thoughts* :

> As he went through Coldbath Fields he saw
> A solitary cell ;
> And the Devil was pleased, for it gave him a hint
> For improving his prisons in Hell.

The darkness defeated us and we had to give up our journey for the day, so we walked along Turnmill Street again and took our map and reference books into the Castle Tavern ; unique among the pubs of London, for it holds two licences—one as a public house and one as a pawnbroker's shop.

While we were drinking our sherry, we opened volume I of *Cunningham* and we read about this part of the Borough, which is known as CLERKENWELL. The name derives from a holy well, of water that was described as especially " sweet, clear and salubrious " ; and it was here, as early as the 12th century, that the Parish Clerks of the City gathered to perform their Biblical plays. The " Clerk's well " was unearthed in 1924, and it is now preserved in the basement of 14–16 Faringdon Road.

Another of these early sources of water was *Godewell* (Goodwell), a word that was twisted through the centuries to Godeswell, then Gosewell, and to GOSWELL, the name of the long, important road that now divides the Borough in two. The Godewell was mentioned in the *Registrum de Clerkenwell*, compiled in the time of King John. Mr. Pickwick lodged in " Goswell Street " and, in 1843, at No. 266 Goswell Road, Thomas Hancock discovered the art of vulcanisation. It might be said that he thus created the rubber trade of the world.

We left the Castle Tavern and walked along CLERKENWELL ROAD, past Britton Street,[1] until we came to ST. JOHN's GATE (Pl. 9). We stood beneath the gate-house which is all that remains of the Priory of St. John of Jerusalem. It was dark enough, with the help of the silent night, for us to imagine the long, brave history of this ancient gate. The Knights Hospitallers, who occupied Jerusalem in 1099, pledged themselves to further the good work of the Hospital of St. John which they found there. Forty-five years later they built their first Priory in England, in Clerkenwell, on land granted to them by " a certain Jordan of Bricett ", remembered today in BRISET STREET, nearby. The Order endured persecution from Henry VIII, and the Priory—all but the gate-house—was blown up in 1550. The estates were confiscated by Elizabeth, in 1559, and almost three hundred years passed before the Order returned to England, as an independent foundation, owing no allegiance to the Roman branch of the original order. In 1873, through the kindness of Sir Edward Lechmere, the remains of the Priory were restored to the Order,

---

[1] See chapter on Holborn, p. 27.

and, fifteen years later, Queen Victoria became its Sovereign Head. The promises made in Jerusalem almost a thousand years ago are being kept, within the gate-house, for it is now the headquarters for the noble work done by the St. John's Ambulance Association. When we returned home that evening, we came on some verses written by Mr. Harold Adshead which seem to end our story :

A grey-stone gateway spans the narrow street,
Where chivalry and modern custom meet,
And here beneath the castellated arch,
The silent shades of old Crusaders march.

The swords and armour hang today in rust,
But still the Order keeps its sacred trust.
And in this peaceful gateway of St. John,
The healing work of modern Knights lives on.

CHAPTER THREE

Holborn

" Now I'm a wretch, indeed. Methinks I see him already in the Cart, sweeter and more lovely than the nosegay in his hand !—I hear the crowd extolling his resolution and intrepidity !—What vollies of sighs are sent from the windows of Holborn that so comely a youth should be brought to disgrace ! . . ."

Polly Peachum in *The Beggar's Opera.*

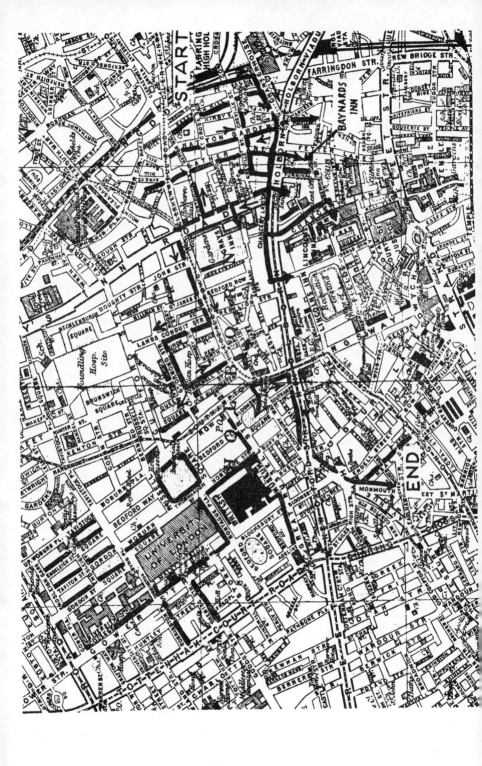

Our next borough was Holborn, and we arranged to begin our journey from the second-hand bookstalls in Farringdon Road. By this time my collaborator used them as a reference library for lunch-time research, as well as for bargain-hunting, and I found him, holding two books and leaning over a tea-chest full of shabby old prints. He had found one of Thos Britton, the Musical Small Coal-man (Pl. 10), and, pinned to it, a bedraggled cutting from The London Magazine for February, 1777.

"You see," he said, "we missed a very good story in BRITTON STREET [1]—which we passed last night on our way to St. John's Gate."

Britton Street was named after an incredible Londoner of the late 17th century, who walked the streets by day, "in his blue frock and with his small-coal measure in his hand", and who by night gave concerts in his humble abode next to Jerusalem Tavern, in what is still JERUSALEM PASSAGE, St. John's Square. In The London Magazine we read, "On the ground floor was a repository for small-coal ; over that was the concert room, which was very long and narrow. . . . Notwithstanding all, this mansion, despicable as it may seem, attracted to it as polite an audience as ever the Opera did. . . . At these concerts Dr. Pepusch and frequently Mr. Handel played the harpsichord. . . ." When passing along the streets with his sack of small-coal on his back, Britton "was frequently accosted with such expressions as these : ' There goes the famous small-coal man, who is a lover of learning, a performer in music, and a companion for gentlemen.' "

Thomas Britton was buried in Clerkenwell Churchyard in October 1714 and, most suitably, a street was named after him within earshot of Jerusalem Passage, where he created the first musical concerts in England, two and a half centuries ago.

The two books my friend had bought, for two shillings and threepence, were the Everyman edition of Evelyn's Diary, and he had already marked four passages to help us in our search.

We walked to the end of the Farringdon Road, west along Charterhouse Street and into HOLBORN CIRCUS—where a bronze Prince Consort sits upon his bronze horse, his cocked hat raised, and withal looking most uncomfortable. Just off the Circus we found ELY

[1] See chapter on Finsbury, p. 22.

PLACE, a short, austere cul-de-sac guarded by a squat lodge, with a sign, " To St. Etheldreda's Catholic Church ". On the left we saw the bombed skeleton of the Church, built in 1252 ; all that survives of Ely House, the early property of the Bishops of Ely. They had possessed wide estates, with vineyards—hence VINE HILL nearby— and, in defiance of the English climate, a garden where saffron grew —hence today's SAFFRON HILL.

In 1576, part of the estate was leased to Sir Christopher Hatton (Pl. 11) by Queen Elizabeth's orders, at an annual rent of "£10, ten loads of hay, and a rose at midsummer ". Richard Barham wrote :

> Sir Christopher Hatton, he danced with grace,
> He'd a very fine figure, a very fine face. . . .

Christopher Hatton was also astute, and he spent big sums of money —advanced by the Queen—in developing the estate. Hatton then proposed that the money he had spent should be repaid to him, or the land forfeited to him entirely. The Bishop protested, and Queen Elizabeth met his demur with all the rich anger of her royal quill.[1]

> Proud Prelate ! I understand you are backward in complying with your agreement, but I would have you know, that I, who made you what you are, can unmake you ; and if you do not forthwith fulfil your engage-ment, by God ! I will immediately unfrock you.

The Bishop withdrew and the name of Hatton was fixed on the land for ever. It was not until the 17th century that the first Baron Hatton (1605–70) created HATTON GARDEN. On June 7, 1659, Evelyn wrote : " To London, to take leave of my brother, and see the foundations now laying for a long street and buildings in Hatton-Garden, designed for a little town, lately an ample garden." Early in the 19th century, Hatton Garden became the diamond and precious stone market of the world.

Forming a cross-road with Hatton Garden is GREVILLE STREET, named after Fulke Greville, 1st Lord Brooke, the poet and friend of Sir Philip Sidney. It was in nearby BROOKE STREET, in August, 1770, that " the marvellous boy ", Thomas Chatterton, " penniless, starving, yet too proud to accept the meal his landlady offered him . . . locked himself in his garret, tore up his papers, and was found the next morning dead—poisoned with arsenic."

[1] Cunningham, vol. 1, p. 290.

At this point in our searches we became perplexed by two problems. Parallel with Hatton Garden was LEATHER LANE which one might suppose to have housed tanners or leather merchants. Its nearness to Smithfield encouraged us to this view, but we found in Henry Harben's *Dictionary of London* that Leather was *Lither*, or *Liver Lane*, in 1606, and *Louerone Lane* early in the 14th century; and Louerone was the name of a citizen of that time.

Our second problem came in Greville Street, turning from Saffron Hill, where we came on BLEEDING HEART YARD (Pl. 12), a little court of drab buildings; the backs of warehouses, a garage, and the shop of a " guillotine knife grinder ".

That evening we searched several books of reference for the story of Bleeding Heart Yard, but even Stow and Cunningham did not mention it; nor was there any help from *The Place-Names of Middlesex*. My collaborator made the next step by bringing me a quotation from Chapter 12 of *Little Dorrit* :

> The opinion of the yard was divided respecting the derivation of its name. The more practical of its inmates abided by the tradition of a murder ; the gentler and more imaginative inhabitants, including the whole of the tender sex, were loyal to the legend of a young lady of former times closely imprisoned in her chamber by a cruel father for remaining true to her own true love, and refusing to marry the suitor he chose for her. The legend related how that the young lady used to be seen up at her window behind the bars, murmuring a love-lorn song, of which the burden was " Bleeding Heart, Bleeding Heart, bleeding away ", until she died. . . .

Dickens gave us one hint : he had written, " Neither party would listen to the antiquaries who delivered learned lectures in the neighbourhood, showing the Bleeding Heart to have been the heraldic cognisance of the old family to whom the property had once belonged ". So we wrote to the College of Arms, and Blue-mantle Pursuivant replied that there were " a great many coats of arms with hearts ", but he had " been unable to find one *gutté de sang* ".

The Borough Librarian gave us our answer, from Thornbury and Walford's *Old and New London*, which we had overlooked. Bleeding Heart Yard is derived from a pre-Reformation tavern sign—the heart of the Blessed Virgin pierced with five swords.

From Bleeding Heart Yard we returned to Holborn Circus and

then walked along HIGH HOLBORN—the *Holburne Strate* of the 12th century. Hol-burne is the simple description of the land, through which a sweet stream or " burn" once ran, in a " hollow ". This road had a nickname in the 16th and 17th centuries ; it was *The Heavy Hill* along which felons from Newgate prison and the Tower were dragged to the gallows at *Tyburn*.[1] On 22 May, 1685, Evelyn wrote, " Oates, who had but two days before been pilloried at several places and whipped at the cart's tail from Newgate to Aldgate, was this day placed on a sledge, being not able to go by reason of so late scourging, and dragged from prison to Tyburn, and whipped again all the way, which some thought to be severe and extraordinary. . . . I chanced to pass just as execution was doing on him ".

There were, however, gestures of charity on this terrible road. At the west of the Borough we were later to pass near ST.-GILES-IN-THE-FIELDS, built in 1733 on the site of a chapel to a leper hospital founded by Queen Matilda and dedicated to St. Egidius (of which the popular form, through Old French, was *Giles*[2]) in 1101. " At this Hospital the prisoners conueyed from the City of London towards Teyborne, there to be executed for treasons, fellonies, or other trespasses, were presented with a great Bowle of Ale, thereof to drinke at theyr pleasure, as to be theyr last refreshing in this life." [3]

We walked along High Holborn until we came to CHANCERY LANE —the road of the law—where barristers, their pockets lined by human folly, walk to and from their chambers. We quote a few phrases from Leigh Hunt's enchanting book, *The Town*. " Chancery Lane . . . built in the time of Henry the Third, when it was called New Lane, which was afterwards altered to Chancellor's Lane, is the greatest legal thoroughfare in England. It leads from The Temple, passes by Sergeant's Inn, Clifford's Inn, Lincoln's Inn, and the Rolls, and conducts to Gray's Inn. Of the world of vice and virtue, of pain and triumph, of learning and ignorance, truth and chicanery, of impudence, violence, and tranquil wisdom, that must have passed through this spot, the reader may judge accordingly."

Half-way down Chancery Lane, we entered the gateway of LIN-COLN'S INN (Pl. 13), where the air is grave and still ; where one's mood

---

[1] See chapter on St. Marylebone, pp. 140–1.

[2] *The Place-Names of Middlesex*, p. 116.

[3] Stow, vol. II, p. 91. There was also the famous inn, The Bowl, where prisoners were comforted with a tankard of ale.

is ordered by the mighty old trees and mellow buildings. Late in the 13th century, " Henry Lacy, Earle of Lincolne . . . builded his Inne"[1] on this land, thus giving it the existing name. The next step in the story seems uncertain and, after reading several books to find out exactly when Lincoln's Inn was " encreased with fayre buildinges and replenished with Gentlemen studious in the Common Lawes ", we were in such a confusion of dates and claims that we felt like two well-meaning rabbits caught in a trap of historian's barbed wire. Mr. James Claude Webster admits, in the thirteenth edition of the *Encyclopædia Britannica*, that " there is little authentic record until the time of Henry VI " of Lincoln's Inn becoming a " place of legal study ". But that the " Gentlemen studious in the Common Lawes " are there today we were quite certain. It was a May afternoon when we went to Lincoln's Inn, and some of the legal gentlemen had opened their windows to observe the first brave buds on the trees.

From Chancery Lane we returned to High Holborn, to see three small streets nearby, before crossing to Gray's Inn. The first of these was GREAT TURNSTILE, where, early in the 17th century, there was a revolving barrier to allow only pedestrians to pass from Holborn to Lincoln's Inn Fields. The second and third were FURNIVAL STREET, and THAVIE'S INN,[2] named after the two Inns of Chancery once attached to Lincoln's Inn. Furnival's Inn, where Dickens later wrote *Pickwick Papers*, took its name from Sir Richard Furnival, who possessed " two Messuages and 13 shops " there during the reign of Richard II.[3] Thavie's Inn recalls an "honest citizen", one "John Thavie, an armourer ", who lived about the time of Edward III.[4] The vast and prosperous-looking building of the Prudential Assurance Company now sprawls over what was Furnival's Inn, and the name survives only in the little street opposite. Thavie's Inn was sold in 1769 and it remains as an ordinary-looking cul-de-sac, opening into Holborn Circus.

We then left High Holborn at Chancery Lane Underground Station, and walked along GRAY'S INN ROAD, to PORTPOOL LANE, and GRAY'S INN. There are 13th-century records of the manor of Port

---

[1] The word *Inn* was then used to describe a great house or mansion. As Leigh Hunt remarks, " The French still use the word *hotel* in the same sense."
[2] Both Furnival Street and Thavie's Inn are just across the boundary, in the City.
[3] Stow, vol. II, p. 37. [4] Cunningham, vol. II, p. 814.

Poole, which belonged to the dean and chapter of St. Paul's. The name of Gray's Inn comes from the family of Reginald de Grey of Wilton who held the land in the next century. But various owners possessed it before it was first leased " to certain students of the law ". Even Stow could not give a date to this and he wrote of " . . . the Inne of Courte, named Grayes Inne, a goodly house there scituate, by whome builded or first begun I haue not yet learned, but seemeth to be since Edward the third's time. . . ."

The two Inns of Chancery associated with Gray's Inn were STAPLE INN and BARNARD'S INN. Both these names survive, but Barnard's Inn (just beyond the Borough boundary) has become the Mercer's School, and Staple Inn belongs to the Prudential Assurance Company who are trying to expiate the crime of their own vast edifice by leaving the ancient Inn buildings as unspoiled as possible.

From grave scholars at their law we walked into THEOBALDS ROAD, to be met by a most revolting ghost : King James I returning from his hunting at Theobalds, in Hertfordshire ; a greedy king, too long in speech and too short in manners, dazed with having eaten three meals as one, and with just enough energy to belch, and blow his nose on his sleeve, as he rides by.

About four hundred yards along Theobalds Road, from Gray's Inn, we turned into LAMB'S CONDUIT STREET ; Holborn's memorial to a charming man from Kent who lived in London in the time of Henry VIII. William Lamb, " for some time a gentleman of the chappels " of St. Paul's and Westminster Abbey, was paid only 7d. a day for his singing. " It is supposed, however, that he got into the good graces of the capricious monarch through his voice " and that he " acquired great affluence " at an early age. He used this affluence to endow a chapel in the City, and to build " a faire Conduit " in Holborn where there was a spring of drinking water, " clear as crystal ". The water " was carried along in pipes of lead from the north fields more than two thousand yards, all at his own cost and charge, amounting to the sum of fifteen hundred pounds ".

William Lamb was imaginative as well as kind ; he gave " pails to one hundred and twenty poor women, wherewith to serve and carry this water as it ran out ". The conduit was removed in 1746, but Lamb's name [1] still catches the lamplight at the end of the street.

[1] There is a short essay on William Lamb and The Old Lamb's Conduit in *The History and Traditions of St. Pancras* by Thomas Coull, 1861.

11. SIR CHRISTOPHER HATTON

10. THOMAS BRITTON,
THE MUSICAL SMALL COALMAN

12. BLEEDING HEART YARD

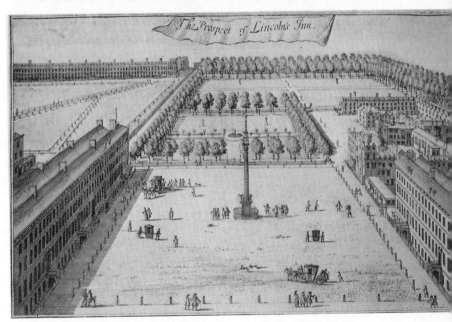

13. THE PROSPECT OF LINCOLN'S INN

We made our way along Great Ormond Street, to QUEEN SQUARE, named after Queen Anne in 1706. (It might be mentioned that Queen Anne's dull Danish husband—of whom King Charles II said, " I have tried him drunk and I have tried him sober, but there is nothing in him "—is also remembered in Holborn ; in DENMARK STREET, and PLACE, near St. Giles, at the west end of the Borough.) The figures that flit among the trees of Queen Square are livelier than these : Edmond Hoyle, the " creator of whist ", walking towards his house in the square, in the early 1760's ; Fanny Burney, at the age of nineteen, hurrying to her " small room up two pairs of stairs ", to write one more page of the diaries that were already three years old ; and William Morris, living at No. 26, where he designed his famous pomegranate wallpaper. None of these is recalled in street-names in the Borough, and we have to cross to Westminster for Fanny Burney's memorial—D'ARBLAY STREET, off Poland Street, in the heart of Soho, where her father lived before the family moved to Holborn.

By this time my collaborator and I had learned to share the writing of this book in just measure : he did all the research during the week, and I merely joined him each week-end, through the spring and summer, to go where he led me, and listen to his recital of facts and authorities. As we walked towards RED LION SQUARE, by way of Boswell Street and Drake Street, Derek Peel alarmed me with the history of the square, which sounded like the list of a felon's convictions.

There was already an Inn—the Red Lion Inn—in this part of Holborn in the early 17th century. After the bodies of Cromwell, Ireton and Bradshaw were taken from Westminster Abbey, they were dragged to the inn where they rested for the night. Next morning they were taken on a sledge, to be hanged at Tyburn, followed on their terrible journey by the " universal outcry and curses of the people ".[1]

In the 1680's there was built on *Red Lion Fields* " a large four-square house, with three galleries round, for the killing of wild bulls by men on horseback, after the manner as in Spain and Portugal ".[2] It seems that the discovery of the Popish Plot interrupted this plan, but the choice of *Red Lion Fields* as a setting for drama went on.

---

[1] There are, nevertheless, twenty-four streets and places named after Cromwell in Greater London.

[2] *The History of the Squares of London*, Chancellor, pp. 172–83.

There were constant duels here, and in one of them, between " Burton and Tankard ", the " latter killed the former basely before he drew his sword " and was most rightly sent to Newgate. And there was " a duell in Red Lyon [Fields] between a person called the Earl of Banbury and Captain Lawson of the Guards, his brother-in-law, and the latter was killed on the spot ".

It might have been hoped that these dark episodes would come to an end, when Red Lion Square was built. But no : Narcissus Luttrell wrote in his diary, on June 10, 1684, " Dr. Barebone,[1] the great builder, having sometime since bought the Red Lyon Fields, near Graies Inn walks, to build on, and having for that purpose employed several workmen to goe on with the same, the gentlemen of Graies Inn took notice of it, and, thinking it an injury to them, went with a considerable body of one hundred persons ; upon which the workmen assaulted the gentlemen, and flung bricks at them, and the gentlemen at them again : so a sharp engagement ensued, but the gentlemen routed them at the last, and brought away one or two of the workmen to Graies Inn ; in this skirmish one or two of the gentlemen and servants of the house were hurt, and severall of the workmen."

Barebone apparently won the day and Red Lion Square was built ; but his enterprise did not bring peace. In 1700 there was a fire in the Square, in which Mrs. Aislaby perished—wife of John Aislaby, who was sent to the Tower for his " notorious, dangerous, and infamous corruption " in connection with the South Sea Company. On the same night Mr. Knightley's house was burned ; the same Mr. Knightley who was " one of those implicated in the plot to assassinate William III on his way to hunt in Richmond Park ".

Distinction and honour came to the Square in the end, with the advent of the Pre-Raphaelites. In January, 1851, Dante Gabriel Rossetti moved into No. 17, with a stipulation from the landlord— that the models be kept " under some gentlemanly restraint ", as " some artists sacrifice the dignity of art to the baseness of passion ". Five years later, Burne-Jones and Morris moved into the same rooms. " We are quite settled here now ", wrote Burne-Jones. " Today Morris has had some furniture (chairs and tables) made after his own design ; they are beautiful as medieval work, and when we have

[1] Dr. Nicholas Barebone or Barebones, son of Praise-God Barebones, was the institutor of fire insurance in England, and a busy builder of new houses after the Great Fire.

painted designs of knights and ladies upon them, they will be perfect marvels." The bloody ghosts of two hundred years departed then and left the Square in peace.

Our next step intimidated us : we walked from Red Lion Square, along PARTON [1] STREET, into BLOOMSBURY SQUARE ; the heart of the immense estates of the Russell family—the Dukes of Bedford—that stretch over almost one third of Holborn and a considerable area of St. Pancras. The actual name, Bloomsbury, presented no problem. Although called *Lomsbery* in the 16th century, the name is directly derived from the *Manerium de Blemund*, of the 13th century. A William Blemund is "mentioned in 1202 in a fine concerning part of *Totenhale*",[2] an early form of Tottenham. All this fitted quite pleasantly, for part of Tottenham Court Road forms the western boundary of Holborn.

Disentangling the story of the Russells, rather than that of the Blemunds, was our problem. There is barely a corner in Bloomsbury where we do not read the name of a member or connection of this great Whig family, or of an estate in their possession. The streets of Bloomsbury are the Russell family tree, spread upon the earth, and it is not easy to trace all its branches in a paragraph or two.

The story begins with John Russell, son of a Weymouth merchant, who was brought into the Court of King Henry VIII by " a happy accident ". The Archduke Philip, son of the Emperor Maximilian, was driven into Weymouth Harbour by a storm, and John Russell, already a traveller and linguist, accompanied him to London where he was recommended to the King. In 1550 he had risen to such authority that he was created Earl of Bedford.

We now turn to the 4th Earl of Southampton—son of Shakespeare's patron—living in his town house off Chancery Lane. In 1638 he replaced the house with tenements—on land now known as SOUTH-AMPTON BUILDINGS—and moved to a " mansion set among spacious meadows " in Bloomsbury. He soon pulled down this mansion also, and in 1665, when Evelyn visited the site of the new Southampton House, he noted that the Earl was " building a noble Square or Piazza, a little towne ".

The widowed daughter of this 4th Earl—the " virtuous " Lady

---

[1] Named after John Parton, the Vestry Clerk whose history of St. Giles-in-the-Fields was published in 1822.

[2] *The Place-Names of Middlesex*, p. 114.

Rachel—married the " patriot " William Lord Russell, second son of the 5th Earl of Bedford. Lady Rachel inherited her father's estates, which ultimately went to her son. He was an heir twice over, for he also came into the Russell fortune, and the titles of his grandfather, who had been created Duke of Bedford and Marquess of Tavistock, in 1694. Southampton House, with its "noble Square or Piazza " and "little towne", became Bedford House in the process. Thus the Russell dominion was established in Bloomsbury, and, as their marriages increased, the streets were named, one by one, to tell the story.

Tavistock Square was named after their manor in Devon ; Endsleigh Street and Taviton Street (both in St. Pancras), from places on the same estate. Woburn Square was named from Woburn Abbey, the family seat in Bedfordshire, and Chenies Street recalls the name of the family estate and ducal burial ground in Buckinghamshire—also of the property acquired by the first John Russell as part of what has been described as " a vast estate of church lands, and lands forfeited by less successful navigators of the troubled sea of Tudor politics". Montague Place, and Montague Street, which links Russell Square with Great Russell Street, both come from Lady Rachel's brother-in-law, Ralph Montagu. Howland Street is named from the family of the second Duchess ; Gower Street from the father-in-law of the 4th Duke ; Keppel Street from the mother of both the 5th and 6th Dukes, who was a daughter of William Keppel, Earl of Albemarle. The pattern is rich but confusing. Torrington Square and Place, and Gordon Square, recall Viscount Torrington and the Duke of Gordon ; fathers, respectively, of the two wives of the 6th Duke. The third son of the first of these was Lord John Russell, twice Prime Minister, and chief architect of the Reform Bill of 1832. It was Lord John who wrote of his family that " in all times of popular movement the Russells have been on the ' forward ' side ".

This monopoly has made it difficult for other great men to achieve the fame of a street-name in Bloomsbury. One of the few instances of a Russell name being overwhelmed by superior forces was when Montagu House became the British Museum. Sir Hans Sloane (1660–1753) is recalled in Sloane Street, Chelsea, but he lived in Bloomsbury Square from 1689–1741, with some of his great collection of 50,000 volumes and 3,560 manuscripts which formed the nucleus of the Museum. Another, similar benefactor also lived in

Bloomsbury Square : Dr. John Radcliffe (1650–1714), who bequeathed the money with which the Radcliffe Library, Infirmary and Observatory were founded, in Oxford. But he has no street named after him in Bloomsbury, although he was apparently called on to pay for the paving of one of them. He was known to be tardy in paying his bills, and one day he was waylaid on his own doorstep by a pavior to whom he owed money.

" Why, you rascal ! " said the doctor, " do you pretend to be paid for such a piece of work ? Why, you have spoiled my pavement, and then covered it over with earth to hide your bad work."

" Doctor ! " said the pavior, " mine is not the only bad work the earth hides."

" You dog you ! " said the Doctor, " are you a Wit ? You must be poor, come in "—and paid him.[1]

We did not explore all these streets but walked back from Bloomsbury Square, towards High Holborn, where we caught a No. 22 bus and went as far as the Prince's Theatre. There was still the last of the four entries marked in Evelyn's Diary to be dealt with. On October 5, 1694, he wrote, " I went to St. Paul's to see the choir, now finished as to stonework. . . . I went also to see the building beginning near St. Giles, where seven streets make a star from a Doric pillar placed in the middle of a circular area."

When we came to the northern end of Monmouth Street, we jumped off the bus and made our way to see the famous intersection of streets, before going home.

The work of building SEVEN DIALS had been begun in 1693, on what were then called the Cock-and-Pie Fields ; a merry enough name, taken from an inn nearby. One Thomas Neale undertook the task of making the great junction, and, in the centre, he erected the pillar mentioned by Evelyn, with seven sundials, one for each of the streets. Seven Dials has survived, as a frantic traffic centre, but both Mr. Neale's pillar, and his name, have suffered during two and a half centuries. The pillar was taken down in 1733, because, according to Cunningham,[2] it was supposed that " a considerable sum of money was lodged at the base ". No fortune was found, and the pillar was transported to ornament " the park of a country gentle-

[1] Dr. Mead, in *Richardsoniana*, p. 317.
[2] *A Handbook for London*, Peter Cunningham, vol. II, p. 735.

man ", in Weybridge, where it still stands, as a memorial to Frederica of Prussia, Duchess of York, daughter-in-law of George III. And so heedless is Holborn of the enterprise of Mr. Neale, that when NEAL STREET was named after him, the enameller omitted the final *e* from the name-plate.

CHAPTER FOUR

Stoke Newington

" My earliest recollections of a school-life, are connected
with a large rambling, Elizabethan house in a misty-looking
village of England, where were a vast number of gigantic
and gnarled trees, and where all the houses were excessively
ancient. In truth, it was a dream-like and spirit-soothing
place, that venerable old town . . ."

EDGAR ALLAN POE, recalling his school-days in
Stoke Newington, in his autobiographical story,
William Wilson.

" My relations had not many congenial friends in the dull
village of Stock Newington when they first went there.
There were a good many Quaker families, nice, kind, respectable people but not inclined to visiting beyond their own set."

MRS. LE BRETON'S *Memoirs.*

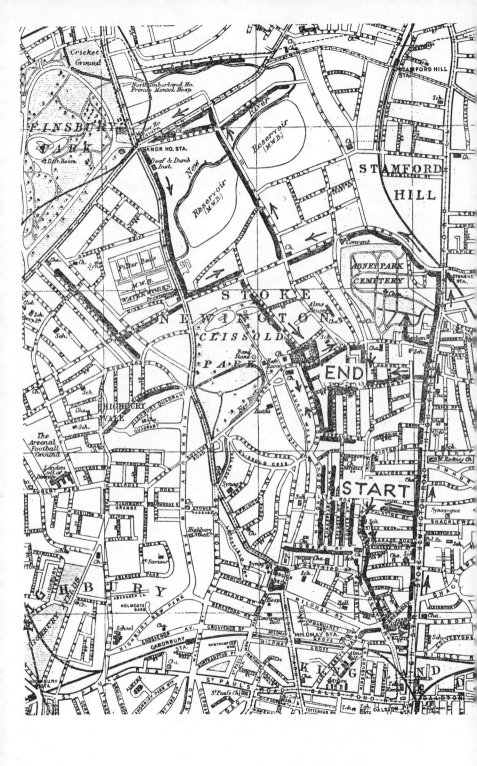

There could be no more delightful way of teaching London children their local geography than with jig-saw puzzle maps. But this complication of interlocked boundary lines makes it difficult for us to present the seventeen boroughs in tidy order, and we must sometimes leap big distances, as now, from Seven Dials in Holborn to STOKE NEWINGTON in the north.

About one hundred years ago, Leigh Hunt wrote in *The Town* :

> In Paris they have streets named after men of letters. There is the *Quai de Voltaire* ; and one of the most frequented thoroughfares in that metropolis, for it contains the Post-Office, is *Jean Jacques Rousseau Street*. It is not unlikely that a similar custom will take place in England before long. A nobleman, eminent for his zeal in behalf of the advancement of society, has called a road in his neighbourhood, *Addison Road*.

The prophecy came true, and streets all over London (birthplace of Chaucer, Spenser, Ben Jonson, Milton, Herrick, Pope, Gray, Blake, Keats and Browning) were named after the more reliable poets and prose writers. Byron heads the list with 19 streets ; next comes Ruskin with 18, Tennyson 15, Shakespeare 13, Addison 12, Chaucer 10, Carlyle 10, Wordsworth and Shelley 9 each, Coleridge 8, Dryden 5, and, most curiously matched, Pepys and Southey with 4. Donne, Defoe, Boswell, Keats, Macaulay, Congreve, Meredith, Galsworthy and Kipling can claim two streets each. Ben Jonson, Bunyan, Leigh Hunt and Barrie are remembered with only one.

When we arrived at the southern end of Stoke Newington, we came on a network of streets named after poets—SHAKESPEARE, SPENSER, MILTON, COWPER and WORDSWORTH. This was no idle Victorian gesture, but a deliberate move in social history. Wordsworth Road had long been *Cut Throat Lane*, the haunt of rapscallions, but the change to Wordsworth seemed to frighten them away. The authorities made doubly sure by directing all the poets' streets into HOWARD ROAD. John Howard (Pl. 15) (1726-90) was a romantic sort of reformer [1] who was left a fortune when young and went

---

[1] In the north-west corner of the Borough is WILBERFORCE ROAD, named after the fighter for the abolition of the slave trade. William Wilberforce did not live in Stoke Newington ; he asked to be buried there, beside his sister, in the churchyard of St. Mary's, but he was accorded a national burial in the Abbey.

travelling abroad. His ship was intercepted and, after being cast into prison at Brest, he returned home and lived in Stoke Newington. He remained so shocked by what he had seen that he devoted the rest of his life to cleansing the prison life in England.

From Wordsworth Road we walked past the end of St. Matthais Road and found BOLEYN ROAD, which marks the southern tip of the Borough. Then we noticed that the adjoining street, across the border, in Islington, was KING HENRY'S WALK, with KINGSBURY ROAD nearby, and KINGSLAND HIGH STREET just across the border in Hackney. The three boroughs meet near the point where King Henry's Walk joins Boleyn Road. These royal names were not dropped on the land by accident. A quarter of a mile away, to the west, we found NEWINGTON GREEN, (*Newyngtongrene* in 1480), where King Henry VIII had a hunting lodge, known in later years as Bishop's Place. When some dismal tenements were pulled down on Newington Green at the beginning of the last century, gilt wainscoting and frescoes of the right date and fashion were revealed out of the dust.

From Boleyn Road we walked, just over the Borough boundary, along JOHN CAMPBELL ROAD—probably named after the early 19th-century Lord Chancellor, John, Baron Campbell, whose efforts as a biographer prompted a contemporary to re-hash the old *bon-mot*, that Campbell " had added a new terror to death ". We then came to Stoke Newington's main street—here named STOKE NEWINGTON ROAD—which follows the line of the Roman road from London to Lincoln.

It is not easy to believe that London covers the rubble of a Roman city. We see mouldering walls, a stone coffin, or a handful of coins, and we are asked to believe that they are the relics of a valiant and lively civilisation ; that dull Claudius once came here, and that his legions once dominated this essentially English earth. It is difficult to realise that the close-packed shops of today thrive where our ancestors once laboured under their Roman masters, making a strategic highway across the woods and fields.

The legions departed ; the Saxons, the Danes, and then the Normans came. In the *Domesday Book* there is a record of the parish of *Neutone* : it is surmised that the prefix, *Stoke*, a common English word deriving from the Saxon *Stok*, a wood, was not added until the time of Richard II. We read of *Stoke Newton*, or *Newnton*, in 1774, as " a pleasant village near Islington where a great number of the citizens of London have built houses, and rendered it extremely populous, more like a large flourishing town. . . ." But the " flourishing town " was no more than a hamlet, with less than two hundred dwellings. It was not until the end of the Napoleonic Wars that real prosperity came ; and, at the time of Queen Victoria's birth, there were more than 1,600 houses in the parish. This was the story of perhaps twenty other sequestered villages about London, that spread until they joined hands and formed the vast circle of suburban hinterland.

The first interesting street that attracted us, opening off Stoke Newington Road, was PALATINE ROAD. The scene and the period change to the Palatinate in Bavaria, at the end of the 17th century, when thousands of Protestant Palatines were forced to accept Catholic oppression, or leave their homes. As has so often happened, England offered a haven to some of the exiles. On 15 August, 1709, at " a vestry held . . . for the Parish of Stoke Newington ", it was agreed " That the Parish is willing to Settle ffour ffamilies of the Palatines to the Number not exceeding twenty persons, at the rate of ffive pounds per head—provided that other parishes do the same ".[1] So the Palatines, and the street-name, came to Stoke Newington.

Near the intersection of Palatine Road, the shopping thoroughfare becomes STOKE NEWINGTON HIGH STREET. The map of the streets opening on the left for the next half-mile seemed so dull that we hurried on, in a taxi-cab. Brighton Road, Victorian Road and York-shire Grove were not tantalising, and we came on only one street-name in this area that made us curious—KYNASTON ROAD. This was once *Pawnbrokers Alley*—hardly a genteel address for the villas that were built here in the 1870's—and Kynaston was substituted, but we could not find any local reason for this choice. The *Dictionary of National Biography* presents a group of possible Kynastons, including Sir Francis, the early 17th-century " centre of a brilliant coterie at Court " ; Herbert, who was " high-master of St. Paul's School ", 1838–76 ; John, who busied himself with controversial pamphlets ; and Edward, the Restoration actor, who was such a female stage beauty that, according to a contemporary,[2] " it has since been disput-

---

[1] *The History of the Palatine Estate and Charity*, J. R. Spratling.
[2] Downes's *Roscius Anglicanus*, 1708, quoted in Cunningham's *Handbook for London*.

able among the judicious, whether any woman that succeeded him so sensibly touched the audience as he ".

We continued northwards for another two hundred yards, and turned into Stoke Newington Church Street to see a cul-de-sac on the right, so small and apparently unimportant that it was not named on either of our maps. This is FLEETWOOD ROAD, which nestles at the southern end of ABNEY PARK CEMETERY. Charles Fleetwood (1618–92) was the Parliamentarian who married Cromwell's second daughter, Bridget. After the Protector's death, Fleetwood was alternately in and out of power as Commander-in-Chief, until 1659, when he withdrew to the quiet and piety of his mansion on the edge of the present cemetery.

The name Abney takes us back two and a half centuries : this is one of the few old family names associated with the Borough that has survived. In 1700 the manor[1] of Stoke Newington came into the possession of the wife of Sir Thomas Abney, and it was given the name of Lady Abney's Land. When the last Abney died, the lease of the manor was bought by a wealthy merchant named Eade. The lands were ultimately broken up, but there are memorials to the early manor in several local place-names—MANOR ROAD, LORDSHIP GROVE, PARK, ROAD and TERRACE, also BARN STREET, and MEADOW STREET, built on the House Meadow. And there is EADE ROAD, by Harringay, in the far north of the Borough, to remind us of the last owner before the estate was scattered.

We kept our taxi-cab, driven by an old hand who, during the first half-mile, had treated us as being mildly dangerous. When we had taken him into our confidence, he eyed our maps, and ourselves, as if we were less dangerous but truly mad. We asked him to drive us to Manor Road, which is north of Abney Park Cemetery ; then up Lordship Road, between the two immense reservoirs, and into SEVEN SISTERS ROAD—a gentle name to have settled on such a long, harsh thoroughfare. It is a pity that we have no more than the misty legend, of a merchant in the late 17th or early 18th century who planted seven elm trees on Page Green, one for each of his seven daughters. John Rocque's Survey marks the spot as 7 *Sesters*, in 1754, but the highway of today was not made until 1831–3.

Seven Sisters Road led us south-west to Manor House Underground

---

[1] The present Town Hall and Library are built on the site of the old manor house which was destroyed in 1695.

Station, on the Borough boundary, where we abandoned the cab and went the rest of the way on foot. Unless one is a devoted scholar one can become weary of the interminable story of early manorial rights in and about London. We did not go very deep into the history of the separate, northern manor of Hornsey, known as the Manor of Brown's Wood. It is one more old name that has been lost, except for BROWNSWOOD ROAD, which crosses Wilberforce Road, at the extreme west of the Borough.

In addition to Seven Sisters Road, there are two interesting thoroughfares that cross at Manor House : the longest of them, stretching from one end of the Borough to the other, is GREEN LANES, formerly *Green Lanes Turnpike Road*. It is amusing to read of these early turnpikes being wrecked, and the wretched toll collectors manhandled, by local residents who hated paying the tolls. Feeling was so violent among the inhabitants of Newington Green, at the other end of *Green Lanes Turnpike Road*, that, in the reign of George III, they gained exemption from the tax ; a privilege they enjoyed until the tolls were finally abolished. The other street, which curves like a boomerang between the reservoirs and the Seven Sisters Road, is WOODBERRY DOWN. Here we have an instance of the way in which place-names have been twisted by use. The original name was *Berrie Down Wood*, but when the trees were felled to make pasture land, the name was no longer relevant, and it became Woodberry Down.

Other descriptive field-names in the Borough include RIVERSDALE ROAD, to the west of Clissold Park : the New River is submerged here, before it comes to light in the Park. On the eastern side of the Park is GRAZEBROOK ROAD, where Hackney Brook once " grazed " this part of the land ; and there is SANDBROOK ROAD in the lower heart of the Borough—with no record of a brook ever having run here, but with a subsoil of clay and sand, indicating that there was water at one time.

We left Green Lanes and turned east along Lordship Park, into QUEEN ELIZABETH'S WALK, which skirts the edge of CLISSOLD PARK. Here were two romantic stories, of a Queen, and of a humble curate. It is certain that Queen Elizabeth sometimes visited the Lord and Lady of the Manor, and that she liked to walk between two rows of elm trees that ran in the direction of the present road ; certain also that one day she took " a jewel of great value from her hair " and " made a present of it " to her hosts' little daughter. But this was not enough for the local historian, Dr. Robinson,[1] writing in 1820. He claimed that " in the memory of two old gentlemen living about the year 1763 ", there was a brick tower in which Elizabeth had been hidden from the treachery of her sister. And one of these old gentlemen " positively asserted that a stair-case had been in existence which led up to the identical spot where the Princess had been concealed ".

The second story concerns Clissold Park, where nature leaps free from the oppression of bricks and tiles, over an area of twenty acres. Here are two lakes, and a stretch of the winding New River, allowed to emerge for half a mile, before it goes back to its prison beneath the pavements. Here is the agreeable setting for an early 19th-century romance. This land was then known as Crawshay's Farm, and the owner, Mr. Crawshay, had a great fortune, great pride, and at least one pretty daughter. She was courted by the curate, the Reverend Augustus Clissold, but the father would have none of it. The Reverend Augustus Clissold had no fortune, but he had patience ; and, when Mr. Crawshay died, the curate married the pretty daughter and changed both her name and the name of the farm.

At the southern end of Queen Elizabeth's Walk we turned into EDWARD'S LANE, named after an important early 18th-century builder. At the far corner of the lane, on the north side of Stoke Newington Church Street, was an exciting find. The shop at No. 176 Church Street stands on ground that once belonged to Manor House School, where Edgar Allan Poe went as a pupil when he was six years old. He remained at the school four years, until his foster father took him back to America. Poe's teacher at Manor House School had been Dr. Bransby, whom the dissolute and brilliant writer afterwards recalled in his short story, *William Wilson*, published in 1840.

There is no Poe Street in Stoke Newington, but the Council recently showed their good sense and imagination by placing a bronze tablet to his memory in the Central Library, four houses away from No. 176.

We turned west, for a few yards, along Stoke Newington Church Street, and then south, along Albion Road, for a diversion. We came on BARBAULD ROAD, named after Anna Letitia Barbauld (Pl. 14) (1743–1825), teacher, poet, and editor of *British Novelists*—some fifty volumes with her own biographical and critical notes. Mrs.

[1] *The History and Antiquities of Stoke Newington*, William Robinson, 1820.

Barbauld's numerous literary works have been largely forgotten, but she shines pleasantly in many reminiscences of the time. Dr. Johnson, who " did not greatly approve of literature as a career for women ", had for her " the highest praise ". Garrick described her as " She who sang the sweetest Lay " ; and Wordsworth went so far as to say that she was the " first of literary women ". She went to live in Stoke Newington in 1802, and there she wrote her life of Samuel Richardson and edited his correspondence.

We began our story of Stoke Newington with the poets : it ends with one of the greatest of all English novelists. After returning along Albion Road, and walking east, we turned into DEFOE ROAD ; shabby in the late afternoon, with signs of the brave, harsh life of the people who live nearby. There was a ragged boy with a home-made trolley ; a sly and hungry cat ; the stark lines of a new building of flats, rising where a bomb had smashed a group of little houses ; and—the touch of pride we usually found in poor streets—scrubbed doorsteps, and washed lace curtains, parted to frame a geranium in an ornamental pot.

Daniel Defoe went to live in Stoke Newington in 1708 : seven years later he was building " a large house on the south side " of Church Street. We read, " It was square in plan, the walls, which were of red brick and very thick, being raised, as the fashion then was, so as to conceal the roof ; it had deep window seats, curious cupboards in recesses, and massive bolts and locks to its doors. . . . The garden, with its ' green walk ' and other pleasure grounds, which covered four acres, was bounded on the south by Pawnbrokers Lane. . . ."

The circle of our day was complete. Pawnbrokers Lane (Alley) was the Kynaston Road we had found, soon after we began. But the garden with its green walk had gone ; also the house " of red brick and very thick " (Pl. 16). There was but this one, undistinguished street, with a tall wall. " If he built the house in 1715 ", said Derek Peel, " he must have been here when he was writing *Robinson Crusoe*. It was published in 1719." We stood on the curbed pavement and looked up at the wall. Defoe Road, with its little houses and bombed site, cut right across what must have been Defoe's garden. Was it possible that he had been sitting behind that wall when he wrote the words, " It happened one day about noon, going towards my boat, I was exceedingly surprised with the print of a man's naked foot on the shore, which was very plain to be seen in the sand : I stood like one thunderstruck, or as if I had seen an apparition " ?

We moved forwards and read, on a plaque, " Daniel Defoe lived here. . . ." We walked to the corner again and read, over a door, " Morris & Stone, Distributors of Toys and Fancy Goods ". So we opened the door of Messrs. Morris & Stone, and rang a bell.

" Yes," we were told, " this is the spot where Defoe wrote *Robinson Crusoe*, but it's changed a good deal since then."

We had a long talk with a friendly man, who did not seem to mind our not being customers. He told us that he liked selling toys from the ground on which Daniel Defoe used to live : that he was sure Defoe would also be pleased with the idea of cowboy hats, holsters, and the like, being sold to boys in love with adventure. When we departed, he gave us a beautiful model of a hansom cab, with movable driver, pliable reins and all, sold in the shops for one-and-elevenpence. " It's a present," he said. " Most everyone who comes in here just comes for business. It's a change, having a talk about *Robinson Crusoe*."

14. MRS. BARBAULD   15. JOHN HOWARD, BY MATHER BROWN

16. DANIEL DEFOE'S HOUSE IN STOKE NEWINGTON,
BY T. H. CRAWFORD

17. MAJOR JOHN ANDRÉ

18. THE QUEEN OF BOHEMIA.
BY HONTHORST

CHAPTER FIVE

Hackney

" With my wife only to take the ayre, it being very warm and pleasant, to Bowe and Old Ford ; and thence to Hackney. There light, and played at shuffle-board, eat cream and good cherries ; and so with good refreshment home."

PEPYS'S *Diary*, 11th June, 1664.

We began to explore HACKNEY more or less where we had ended our searches in Stoke Newington. It was a wet and horrid Saturday morning, so we guarded ourselves, our maps and books, in a hired car. As I stepped in, I commented on the sign *hackney carriage*, beside the tail light, and suggested that the first hackney carriage perhaps came from the Borough. But Derek Peel had not wasted his evening : he handed me Mr. Ivor Brown's *Having the Last Word*, in which I read, " A Hackney horse is not named after a portion of the East of London ; indeed the animal ' came over with the Conqueror ' and began most loftily. He, or more commonly she, was an ambling horse for the use of ladies (haquenée) . . . the hackney-horse became the hired horse, a tame and tired beast with no troublesome show of mettle."

Then came a footnote from *The Town* : " Captain Bailey, said to have accompanied Raleigh in his last expedition to Guiana, employed four hackney coaches, with drivers in liveries, to ply at the May-pole in the Strand, fixing his own rates, about the year 1634. Bailey's coaches seem to have been the first of what are now called hackney coaches ; a term at that time applied indiscriminately to all coaches let for hire."

The origin of the name of the Borough is different, and less clear. It has survived, in varying forms, since the 12th-century *Hakeneia*, and is believed to refer to the " well watered land or marsh " that belonged to one *Haca* ; another ancient personal name with a topographical suffix.[1]

The weather had improved in temper when we came to Stoke Newington Road, so we made our way on foot. My collaborator offered one more piece of etymological information. He said, " There is, of course, another corruption of the word *hackney*." He shook his notes in my face and added, " We have the word *hack*— the one who does all the work ! "

We were near the end of Kynaston Road, just south of where Stoke Newington High Street becomes STAMFORD HILL, within the Borough of Hackney. As this lies along the old Roman road between London and Lincoln, we supposed that it might take its name from Stamford Bridge in Yorkshire—the scene of King Harold's victory

[1] *The Place-Names of Middlesex*, p. 105.

in 1066. But we had to bow to the ruling of the scholars ; that Stamford Hill was *Sanford* in 1255, and later *Sandfordhull,* "a hill by a sandy ford ".[1] The ford was across the river Lea, which still forms more than a mile of the boundary between Hackney and Leyton ; the hill is the one on which James I paused, after his long journey from Scotland, to look towards London and exclaim, " At last, the richest jewel in a monarch's crown is mine ! "

When one finds a well-known place-name on the map, like Stamford Hill, it is interesting to run the magnifying glass over the surrounding district and seek for survivals of the same name in ancient forms. There are SANFORD TERRACE and SANFORD LANE, both in Hackney. But we tread warily here, for we know now that many writers on London have set down, as facts, notions that have no roots in history. Among our books was *Glimpses of Ancient Hackney* by Benjamin Clarke, who modestly wrote under the initials F. R. C. S. He claimed that Sanford Lane in Hackney was named after Thomas Day (1748–89), author of the famous old children's book, *Sanford and Merton.* But the title of the book is *Sandford and Merton,* and there is no Sandford Street, Road or Lane, anywhere in the Borough.

We walked south along Stoke Newington High Street, to find a suitable side street by which to assault Hackney. We were fortunate : we came on TYSSEN ROAD;[2] then, about three hundred yards south, was AMHURST ROAD, which curves south-east into the heart of the Borough. The Tyssens, of Dutch origin, became powerful and rich in Hackney in the 17th and 18th centuries : when Francis Tyssen died in 1717, his funeral was " so sumptuous as to call forth a special notice in the Gazette . . . animadverting upon the style, and setting forth what should be done, according to the grade in society of the deceased. . . ."[3] In 1766 Mary Tyssen was married to Captain John Amherst, R.N., and the name Tyssen seems to have been absorbed into the Amherst family, who became barons of Hackney in 1892. It is curious that although they spell their name with an *e,* the places named after them, AMHURST PARK, AMHURST ROAD and AMHURST TERRACE, are all spelled with a *u.*

We walked a long way down Amhurst Road before we came on a name that stirred our imagination—ANDRÉ STREET, named after

---

[1] *The Place-Names of Middlesex,* p. 107.

[2] There is also TYSSEN STREET, in the south-west of the Borough.

[3] *Glimpses of Ancient Hackney,* by F. R. C. S. (1893), p. 73.

Major John André (Pl. 17), Hackney's greatest hero, born there in 1751. At twenty-three he joined the Seventh (Royal Fusiliers) in Canada, and soon began the adventures—secret negotiations with the traitor Benedict Arnold ; escape, capture, and the discovery of the secret plans in his boots—that led to his being hanged as a spy by Washington's orders. The sentence was considered to be so harsh that all the British Army went into mourning for him. In 1821, André's body was brought back to England and buried in the Abbey ; and Hackney gave his name to a street, leading from Amhurst Road to the southern edge of Hackney Downs.

At the end of Amhurst Road we came to the heart of the Borough, and of its more ancient history.

We turned into busy MARE STREET[1]—not recalling a horse, but corrupted from *Merestret* (1443)—which took its name from an ancient hamlet on the south edge of the parish, and its meaning from *mere*, a boundary. Then into BOHEMIA PLACE, where one might have wept for the ingratitude of history. This blind little street, with bombed houses on one side, waste land so sour that no grass would grow on it, and, at the end, a tram depot, is named after the " Queen of Hearts " (Pl. 18).

Princess Elizabeth was not yet seven years old when her father became King James I of England. In 1613 she was married to Frederick V, the Elector Palatine, and five years later she was crowned Queen of Bohemia. Then came her romantic and pathetic story ; of escape, miseries, and secret romances,[2] until she returned to England at the Restoration. On February 17, 1662, Evelyn wrote in his Diary that, during " such a storm of hail, thunder, and lightening, as was never seen the like in any man's memory, was buried in West-minster-Abbey the Queen of Bohemia, after all her sorrows and afflictions being come to die in the arms of her nephew, the King. . . . "

The Hackney tram depot, rising in supreme ugliness from the rubble and dead earth, is built on the site of a mansion in which Princess Elizabeth lived for a brief spell, before she went to Heidelberg, to be carried into the castle as a bride.

---

[1] Other Hackney streets, with animal names, might easily have deceived us. RAM PLACE was named after Stephen Ram, who built Ram's Chapel in 1723. SHEEP LANE was *Ship Lane*, in a mid-16th-century survey ; and LAMB LANE recalls the heraldic emblem of the Knights Templars—the Lamb and Flag.

[2] See Craven Hill, Road and Terrace, chapter on Paddington, p. 148.

There was one redeeming view in this jumble of trams, ruins and dust : to the north lay the churchyard, and, at the nearest corner of the sheltered grass, we saw ancient HACKNEY TOWER. We walked over and found a street dustman brushing the steps. "Yes", it was "a rare old history place", he said.

The Tower, and the Chapel of the Rowe (Roe) family, are all that remain of the early Tudor parish church of St. Augustine. Sir Thomas Roe was a Merchant Taylor, and Mayor of London in 1568. He is mentioned by Stow[1] because he "inclosed with a wall of bricke nigh one acre of ground, pertayning to the Hospital of Bethlehem, to be a buriall for the dead", but he was himself buried in Hackney, and honoured in the name of ROWE LANE, immediately north-east of the churchyard. The ancient church was pulled down in 1798, and the present Parish Church of St. John at Hackney was built in its place.

We paused in the churchyard, looked at our maps, and found that the surrounding streets were full of promise, and not without humour. To the north-east of the churchyard, URSWICK ROAD and LESBIA ROAD meet, almost in front of the public baths.

From the churchyard we walked along ST. JOHN'S CHURCH ROAD, into Urswick Road, named after Christopher Urswick (1448–1522), the diplomatist, who held the rectory of Hackney for the last twenty years of his life. It was a curious demand on our imagination, to link this quiet little street of villas with the friend of Erasmus and Sir Thomas More ; the man who helped to secure the throne for Henry VII, and who was sent to Spain to arrange the marriage between Prince Arthur and Catherine of Aragon. The name of Lesbia Road seemed even more incongruous, for we could find no reason why Catullus of Verona—Tennyson's "tenderest of Roman poets nineteen hundred years ago"—should be celebrated with a street-name in Hackney.

Lesbia Road turns south into TRESHAM AVENUE, named after Sir Thomas Tresham (d. 1559), Grand Prior of the Order of St. John— to which estates in Hackney were given when the Order of the Knights Templars was dissolved in 1312. Both orders have left their mark in the Hackney street-names. Tresham Road leads into TEMPLAR ROAD, and, in the far east of the Borough, are TEMPLE MILLS ROAD and TEMPLE MILLS BRIDGE. After the dissolution of the Knights

[1] Stow, vol. 1, p. 165.

Templars, names associated with the Order of St. John were used for many of the streets : among those that survive are PALACE ROAD and PRIORY PLACE—near the site of the palace of the prior, half-way between St. John's Church and the southern boundary.

We walked down Templar Road into HOMERTON ROW—derived from the name of an ancient farm—and then returned west, to the southern end of Urswick Road. We had a choice here, between SUTTON PLACE (no doubt named after Thomas, founder of Charter-house School) and Isabella Road, which we took, to find ourselves in Mehetabel Street, for which we can offer no explanation. The morning had gone, so we walked back to Mare Street—by way of the tram depot and Bohemia Place—and found a public house where we lunched well enough. When we came out, rain was threatening, so we made the rest of the journey in a taxi-cab.

South of Bohemia Place was MORNING LANE, which has a curious etymological history, according to the editors of *The Place-Names of Middlesex*. It was *Mourning Lane* in 1732, and *Money Lane* 1741-5. We drove this way and soon found, on the right, STOCKMAR ROAD. Baron Stockmar was the Coburg doctor who became the devoted adviser and friend of both Prince Albert and Queen Victoria. Lord Melbourne described him as " one of the cleverest fellows " he had ever seen, and Queen Victoria wrote that Stockmar had her " *most entire* confidence ", so it is suitable that he should have a memorial in London.

We turned down Stockmar Road, into FRAMPTON PARK ROAD. Major Heathfield Frampton was another Hackney hero, of a different sort : he went to fight in the Crimean War with only one arm. When the Russians took him prisoner they were so touched by his gallantry that he was spared and taken to St. Petersburg, where he was treated with kindness by the Tsar and his family.

We returned to Morning Lane and drove east, to WICK ROAD, which is surrounded by the district of HACKNEY WICK ; an odd name with a fascinating origin. Wick simply means "dairy farm", and the name goes back to the 13th century, when the Knights Templars granted some three hundred acres of pasture land to a man named Robert, who took the surname of *de la Wike*. This is an example illustrating the practice of taking surnames from the nature of the lands held by their owners. Robert de la Wike was " Robert of the Dairy Farm ", just as the early owners of HACKNEY DOWNS and

HACKNEY MARSH were called William atte Doune and John de Mersshe.[1]

We found no streets opening off Wick Road to make us curious, so we turned south-west along CASSLAND ROAD—an important name in the history of the Borough. Sir John Cass (1666–1718) bequeathed enough money to endow the Sir John Cass Institute ; still a significant educational force among the youth of Hackney. About half a mile along Cassland Road we came to the edge of Hackney Common. Here turned south-west again, along Meynell Road, and, still skirting the common, we made our way to LAMMAS ROAD—a name which had excited our interest when we first scanned a map of Hackney.

The word " Lammas " is derived from the old-English *hlaf-maesse*, meaning *loaf-mass*—the mass or festival of the wheat harvest when, as in the Harvest Thanksgiving services of our time, the parishioners brought to their church a loaf made from the new wheat of the year. Lammas Lands were a relic of the " open-field " method of agriculture, whereby the owners had the right to grow and gather crops from Lady Day (March 25) to Lammas Day (August 1). All the fences had then to be taken down and the fields opened to those with the common rights of pasturage. As late as 1875, there were quarrels in Hackney over these privileges. The lord of the manor in that year had set up wooden posts and iron railings to protect what he considered to be his rights, but the angry inhabitants pulled them down. Today, what were Lammas Lands in the Borough are under the control of the municipality, and the lord of the manor is a powerless and almost mythical figure.

From Lammas Road we sped west along Victoria Park Road at thirty miles an hour. The district was already settling into its week-end quiet and there was nothing to divert us until we came again to Mare Street. Here we turned north until we reached Lamb Lane (see footnote, p. 54) which led us to the pleasant edge of London Fields. Then to Martello Street, Eleanor Road, Richmond Lane, NAVARINO ROAD (the naval battle of Navarino, which established the independence of Greece, was fought in 1827), and on to Dalston Lane and RIDLEY ROAD, which brought us back to the western boundary, but also back to the beginning of Hackney's street history.

In 1290, King Edward I had granted the lordship of the manor to the Bishops of London, who held it until the time of Nicholas Ridley,

[1] *The Place-Names of Middlesex*, p. 108.

who was Bishop in 1549. In 1550, the lands in Hackney reverted to the Crown, and, five years later, Ridley, with Latimer, was burned at the stake in Oxford, for heresy.

There were two more names of interest, in the south-west of the Borough, contained in a rectangle that juts, like a step, into Islington. This rectangle is called DE BEAUVOIR TOWN—named after Richard de Beauvoir, a native of Guernsey, who came here in 1680. (DE BEAUVOIR ROAD, SQUARE and CRESCENT are all contained within this area.) Until 1840 this was open country, with a few grand houses : then De Beauvoir Town was built, to accommodate some of the growing early-Victorian population. Before Richard de Beauvoir, the land was owned by Sir George Whitmore,[1] master of the Haberdashers' Company, Sheriff of London in 1622, Lord Mayor in 1631, and knighted in 1632; but withal a man of fine independence, for he was twice imprisoned for not paying his taxes.

During the reign of Henry VIII, the land belonged to two brothers —Spanish merchants called Balmes, who named their mansion Balmes House. (They are remembered in one small thoroughfare, BALMES ROAD, parallel with De Beauvoir Crescent, in the south.) It was in the garden of Balmes House, more than a hundred years later, that King Charles I was met by the Lord Mayor and Aldermen of London, after his fruitless journey to Scotland where he had hoped to enlist the help of the Scottish army against the English Parliament. It was on November 25, 1641, that he paused in Hackney, before driving on to London where Evelyn saw him " ride through the City . . . with great acclamations and joy of the giddy people ".

[1] There is a WHITMORE ROAD, just over the southern boundary of Hackney, in the Borough of Shoreditch.

CHAPTER SIX

Shoreditch

"Courage, I say; as long as the merry pence hold out, you shall none of you die in Shoreditch."

JOHN DRYDEN, *The Kind Keeper,*
or Mr. Limberham, 1680.

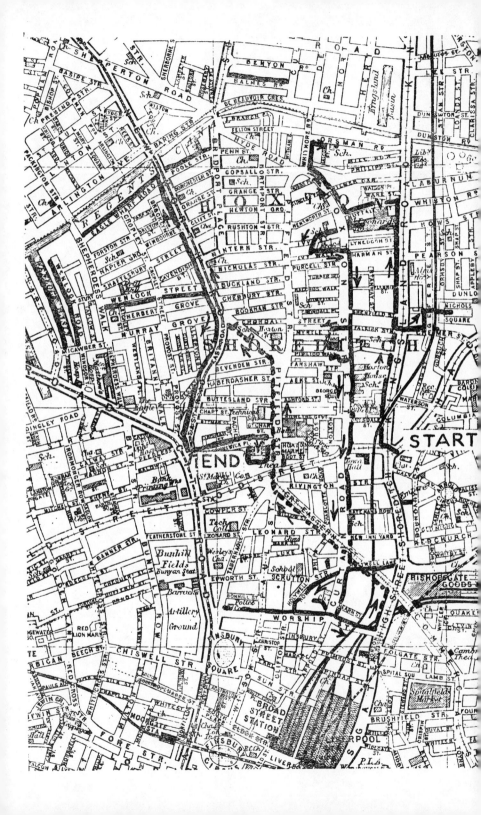

Jane Shore (Pl. 19) must have been a charming woman, not unlike Nell Gwynne in character, but marked for a sad and different fate. About the year 1470 she left her husband—a goldsmith—to become a mistress of King Edward IV, and, although she enjoyed both luxury and power, according to Sir Thomas More she never " abused it to any man's hurt, but to many a man's comfort and relief ". When the King died she found other sponsors ; but after Richard III came to the throne he treated her mercilessly, in memory of the hatred he had borne his brother. Jane Shore was made to walk through the streets, taper in hand, dressed only in her kirtle. She lived long into the reign of Henry VIII, " lean, withered and dried up ", and forced to " beg a living of many that had begged if she had not been ". It is believed that she died, in what is now the Borough of Shoreditch, about 1527, in miserable poverty. Out of her story came a fictitious explanation of why the Borough was given its name. The old ballad in Percy's *Reliques* credits Jane Shore with this unhappy song :

> Thus weary of my life, at length
> I yielded up my vital strength
> Within a ditch of loathsome scent
> Where carrion-dogs did much frequent.

> The which now since my dying daye
> Is Shoreditch call'd, as authors say ;
> Which is a witness of my sinne
> For beinge concubine to a King.

The more reasonable explanation of SHOREDITCH is less dramatic than this. The lord of the manor, in the reign of Edward III, was named Soerdich : there was Sir John de Soerdich, warrior, lawyer and statesman, who had fought beside the Black Prince, against the French. There is a third, less pretty alternative : that Shoreditch is merely a modified form of Sewerditch, as the word *sewer* was often spelled *shore*.

An old nursery rhyme, *The Bells of London*, to which we have all played the game of *Oranges and Lemons* in our time, gave us the clue we needed for a starting point in our walk through Shoreditch.

Gay go up and gay go down,
To ring the bells of London town. . . .

When will you pay me ?
Say the bells of Old Bailey.

When I grow rich,
Say the bells of Shoreditch. . . .

The bells, a peal of twelve which Queen Elizabeth liked to hear, were those of St. Leonard's Church (Pl. 20), first built in the 9th century. We drove to the intersection of the four main roads of the Borough—High Street, Old Street, Kingsland Road and Hackney Road. Here we found the present church, opened in 1740, with a lofty steeple, and masses of poplar and plane trees in the surrounding churchyard ; one of the few green open spaces in the Borough. This is the third church to be built on the site : the second, built in the 13th century and demolished in 1736, was known as the " Actors' Church " —for a very good reason. The earliest theatres in London were built in Shoreditch, by James Burbage, father of the great Richard. They were The Theatre, and the Courtein (Curtain), and the first of these was opened eighteen years before the Globe in Southwark.

We went into St. Leonard's Church and found the Burbage Memorial, on which we read the inscription :

This stone is placed here to the glory of God, and in acknowledgement for the work done in English drama by the players, musicians and other men of the theatre who are buried within the precincts of this church. . . .

Then followed a list of names, including those of three members of the Burbage family ; Richard Tarlton, the great Elizabethan comic actor, and Gabriel Spencer, who was killed " in the fields at Shoreditch . . . with a certain sword of iron and steel " by Ben Jonson. The association with the early theatre gives Shoreditch its chief historical flavour, but there is scant record of this in the street-names, and we could trace only Curtain Road, named after Burbage's second theatre.

Up to Queen Elizabeth's time, plays and interludes were considered suitable for the gentry, but a dangerous diversion for the poor, who could be better improved by toil. Queen Mary had gone so far as to suppress all performances of plays within the City of London.

But there was a way out, and the way led to Shoreditch ; near enough for a carriage drive, but beyond the jurisdiction of the Lord Mayor.

In 1576, James Burbage, a joiner and one of the Earl of Leicester's players, secured the lease of a barn in Shoreditch, with adjoining land on which he built The Theatre. There, and at the Curtain, built some time later, Burbage's son, Richard (Pl. 22) (1567–1619), made his name as the greatest tragedian of his time ; there also, it seems certain, Shakespeare arrived from Stratford to work as a call boy in the theatre. It was at the Curtain that Shakespeare later sponsored the first production of Ben Jonson's *Every Man in His Humour*.

But Shoreditch has taken little heed of all this : the nearest Shakespeare street is in Stoke Newington ; there is a Ben Jonson Road in Stepney, and a Burbage Road in Camberwell ; but no reminder of them in this borough where there are so many dull street-names that might be changed, in memory of these exciting Elizabethans.

We paused in the churchyard—where the ancient stocks and whipping-post have been retained as an unfriendly warning to the children who play there—and we studied our maps. We had recently found a copy of " Smith's new & correct pocket plan " of London, dated 1805, and it revealed a charming impression of what Shoreditch must have looked like at the beginning of the 19th century—with a handful of little streets and lanes, spreading tentatively between gardens and the countryside.

Part of the refreshing plantation of trees and lawns about St. Leonard's Church is named the FAIRCHILD GARDEN,[1] after Thomas Fairchild, who was one of the great London botanists of the early 18th century. His gardens and vineyards were in Hoxton. " I cannot omit to mention with applause the name of Fairchild," wrote Dr. Pulteney, a contemporary scientist. Thomas Fairchild's skill as a gardener was close-wrapped with his religious convictions. When he died, in 1729, he left funds for the Botanical Sermon which is still preached each Whitsun Tuesday, at St. Leonard's. In Fairchild's own words, this sermon must be based on " The Wonderful Works of God in the Creation, or on the certainty of the resurrection of the dead, proved by the certain changes on the animal and vegetable parts of the Creation ".

[1] There is also a FAIRCHILD STREET and a Fairchild block of flats in Shoreditch.

There were several names on our 1805 map that demanded attention —Ivy Lane, Dirty Lane, and Land of Promise—so we made our way up Kingsland Road, which divides the districts of HAGGERSTON and HOXTON. These Ugly Sisters of London place-names are both old, and are listed in the *Domesday Book* as *Hergotestane* and *Hochestone*.

About half-way between St. Leonard's Church and the northern boundary, we were diverted from our quest for the Land of Promise and Dirty Lane, first by CREMER STREET,[1] then by the splendid sight of the GEFFRYE MUSEUM and almshouses which were damaged during the war. This remarkable museum, set among trees and lavishly surrounded by flowers, includes period panel rooms, exhibits illustrating the evolution of domestic architecture, and two pieces of the keel of what is "supposed to be the Great Harry"—the first ship of the Royal Navy, built in 1488. But our mission was to find place-names, so we walked to the back of the museum, to the little old chapel of the almshouses, and there we saw, in a niche, a statue of "Sr. Robert Geffrye, Knt., Alderman and Ironmonger, and founder of this hospital". Sir Robert Geffrye lived from 1613 to 1703, and he was one of the great benefactors of his time.

We walked then into GEFFRYE STREET, behind the museum, and found NICHOLS SQUARE, named after John Nichols (1745–1826). He edited the *Gentleman's Magazine* for thirty-eight years, and also gave us his edition of Swift's works, the *Bibliotheca Topographica Britannica* (10 vols.), *The Progresses and Public Processions of Queen Elizabeth*, and, to the abounding joy of all writers, *The Biographical Dictionary*. I don't suppose anyone this side of sixty has time nowadays to read the *Gentleman's Magazine*, copies of which pop up in the second-hand shops quite frequently, for a few pence. But they are invaluable to anyone who wishes to study the literature of the 18th century.

The greatest name that comes from Haggerston is that of Edmund Halley (Pl. 21), the astronomer (1656–1742). His father was a rich soap-boiler who sent his son to St. Paul's School and then to Oxford. From the beginning, Edmund Halley was as brilliant as his own comet. He was only seventeen when he "observed the change in the variation of the compass": at nineteen "he supplied a new and improved method of determining the elements of the planetary

[1] Sir William Cremer was Member of Parliament for Haggerston for eighteen years. In 1903 he was awarded the Nobel Prize for his work on behalf of international arbitration.

19.   THE PENANCE OF JANE SHORE

20.   ST. LEONARD'S CHURCH, ABOUT 1810

21. EDMUND HALLEY   22. RICHARD BURBAGE

23. BEN JONSON

25. BARONESS BURDETT–COUTTS,
BY W. C. ROSS

24. GEORGE DORÉE AT HIS LOOM,
BY DEREK MYNOTT

26. "THE BLIND BEGGAR OF BEDNALL GREEN",
BY WILLIAM OWEN

27. COATE'S FARM AND THE OLD GEORGE INN, 1773

orbits ". In later life, Halley lived in Islington, but Shoreditch recently honoured him by naming a building of flats after him—HALLEY HOUSE—within his native district of Haggerston.

We turned back from Nichols Square to Kingsland Road, and continued our search for Dirty Lane and Land of Promise. Dirty Lane is no more ; it now enjoys the duller name of Nuttall Street. But we found Land of Promise, leading from the east side of Hoxton Street to St. Leonard's Hospital. Nearby we came to ORSMAN ROAD by which we crossed from Kingsland Road to Whitmore Road,[1] to travel south again. William Orsman, J.P., must have been a kindhearted old eccentric. He lived until he was almost eighty-five and was known as " The Coster's Friend ". When he was very young he had been horrified by an act of injustice against the costers, so he spent the rest of his life in helping them ; by promoting donkey shows in Victoria Park, building the Costers' Hall, and gaining the trust of the poor with his rare gift of sympathy. When he died, in 1923, costers made up the greater part of those who followed him to his grave, in Abney Park Cemetery.

It became as exciting as any table game, spreading out the old and new maps side by side, and tracing the changes that have come to the land in the past one and a half centuries. We walked from Whitmore Road, and then south, along HOXTON STREET. The street formation here is old and, on our left, we found four names more or less unchanged. The Ivy Lane on our 1805 map appears twice, as Ivy Street and Ivy Walk ; Turner Square survives, then Myrtle Street, and, most fortunately, Pimlico Gardens, with the slight change to PIMLICO WALK.

Here again was an area with the pungent smell of theatre history. Nearby was No. 73 Hoxton Street, the toy-theatre shop patronised by Robert Louis Stevenson ; where his tall hat was once knocked off by a model hanging from the ceiling, and where he gathered the impressions that were written into his essay, *A Penny Plain and Twopence Coloured.*

Ben Jonson (Pl. 23) referred to Pimlico [2] in three of his plays : in *The Alchemist, Bartholomew Fair,* and *The Devil is an Ass.* In his day,

---

[1] See chapter on Hackney, p. 58.

[2] Pimlico, the district in Westminster, " was presumably copied from the Hoxton one, though there is no actual proof of this ". *The Place-Names of Middlesex,* p. 171.

the Pimlico was a drinking place used by the actors from the old Burbage theatres, and the official guide to Shoreditch comforts us with the thought that Shakespeare sometimes drank porter there. Ben Jonson wrote :

> " I'll have thee Captain Gilthead, and march up,
> And take in Pimlico, and kill the bush
> At every tavern."

And Sir Lionel, in Grene's *Tu Quoque*, published in 1614, has to say, " I have sent my daughter this morning as far as Pimlico to fetch a draught of Derby ale, that it may fetch a colour to her cheeks."

The tavern, owned by an Italian named Pimlico, was later called the *Britannia*. " In 1814 it was acquired by Mr. Samuel Lane, who . . . erected a saloon in the old Pimlico Gardens, and formed a variety company. . . . Not a few notable personages appeared there. . . . In 1851 James Anderson, the tragedian, was engaged, at a salary of £120 a week. . . . The old saloon closed its doors for ever in June, 1858, and Mr. Lane then erected the present huge building on the site, and opened the new Britannia Theatre. . . ." [1] For many years the Britannia was one of the finest theatres for melodrama in London. Afterwards it became a cinema, but it was destroyed by a bomb in 1941. There is a polite street, BRITANNIA WALK, in the south-west of the Borough, in memory of the great days when the stage of the old playhouse was alive.

The theme of the theatre continued. We walked on down Hoxton Street, which becomes Curtain Road in the south of the Borough, and we found an inscription on a modern façade, " Within a few yards stood, from 1577 to 1598, the first London building specially devoted to performances of plays, and known as ' The Theatre ' ". There was another inscription, on the same plaque, that led us to our next street-name. It read, " The site of this building forms part of what was once the Precinct of the Priory of St. John the Baptist, Holywell ".[2]

We continued south along Curtain Road and found both HOLYWELL LANE and HOLYWELL ROW—the name being derived " from a certain sweet wholesome and clear fountain or well, which, for the virtue of its water, amongst the common people was esteemed ' Holy ' ".[2]

---

[1] *The Official Guide to the Metropolitan Borough of Shoreditch*, 1940.
[2] *History and Antiquities of Shoreditch*, Henry Ellis, 1798.

We had been directed to a small alley nearby—MOTLEY COURT—by Mr. C. M. Jackson, the Borough Librarian, who has done much original research into the history of Shoreditch. Motley Court, between Scrutton Street (which leads to Holywell Row) and Christina Street, may be related to the great theatre period of the Borough's story, but its interest now is in the old holy well—discovered by Mr. Jackson—the same well that watered the lawns and supplied the needs of the 12th-century Priory.

From Motley Court we walked to WORSHIP STREET, which has nothing to do with the Priory, but was named from John Worsop, who held lands here in the 16th century. This was the southernmost point in our search. We walked along Worship Street to NORTON FOLGATE, " anciently a manor of St. Paul's ", named, perhaps, " from Richard Foliot, a canon of St. Paul's in 1241 "[1] ; then we crossed the Borough from east to west by taxi-cab, and came on an entirely different world of names, with the sound of the sea in some of them. Here, in the heart of suburban London, were EAGLE WHARF ROAD, POOLE STREET, and WENLOCK BASIN. This seafaring note was explained by a slim blue line on the map, bordering the north-western edge of the Borough, and tracing the course of the Regent's Canal, opened in August 1820. Of these names, Wenlock is old, and has been given also to a street, and a road, in Shoreditch. *Wenlocks Barn* appears on our 1805 map, but there are records of the name in this part of the country as early as the mid-13th century.

A new fact was impressed on us as we walked among the streets in this north-western part of Shoreditch. Dealing with each borough individually, for the sake of tidiness in our minds and clarity for our readers, we had been inclined to think of them as if they were separate rooms in a house. But we had come to realise that the boundaries of these northern boroughs exist on the charts of the cartographers rather than in fact. We have an example of this in the stories of Balmes House, which was actually just over the border of Hoxton, and Colebrooke Row, to which we referred in writing of Charles Lamb, in Islington. They are in different boroughs, but they become closely related when we recall Lamb, leading his sister Mary across the green fields, from the little house in Colebrooke Row, to Balmes House—then a lunatic asylum—at those terrible times when they both realised that her mind was once more becoming dark with

[1] *The Place-Names of Middlesex*, p. 147.

madness. The other link between these adjoining boroughs is less melancholy. In our chapter on Finsbury, we described the relationship between John Wesley and the place-names of that Borough. His Chapel was within a short distance of Shoreditch, and sometimes he came across the border to conduct his rousing mission.

On one occasion he chose to address a multitude in CHARLES SQUARE (believed to have been named after Charles II), which is near the western boundary of Shoreditch. Long before this, the square was famous as a healing place for the flesh : eighteen feet below the surface of the earth was revealed a strange white-coloured water, containing " no less than the original property of salt and sulphur digested with the finest vitriol of Mars ". Dr. Byfield, in 1687, extolled the virtue of these wells as " admirable against dropsies, justly recommended against the jaundice, yellow and black, melancholy and fearful passions, colick, diarrhoea, dysenterea, and the distempers called *Vapours* offending head and heart. . . ." These magic waters enjoyed their brief season of fame, and Charles Square then settled down to being a peaceful residential area. It suffered only one more disturbance, in the summer of 1741, when John Wesley held his open-air service in the square. " The persecuting rabble arranged as good as murder. A bullock was brought, in the hope of getting up a scene of wild disorder. When let loose, he quietly surveyed the crowd, but, instead of attempting to disperse it, he ran round and round, and then broke through and ran clean away, leaving Wesley calmly rejoicing and praising God." [1]

[1] *John Wesley at Charles Square*, by the Rev. W. Cuff of Shoreditch Tabernacle.

CHAPTER SEVEN

Bethnal Green

"My father," shee sayd, "is soone to be seene ;
The seely blind beggar of Bednall-greene,
That daylye sits begging for charitie,
He is the good father of prettye Bessee.

"His markes and his tokens are known very well ;
He always is led with a dogg and a bell ;
A seely olde man, God knoweth, is hee,
Yett hee is the father of prettye Bessee."
                    The Beggar's Daughter of Bednall-greene.

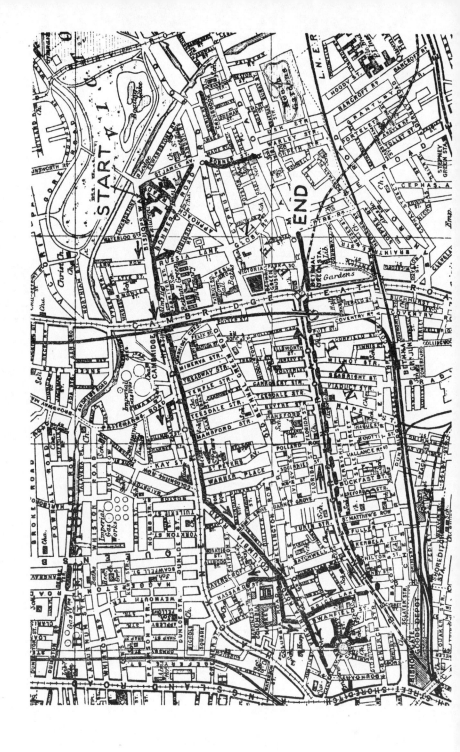

There are few monuments to wicked men, and our daily drudgery might be that much merrier if we had statues of Nero and Bluebeard in our parks, and a Bloody Mary Crescent, or an Ivan the Terrible Square, to pass through on our way to work. It must be confessed that the parade of bronze statesmen which we endure, and the names of so many noble and famous men on the plates at the ends of streets, make most of us feel that our own efforts in life's battle are not worth while.

The Borough of Bethnal Green could produce a lively company of wicked men, from George Smith, the " Brides in the Bath " murderer, and Bishop and Williams, the notorious body-snatchers of the early 1830's, to Peter the Painter, leader of the criminals besieged in neighbouring Stepney, in January, 1911. But Bethnal Green is sturdy Cockney and respectable at heart, and these startling figures are not remembered with pride. Yet there is one famous villain immortalised in its place-names ; in BONNER ROAD and BONNER STREET, near the Regent's Canal, in the north-eastern part of the Borough. Bonner Road adjoins BISHOPS WAY, a convenient place from which to begin our journey.

We have written in the chapter on Hackney of Nicholas Ridley, appointed Bishop of London in 1549. Before him came Edmund Bonner, undistinguished as a scholar, but so clever as an administrator that Wolsey made him Commissioner of the Faculties. Wolsey fell, but Bonner survived, and in 1532 Henry VIII sent him on a mission to the Pope, to obstruct the proceedings over the dissolution of his marriage with Catherine of Aragon. Bonner was made Bishop of London in 1540, when his association with Bethnal Green apparently began. He presumably lived in Bishop's Hall, near the site of the present Church of St. James-the-Less. Bonner was all things to all princes, and when Mary Tudor was crowned he was as fervent in restoring papal supremacy as he had been in denouncing it for King Henry. Under Queen Mary, his villainy became complete and, with his connivance, two hundred " heretics " were burned at Smithfield within three years. Bonner lived in a cruel age, but his scornful character aggravated that cruelty. It was something that Queen Elizabeth would not allow him to kiss her hand when she acceded in 1558. In 1559 Bonner was committed to prison, where he died ten years later, but his ghost remained to haunt the inhabitants of Bethnal Green.

In the gardens of Victoria Park Hospital there still stands a mulberry tree [1] beneath which, according to tradition, Bonner used to sit and plan his infamies ; and there, his ghost was reported until as late as 1832. " Riding in a black coach, he drove three times round Bonner's

BISHOP BONNER

Fields, and it was said that any person who saw this apparition would die." [2]

We left our cab in Bonner Road, at the junction of APPROACH ROAD (the main " approach " to Victoria Park) and Bishops Way, along which we walked west. We immediately fell into a trap, with

[1] The tree was stunted for some years after being blasted by a bomb, but in the summer of 1951 it was in foliage again.

[2] *Old Bethnal Green*, by George F. Vale (1934), p. 71.

72

the road leading south, called RUSSIA LANE. The Cockney likes to twist words on his tongue and swallow them into his own language : the Neapolitan ice-cream sellers of Hatton Garden soon became *Appletons* to the locals, and, similarly, the once simple *Rushy Lane*, of two and a half centuries ago, became Russia Lane on the tongues of the people of Bethnal Green.[1]

We continued along Bishops Way, to CAMBRIDGE HEATH ROAD, which runs north and south, and divides the Borough in two. Although the road points towards Cambridgeshire, some authorities claim that the *word* Cambridge here is a variant of an old personal name—perhaps of the farmer to whom the heath belonged, as early as the 13th century. We walked south along Cambridge Heath Road for a few paces, to see PARMITER STREET, named after Thomas Parmiter, a local jobmaster who died in 1681, leaving " lands and money to provide six almshouses and one free school for ten poor children ". Then we turned back, making our way, still west, along Hackney Road.

Mr. George F. Vale wrote in *Old Bethnal Green*, " A curious thing . . . is that there are no standing monuments of its past. There are, in fact, no old buildings and, with few exceptions, no antiquities of any kind." This is true, but there is enough evidence in the street-names to trace the chief themes in the Borough's history. Parallel with the southern boundary of Victoria Park runs OLD FORD ROAD, and south of this is ROMAN ROAD. We read in the *History of East London*, by Sir Hubert Llewellyn Smith, of the " pre-Roman road by which in A.D. 43 the Emperor Claudius with his legions and elephants crossed the Old Ford [2] to the conquest of Colchester." On the right and parallel with Hackney Road, where we were walking, was a dull little thoroughfare, COATE STREET. In the same book was a reproduction of a water-colour drawing of " Coate's Farm and the Old George Inn, Bethnal Green " (Pl. 27), in 1773. It shows a pleasant farmhouse, with a man working the water pump, a farm wagon, and a shepherd with his dog. Thus, without " standing monuments " or " antiquities ", one builds up the history of the land as one walks on.

We came to the point where Hackney Road becomes the boundary between Bethnal Green and Shoreditch, and we turned south-west

[1] From information supplied by the Borough Librarian.

[2] The Ford lay to the east, across the River LEA, in what is now the Borough of Poplar.

along COLUMBIA ROAD, into a network of small streets surrounding COLUMBIA MARKET ; a memorial to the stubborn conservatism of the East Londoner, and to the generosity of Baroness Burdett-Coutts. We walked to BARONESS ROAD, north of the market, and my collaborator produced his notes.

Baroness Burdett-Coutts (Pl. 25) was born in 1814 and she lived until 1906 : perhaps the best tribute to her was from King Edward VII, who said that, after his mother, she was " the most remarkable woman in the kingdom ". She was the daughter of Sir Francis Burdett— one of the most popular English politicians of his time—and the granddaughter of Thomas Coutts, the banker, whose fortune of two million pounds she inherited when she was twenty-three. Her life story was an epic of charity : she endowed the bishoprics of Capetown and Adelaide and founded the bishopric of British Columbia ; she helped the Zulus and the Australian aborigines, and she bought boats for poor Irish fishermen. When the silk trade waned, she began sewing schools in Spitalfields,[1] and she helped to found the shoe-black brigade, and placed hundreds of destitute boys in the Navy. She advanced a quarter of a million pounds to buy seed for the starving Irish, and built stables for costermongers' horses. In 1871 she was made a peeress in her own right. Baroness Burdett-Coutts was the first woman to be given the freedom of the City of London, and she was buried in Westminster Abbey. Baroness Road was named after her because it was there that she made the greatest experiment of her career in kindness. In the late 18th century there was an area in Bethnal Green named *Nova Scotia Gardens* ; once a pretty place, which had become the most squalid part of London. When she was about fifty-two, Baroness Burdett-Coutts became interested in changing this terrible spot, so she spent almost a quarter of a million pounds in building a fantastic Victorian-Gothic covered market where the poor people could buy their food. It was to be an example in cleanliness and self-respect to a forlorn district : but the inhabitants would not desert the old-fashioned street stalls, and the market failed.

The Cockneys may be conservative, but they are also imaginative, and there are two streets in this area for which the editors of *The Place-Names of Middlesex* suggest a curious origin.[2] They are VIRGINIA ROAD and GIBRALTAR WALK—named, not to celebrate imperial con-

[1] See chapter on Stepney, p. 84.
[2] *The Place-Names of Middlesex*, pp. 84-5.

quests, but merely because, being on the outskirts of London, they were, to the Cockney, as remote as Virginia and Gibraltar.

From Baroness Road we walked back to Columbia Road, and down BRICK LANE (so named because it led to the district of Spitalfields, which provided clay for bricks, as far back as the 16th century) ; then into Virginia Road, and ARNOLD CIRCUS, named after Sir Arthur Arnold, an alderman in the late 19th century. Six streets stretch out, like spokes, from the circus, and some of them yielded good stories.

First in local interest is CLUB ROW, with its animal market, where the inhabitants of Bethnal Green gather on Sunday morning, to buy and sell their birds, cats and dogs. Here we come on the roots of the Borough's industrial history, for the animal market was begun by Huguenot weavers in the 17th century. There were weavers in Bethnal Green in the year after Queen Elizabeth's death, but the real stimulus came to the trade with the Huguenot exiles who settled in Spitalfields and the surrounding district after 1685, and who left many street-names as a record of their life and industry. There is WEAVER STREET, in the extreme south of the Borough, where some of the houses retain the big first-floor window-frames that provided extra light for the looms. In his book, *London's Markets*, Mr. W. J. Passingham describes how, as late as 1935, he came on the last of these weavers working in such old houses, just off Green Street. " Every machine and tool in the room is an antique—a relic handed down by Huguenot ancestors. It might be a scene from Dickens's London ; the weaver bends over the loom throwing shuttles of different-coloured thread from either side along the grooved race-board, and the steady thud of the batten as each shot of weft is driven into position shakes the floor."

It must have been some satisfaction to the descendants of the Bethnal Green Huguenots that they were called on to make the vestments for Pope Pius IX when he pronounced the decree of papal infallibility in 1870.

There are at least three more names in Bethnal Green associated with the Huguenots : one of them is PALISSY STREET, off Arnold Circus. Bernard Palissy was the 16th-century potter who spent so many years of his life in discovering how to make enamels, and whose talents at first saved him from religious persecution. He was ultimately cast into the Bastille where he died, but his people remembered him when they settled in Bethnal Green. They remembered also the port from which so many of them had sailed, in ROCHELLE STREET, which is the next spoke in the wheel of streets opening into Arnold Circus.

The third of these names of Huguenot origin is DORIC ROAD, in the far east of the Borough, leading from Bonner Street to the bank of the Regent's Canal. Doric is a curiously corrupted form of (George) Dorée (Pl. 24), after whom the street is named. He was born here in 1845, when the weavers were already succumbing to the rivalry of machines. The trade slowly died, but Dorée—one of the last of the celebrated weavers—lived long enough to make the velvet for the coronation robes of King Edward VII.

From the streets opening into Arnold Circus we walked to Bethnal Green Road, by way of Brick Lane. Feeling lazy at the sight of the long road, we found a taxi-cab to carry us to Roman Road and the site of *Bethnall House* ; a mansion long since demolished, in which Pepys lodged the manuscript of his diary during the Great Fire of 1666. He wrote, " About four o'clock in the morning, my Lady Batten sent me a cart to carry away all my money, and plate, and best things, to Sir W. Rider's at Bednall Green. Which I did, riding myself in my nightgowne in the cart ; and Lord ! to see how the streets and the highways are crowded with people running and riding, and getting of carts at any rate to fetch away things . . . I am eased at my heart to have my treasures so well secured."

The origin of the name BETHNAL is doubtful. Some scholars have claimed that it comes from the family of *Bathon* who lived at *Bathon Hall* in the 13th century. Others like the notion that the word was formerly *Blithehale*—a blithe, or happy retreat. The Borough Librarian is cautious with these " too-facile " explanations, and advises us to " keep an open mind ".

Bethnall House marked an important change in the history of domestic architecture in London. When the use of gunpowder made thick-walled defences obsolete, the building of splendid mansions began. Bethnal Green was near enough to the City to attract many new-rich builders, who were teased in their day for their ostentation. Stow wrote in 1598, " . . . wee saw builded many faire summer-houses . . . with towers, turrets, and chimney tops, not so much for use or profits as for shew and pleasure, and bewraying the vanite of men's mindes." Among these follies was Bethnall House, built by John Kirby, an Elizabethan business man, whose enterprise was given the nickname of " Kirby's Castle ". In 1660 it became the property of Sir William Rider, Pepys's friend, and we read of the diarist going there on many occasions. Then the house fell on sad times : for two hundred years it was a private lunatic asylum—with Alexander Cruden as an inmate, in 1737.[1]

Among the papers we carried through Bethnal Green was a letter from the Librarian, on which was printed the Borough crest with its drawing of a blind beggar and his daughter Bessy. They are the figures in the local legend, to which Pepys referred one evening after dining with Sir William Rider. He wrote, " This very house was built by the Blind Beggar of Bednall Green (Pl. 26), so much talked of and sang in ballads." Pepys was wrong, for the legend began long before Bethnall House was thought of. Opening off Roman Road, between Victoria Park Square and Burnham Street, we found BESSY STREET, which yields a romantic story with which to end our journey in Bethnal Green.

The first scene was the Vale of Evesham, on the afternoon of August 4, 1265. All day the armies of Prince Edward and Simon de Montfort, Earl of Leicester, had fought mercilessly across the lovely valley, and they had met, in the final struggle, on the slopes of Green Hill. Prince Edward won the day ; Simon de Montfort was slain, and it was believed that his son, Henry, fell by his side. There history closes and legend begins.

That night, while the daughter of one of the warring barons was searching for the body of her father, on the slope of the hill, she stumbled over the dying body of Henry de Montfort. She carried him into hiding, and nursed him to health again. But he was blind, and his fair rescuer durst not leave him. They were married in secret and, disguised as beggars, they fled the valley.

Years passed, and the scene changed to Bethnal Green. Henry's wife seems to fade from the legend, for when he next appears, he is poor and old, and guarded always by his daughter, " prettye Bessee ". She was so beautiful that the hearts of all were startled at the sight of her, but she answered her suitors—a Gentleman, a Merchant, an Inn-keeper and a Knight—with the modest plea, that they must ask her old father—the Blind Beggar of Bethnal Green—before she could marry. Only the brave Knight dared, for his love was stronger than his pride. The blind old man bade him take his daughter and make her happy : then he confessed that he was the rightful Earl of Leicester and he

[1] See chapter on Islington, pp. 8–9.

endowed his daughter with a vast fortune, the source of which is not explained. "Prettye Bessee" and the brave Knight were married, and the day—and the legend—closed with great celebrations.

> Thus was the feast ended with joye and delighte,
> A bridegroome most happy then was the young Knighte,
> In joye and felicitie long lived he
> All with his faire ladye, the prettye Bessee.[1]

[1] The story forms the basis of Chettle and Day's *Blind Beggar of Bednal Green* (1600, printed 1659). J. S. Knowles also wrote a comedy called *The Beggar's Daughter of Bethnal Green* ; and R. Dodsley wrote a musical play, *The Blind Beggar of Bethnal Green.*

CHAPTER EIGHT

Stepney

There is an old tradition that any child born on the high seas may claim to be a native of Stepney, in respect of which an old rhyme runs thus :

> " He who sails on the wide sea
> Is a parishoner of Stepney."
>
> *The Official Guide to the*
> *Borough of Stepney.*

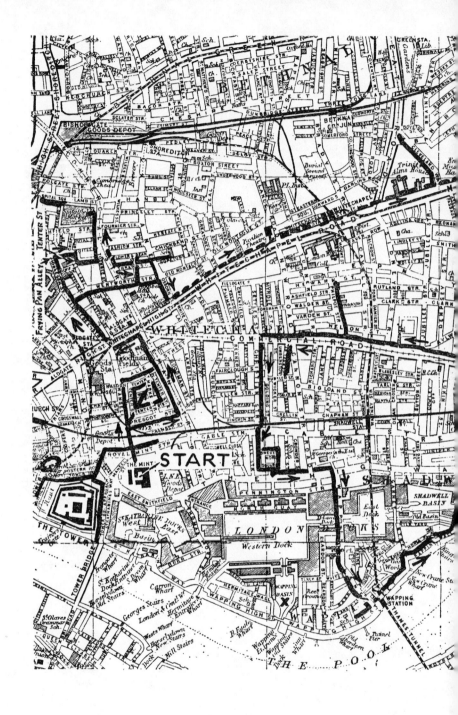

STEPNEY is the ancient mother of East London : from her sprang Hackney and Bethnal Green to the north and Poplar to the east. When the parent parish became too immense for comfort, these brats had to be born, weaned and taught to take care of themselves. On the west was the City ; but Stepney kept her own identity, because, from her southern boundary, she sent ships out into the world and received them back again. While the inland boroughs passed from agriculture to industry, and the City filled up with the money-changers, Stepney—and neighbouring Poplar—were helping to challenge the frontiers of the world.

The history of Stepney goes beyond the Domesday Book, in which the population was entered at eight hundred. It was one of the first Saxon settlements to be built—daringly—without the City Wall. It slowly grew into a parish which was owned by the Bishops of London for almost one thousand years ; from the time of Saint Augustine to the Reformation. King Edward VI gave the manorial rights to his Lord Chamberlain, Thomas Lord Wentworth, whose descendants retained their hold on the lands until early in the 18th century. Two small streets recall their long reign—WENTWORTH STREET, in the north-west of the Borough, and CLEVELAND WAY, which curves up from Mile End Road, commemorating the earldom conferred on the 4th Lord Wentworth, by King Charles II.

But the Borough belongs to the river and to sailors, rather than to earls with grand titles. Its very name, confused by the speech of perhaps forty generations, belongs to the sea. *Stebunhithe*, the Saxons called it : the first part was a personal name, and *hithe* meant " a small landing place on a river ". And a landing place it has remained. If you run a magnifying glass over the map, you come on TRINIDAD STREET, JAMAICA and BERMUDA STREETS. In Stepney, the Regent's Canal ends its course of eight and three-quarter miles : there the barges muster in the REGENT'S CANAL DOCK, to load the cargoes they are to distribute, as they travel inland through town and field. Close beside the river is ROPEMAKERS FIELDS, where the great cables were stretched before they were taken abroad, to tie Stepney's ships to the docks of Zanzibar and Vladivostock, Durban and Shanghai.

At the extreme west of the Borough, near the river, are HER MAJESTY'S TOWER—known to the world as the Tower of London—

the Royal Mint and Trinity Square. Stepney's boundary line suddenly juts out to embrace these austere places, which have little in common with the harsh life of the river front : the familiarity of tenements, the screams of ragamuffins at play, and the bawdy jokes of the four-ale bar. The Tower and the Mint seem to belong to the City, from which they are separated by only a few yards. In this narrative, they must be considered only in relation to the place and street-names they have given Stepney; and these are few. There are Tower Hill, Tower Bridge Approach, and Royal Mint Street, which need no explanation.

Trinity Square takes its name from Trinity House, which was incorporated by Henry VIII in 1514 to increase and augment " the shipping of this our realm of England ". Its powers became great under Elizabeth : the Master and Wardens superintended the building of the Navy, supplied pilots, and were, in fact, overlords for all English shipping, except when Her Majesty's naval vessels went into battle. They also had the right to erect sea-marks ; an office that survives in the control of lighthouses, which is still one of their duties. There is a nice, human touch in the Act of Elizabeth's time, permitting Trinity House to license mariners home from sea to be employed as watermen on the river, " the better to keep and refrain themselves from folly, idleness and lewd company and for the relief of their wives and children ". As the Navy, and merchant shipping, became so immense through the centuries, Trinity House lost much of its power and assumed, instead, the calm look of history. Its headquarters, which have twice been moved, are now just across the boundary, in the City ; near enough to give two names, Trinity Square and Trinity Place, to Stepney.

Having arrived near the Mint by car, we drove along Mansell Street,[1] east into Prescot Street, where we began our journey on foot, with four small streets forming a square and all bearing the same name—North, South, East and West Tenter Streets. They lie just south of the district of Spitalfields, and they reminded us that here also—as in Bethnal Green—the Huguenot weavers had settled, and left their mark in the street-names.

---

[1] Mansell Street, Prescot Street, Leman Street and Alie Street, roughly forming a square, are named after various branches of one family. The Borough Librarian states that there are records of their association with Stepney as early as the 15th century.

We might begin with an explanation of SPITALFIELDS, for which we go back to 1197, when " *Walter Brune*, a Citizen of London, and *Rosia* his wife, founded the Hospital of our Ladie called *Domus Dei*, or Saint *Marie* Spittle without Bishops gate of London. . . ."[1]

The " Spittle " in the " fields " became known as Spitalfields.[2] Its being " without " the City boundary explains why the vanguard of the persecuted Huguenots settled there ; close enough to compete in their trades, but " without " the jurisdiction of the City's protective guilds. The exiles were not wholly welcome. " This set of rabble ", complained Dr. Welton (who held the living of Stepney at the end of the 17th century), " are the very offal of the earth ". Less indignant observers watched the population of Stepney growing, until it trebled within a hundred years, and they named the exiles " The Profitable Strangers ".

So the Huguenots found the Four Freedoms which they sought, and they prospered : at one time there were as many as 10,000 hand-looms being worked in the district. Part of the final process of weaving was to stretch the cloth on frames, to dry evenly. The wooden frames, or tenters (Latin *tentorem*, stretcher, from *tendere*, to stretch), were kept in tenter-grounds, or yards—hence the four Tenter streets forming the square. The cloth was held to the frames by tenter-hooks, and thus, as the *Oxford English Dictionary* so amiably explains, to be " on tenter-hooks " is " to be in a state of anxious suspense ".

One street, in the north-west of the Borough, has a name that fascinated us—Frying Pan Alley. It was not on our 1805 map, and the chroniclers, from 16th century Stow to the 1942 editors of *The Place-Names of Middlesex*, gave us no clue as to its history. But we wished to see it, so from Prescot Street we turned north into Leman Street, and then west along Whitechapel High Street to the Borough boundary. On the map this part is called MIDDLESEX STREET, but it is known to everyone as *Petticoat Lane* (Pl. 28)—the site of a Sunday trading bazaar since the days of Charles I.

As we walked up Petticoat Lane we passed Wentworth Street, and then STRYPE STREET. John Strype, the son of a Huguenot weaver,

[1] Stow, vol. I, p. 105.

[2] This land was originally known as *Lollesworth Fields* : the name survives in LOLESWORTH STREET, a small thoroughfare leading north from Wentworth Street.

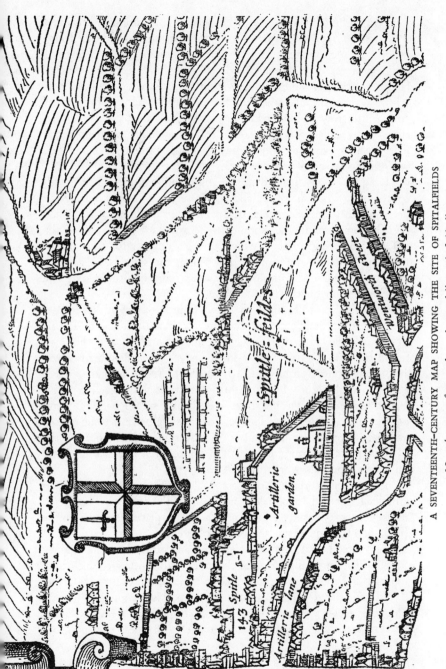

Spittle-feilde

Spittle 143

Artillerie garden.

Artillerie lane

wentworth street

A SEVENTEENTH-CENTURY MAP SHOWING THE SITE OF SPITALFIELDS

Note the tenter-frames above the word "Spittle-feildes"

was born in Spitalfields in 1643. He became an " antiquary, historian and parson ", and he wrote of Petticoat Lane (formerly called *Hog Lane*), " In ancient times, on both sides of this lane, were hedgerows and elm trees, with pleasant fields to walk in. . . . Here was an House on the west side, a good way in the lane, which, when I was a boy, was commonly called the Spanish Ambassador's House. . . . And a little way of this on the east side of the way, down a paved alley, (now called Strype's Court, from my father who inhabited there) was a fair large house with a good garden before it . . . wherein I was born."

This quiet scene changed in the following century. The Jewish community, which had been allowed to settle in Stepney during the Protectorate, soon made the district of Whitechapel their own. They busied themselves in the clothing trade and soon monopolised the old Petticoat Lane market, which is still a magnet for the junk of London—with the noise of the hoi polloi, the spite of bargaining, and the busyness of a thousand clawing fingers, turning over the conglomeration on the stalls.

We walked on to Frying Pan Alley ; a little tunnel of dull façades that left us as bewildered as ever by the name. It led to BRUNE STREET, named after the founders of the " Spittle ", and there we found the fifth TENTER STREET in Stepney. Then Shepherd Street, and north along Commercial Street to SPITALFIELDS MARKET. Here is an incredible sight : hundreds of tons of fruit and vegetables arriving each day from the provinces and abroad, spread over $10\frac{1}{2}$ acres of floor space, with cellars equipped for ripening bananas to be offered and bargained for by the traders. In Brushfield Street nearby, the London Fruit Exchange controls the importation and sale of many millions of pounds worth of fruit each year.

This immense organisation goes back to July, 1682, when King Charles II granted John Balch and his heirs the right to " keep two markets every week . . . in or next a certain place called the Spittle [now SPITAL] Square, in the parish of Stepney ".

We walked back to Commercial Street and turned left into THRAWL STREET (from a family name of the early 17th century), which took us to Brick Lane, already mentioned in the chapter on Bethnal Green.

We had stirred ghosts of Saxons, Stuarts, Huguenots and Jews in Stepney street-names up to this. From Brick Lane we walked into HOPETOWN STREET, which takes its name from a less romantic, but more practical and perhaps more noble influence than any of these, in the affairs of Stepney—the Salvation Army. It was a touch of imagination that urged Queen Mary to go to the Borough in 1931, to open a home for needy women ; and a touch of equal imagination on the part of the Borough authorities when they changed the name of the street to Hopetown Street, in recognition of " the Army's " work in Stepney.

From Hopetown Street we walked down Osborn Street, into WHITECHAPEL which, continuing into WHITECHAPEL ROAD, then Mile End Road, forms the main thoroughfare across the Borough. Stow wrote, " both the sides of the streete bee pestered with Cottages, and Allies, euen vp to White chappel church : and almost halfe a mile beyond it, into the common field : all of which ought to lye open & free to all men ". His emotions if he saw Whitechapel High Street on a Saturday afternoon in the 1950's are not to be measured.

We made the journey across the Borough on a No. 96 bus and watched the main river of week-end shoppers, increasing from the tributaries of Sidney Street, Jubilee Street, Stepney Green and White Horse Lane : so many " characters " for Phil May to sketch, with his touch of Cockney merriment adding vigour to their shabby clothes. And, like elves in a world of realism, there were quick-footed children, with ice-cream cones, scampering among the crowd ; the lively tatterdemalion of an East London Saturday afternoon.

Then MILE END ROAD, the route of the pre-Norman way from London to Colchester ; *La Mile ende* in the 13th century, when it was a hamlet one mile distant from Aldgate, the nearest entrance to the walled city.

The Cockney voices died on the air ; the close, stifled shops fell back into the dust from which they rose, and Stow's " common field " lay " open & free to all men ". The meadow-sweetened air of the land blew down to meet the salty breath of the river. It was the morning of June 14, 1381. All night long the boy king, Richard II—then fourteen—had watched the flames of the outraged city, and listened to the cries of the wild mob, beneath the battlements of the Tower. In the morning, "being threatened by the rebels of Kent", King Richard " rode from the Tower of London to the Myles end, and with his mother, because she was sick and weak in a Wherlicote ". They found the rebels, who were encamped without the City.

" I am your King and Lord, good people," the boy began, with a fearlessness which marked his bearing throughout the crisis. " What will ye ? "

" We will that you free us for ever," shouted the peasants, " us and our lands ; and that we will never be named nor held for serfs."

" I grant it," replied Richard.

Thus, simply, the history books tell the story of a promise that could not be kept. Again, in 1450, there was a rebellion in this part of London, fomented by soldiers returned from the French Wars, led by Jack Cade. Like the rebels of 1381, they gathered in " a field upon the plain of Mile End ".

There was no hint of these alarming episodes in the broad 20th-century thoroughfare, and we became weary of the scene ; so we left the bus when we came to the bridge crossing the Regent's Canal, and turned down CANAL ROAD, on foot, to seek the river again. We turned west along BEN JONSON ROAD,[1] then south, by way of WHITE HORSE ROAD—a survival from the 14th century. Half-way down there was an interesting name, on the left—SALMON LANE, after Captain Robert Salmon (Pl. 29), Master of Trinity House at the time of the Spanish Armada. It was he who wrote, when the peril threatened, promising that within four days " near 30 sail of service-able merchant-ships " would be " ready to set sail ".

Before returning to the river bank we made one more excursion, along Commercial Road, which is as dull as its name, and then south along CHRISTIAN STREET. This is a royal, and not a holy name, recalling King Christian V of Denmark, who gave Stepney a church, in Wellclose Square, in which his sailors could worship. The name led us to realise that this part of the Borough has a Scandinavian air : at the southern end of the street we crossed Cable Street and found ourselves in SWEDENBORG SQUARE, named after the great Swedish scientist, philosopher and mystic, Emanuel Swedenborg (1688–1772) (Pl. 30). He is remembered mostly for his philosophy and religious teaching ; but he must also have been a romantic character. At the age of thirty he invented machines for transporting boats and galleys 14 miles overland, for the siege of Frederickshall. He " even sketched a flying machine ". In middle age he felt compelled to devote his life to more spiritual purposes and he became the founder of the Swedenborgians, of whom there are 5,000 in Britain today. He spent many years teaching in England, and when he was dying he

[1] See chapter on Shoreditch, p. 63.

28. SUNDAY IN PETTICOAT LANE

29. TOMB OF CAPTAIN ROBERT
SALMON, ST. CLEMENT'S CHURCH,
LEIGH-ON-SEA

30. EMANUEL SWEDENBORG

31. WAPPING, BY GUSTAV DORÉ

32. GEORGE LANSBURY

33. CHARLES COBORN

34. SAMUEL PLIMSOLL

35. CHARLES BLONDIN CROSSING
NIAGARA FALLS

36. WEST FERRY ROAD DISTRICT—ISLE OF DOGS, 1928

37. BOW BRIDGE IN 1832

asked to be buried in the Swedish Church in Prince's Square, Stepney. There his body remained from 1722 until April, 1908, when the church was demolished. His body was then removed to Upsala Cathedral ; and the square was re-named Swedenborg Square, in his memory.

From Swedenborg Square we crossed The Highway, and walked down WAPPING LANE into WAPPING HIGH STREET. The name WAP-PING (Pl. 31), which sounds like the lapping of water, occurs here eight times, and seems to be rooted in the river mud. There are WAPPING BASIN, WAPPING OLD STAIRS and WAPPING WALL. We found that the name *did* grow out of the river ; that in the 14th century it was *Wappingge atte Wose*—very likely derived from Old English *wapol*, a marsh, and *wāse*, meaning mud, or " ooze ".

Wapping has enjoyed its hours of distinction. In July, 1629, " King Charles having hunted a Stag or Hart from Wansted in Essex, killed him in Nightingale Lane in the hamlet of Wapping ". The owner of the garden nearby " had some damage among his herbs, by reason of the multitude of people assembled there suddenly ". And Dr. Johnson, talking one day " of the wonderful extent and variety of London ", recommended Boswell to " explore Wapping ". Boswell went there with some friends, but they were " disappointed ".

Boswell would not have been disappointed had he been able to go there towards the end of the 14th century, when the river was so rife with pirates that the land-lubbers had to protect themselves behind chains and barriers across the river streets. These exciting times are linked with PHILPOT STREET (a corruption of Philipot), which runs between Stepney Way and Commercial Road. Sir John Philipot was knighted in 1381 for his valour during the Peasants' Revolt ; but his real conquests were on the river, where he " fitted up a fleet at his own expense ", and captured " the ringleader of the pirates ". Sir John Philipot had imagination as well as courage, and he offered to build a stone tower on one bank of the river, if the Corporation would build one on the other. Between them he proposed stretching a mighty iron chain, to keep the marauders back. Stow describes the gloomy end of these audacious robbers, at Wapping in the Woze, which was " the vsuall place of execution for hanging of Pirats & sea Rouers, at the low water marke there to remaine, till three tides had ouerflowed them. . . ."

We made our way along Wapping Wall, which runs parallel with the river bank, and passed Pelican Stairs, for which nobody seems able to offer an explanation. Then we came to the entrance to SHADWELL BASIN, taking its name from the district of SHADWELL, meaning "shallow spring or well".[1]

The next district is RATCLIFF—merely a corruption of *La Rede Clive*, the red cliff—at the point where the Wapping mud ended in a stretch of red stone foreshore. And then the district of LIMEHOUSE, for which we can do no better than quote from our refuge in times of despair—Samuel Pepys—who wrote, "9 Oct. 1661—By coach to Captain Marshe's at Limehouse, to a house that hath been their ancestor's for this 250 years, close by the lime-house, which gives the name to the place."

We crossed the KING EDWARD VII MEMORIAL PARK and followed the course of the river along The Highway, passing GLASSHOUSE FIELDS, the site of the first crown glass industry in England. Then, nearer the water, along Narrow Street and past Ropemakers Fields, which we have already described, to PHOEBE STREET, on the Stepney-Poplar border.

We end our story with two remarkable people.

Near Salmon Lane, which we passed on our way down White Horse Road, we had overlooked BLOUNT STREET, named after Sir Charles Blount, afterwards Earl of Devonshire, who was "a very comely young man". His "prowess at the tilt" caught the eye of Queen Elizabeth, who sent him "a chess Queen of gold enamelled, which he tied upon his arm with a crimson ribband". This touch of the macaroni so shocked the Earl of Essex that he remarked, "Now I perceive, every fool must have a favour", which so angered Sir Charles that he challenged Essex to a duel in Marylebone Park, where he "disarmed him, and wounded him in the thigh."[2]

Phoebe Street, coupled with HESSEL STREET and AMAZON STREET, elsewhere in the Borough, are in memory of our second remarkable person—Phoebe Hessel, an "Amazon" who was born in Stepney in the reign of Queen Anne. She served in the 5th Regiment of Foot throughout Europe for a great part of the 18th century, and died at the age of one hundred and eight. During her years of rough campaigning she withheld her secret from her comrades-in-arms, until she was wounded. Phoebe Hessel was invalided out of the army

[1] *The Place-Names of Middlesex*, p. 151.
[2] From Lord Orford's *Royal and Noble Authors*.

PHOEBE HESSEL : A SKETCH FROM LIFE IN "THE CIRCULATOR"

She is represented with a pocket hanging at her side, from which a fife protrudes. She has a bundle of windfalls under her right arm, and her left rests on a T-shaped stick

and she retired to Brighton with a pension. There she lived, as something of a character : she was sketched by artists, and King George IV was very amiable to her. When she died, in 1821, she was buried with honours in the parish churchyard, where her tombstone survives to tell her story.

CHAPTER NINE

Poplar

" Popler, or Poplar, is so called from the multitude of Poplar
trees (which love a moist soil) growing there in former times.
And there be yet (1720) remaining, in that part of the
hamlet which bordereth upon Limehouse, many old bodies
of large Poplars standing, as testimonials, of the truth of that
etymology."

DR. JOSEPH WOODWARD, in Strype, Circuit Walk.

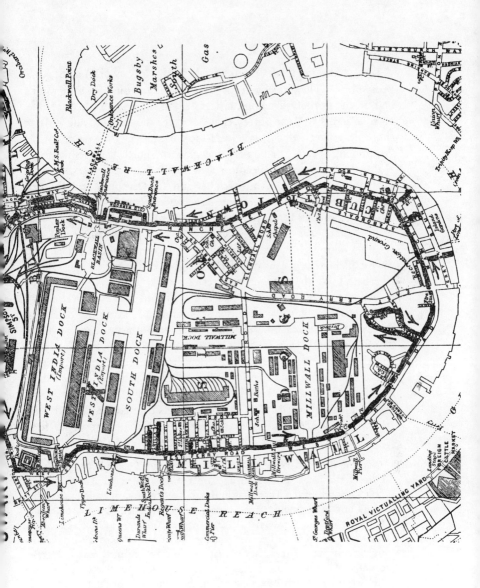

Late in the reign of Queen Elizabeth the River Thames became prosperous. The pirates and cut-throats were less busy for some time, and, in the summer evenings, citizens along the river bank were able to row across to " the Surrey side " [1]: there they could walk on the shore near Greenwich Palace, and look back over the water, to the " trembling spears " of poplars that gave the north bank its name. POPLAR had already become a seamen's hamlet. ". . . of late years ", wrote Stow, " ship-wrights and (for the most part) other marine men haue builded many large and strong houses for themselues, and smaller for Saylers . . . almost to Poplar, and so to Blake wal." *Blake wal*—the BLACKWALL of today—was convenient for wharves, although it was on a windy bend of the river ; a fact that may explain why it was called *Bleak wal* in earlier times. In Queen Elizabeth's day the treacherous acres of mud were already being controlled and a great river wall had been built, so that *Blake wall* grew into a busy loading place for overseas shipping. After the defeat of the Spanish Armada in 1588, these foreign enterprises became more daring, and on December 19, 1606, the *Sarah Constant*, the *Goodspeed* and the *Discovery* set sail from Blackwall with orders to go by way of the Azores and the Canaries, and on, " until such time as they shall fortune to land upon the said coast of Virginia ".

At the end of April, 1607, the adventurers entered the James River and went ashore, thus beginning the romantic and dangerous first episode in the history of English settlement in America.

> To the first settlers the colony was a miniature London, lying on both sides of the James as London does on the Thames ; and as that part of London south of the Thames is in the shire of Surrey, the colonists on the Island in writing home, came to speak of the settlements on the south side as " over on the Surrey side ". The name " Surrey " as thus applied to the south side (but spelled without the " e ") was retained by it when it was cut off from James City County in 1652 and formed into a separate county. Likewise, London, south of the Thames is in Southwark Parish and when a new parish was cut off on the south side [of the James River] it was called " Southwark ".[2]

[1] Greenwich Palace is actually in Kent, although the river bank here is colloquially called " the Surrey side ".
[2] *Old Surry*, by A. W. Bohannan, p. 8. Petersburgh, Virginia, Plummer Pub. Co., 1927.

Thus the first English place-names were planted on the new earth of Virginia. The three ships came back to Blackwall, and the talk in the " many large and strong houses " and the " smaller for Saylers " must have been lively with tales of the New World. But Poplar did not yet absorb the story into her street-names. There are now CONSTANT HOUSE in Harrow Lane, Poplar High Street, and GOOD-SPEED HOUSE in Simpson's Road ; but they were not named until the 1930's. Strangely, in the north-east of the Borough, are FRANKLIN STREET, WASHINGTON STREET and JEFFERSON STREET, side by side ; but the first valiant seamen who sailed for America from Blackwall, and who belong to Poplar's history, are not remembered.

On April 17, 1610, the marine men and Saylers gathered upon the river bank by Blackwall again, to see Henry Hudson setting out on his last attempt to find a North-West Passage. This tragic voyage, during which Hudson was abandoned to his death, is also recalled— in HUDSON BUILDINGS in Gaselee Street.

Slowly, as the great trade routes of the world were opened up, Poplar grew and the names of the world came home and spread through the Borough. There are CUBA, MANILLA, HAVANNAH and MALABAR STREETS, all running at right angles from West Ferry Road. Poplar became famous also for its sailing ships : between 1612 and 1866, 82 wooden ships for the Navy and 275 merchantmen, many of them East Indiamen, were built in Blackwall Yard. By the end of the 18th century the trade through the Poplar docks was so great that ships had to drop their anchors and wait their turn in the river, before they could disgorge their cargoes into the high-packed ware-houses. In 1802, the WEST INDIA DOCKS were opened by William Pitt ; and four years later the EAST INDIA DOCKS were built, to handle cargoes from India and the China Seas. The great age had come : Britannia ruled the waves, and acquired both profit and power.

The map (see pp. 94–5) reveals aspects in which Poplar is different from the neighbouring boroughs. The northern half, with Stepney and Bethnal Green to the west, Hackney to the north, and West Ham [1] to the east, is mainly industrial—manufacturing a thousand things, from chocolates to oakum. In character, Poplar here is much like her neighbours. But the southern half is almost surrounded by the river. This was *Stepheneth* (Stepney) *mershe* in the 14th and 15th centuries, but the name ISLE OF DOGS (Pl. 36) was established in the

[1] Outside the scope of this book since it is not a Metropolitan borough.

16th century, for any one of the following reasons that may please. One chronicler holds that countless dead dogs were washed up here by the tide ; another, that when King Henry VIII, then Queen Elizabeth, were at Greenwich Palace, they kept their kennels in the marshes. Strype offers a tabloid thriller as an explanation. A man was " murthered " here by a ruffian from the river, but the victim's faithful dog led some honest watermen to the body of his master. " Soon after, the dog swimming over to Greenwich bridge, where there was a waterman seated, at him the dog snarled and would not be beat off ; which the other watermen perceiving (and knowing of the murther), apprehended this strange waterman ; who confessed the fact, and was condemned and executed."

But one must not take these fanciful explanations of simple names too seriously, and it is feasible that five hundred years hence some prying scholar might say that the " Isle of Dogs " is a corruption of the name " Isle of Docks ", for the docks are so immense on the peninsula that they stretch from boundary to boundary, cutting the Borough in two. Once again, it is Pepys who makes the scene lively for us, in one or two sentences—written after his coach had not appeared to take him home. " I, being in my new coloured silk suit and coat trimmed with gold buttons and gold braid lace round my hands, very rich and fine. . . . So we were fain to stay there, in the unlucky Isle of Dogs, in a chill place, the night cold, to our great discomfort."

The Isle of Dogs is divided into two districts—MILLWALL in the west and CUBITT TOWN in the east. Until the middle of the 18th century Millwall was *Marsh Wall*, named after the wall that guarded the *Stepheneth mershe* from the flooding of the river. But many mills were built here in the late 1700's and the name was changed. Cubitt Town is named after the enterprising William Cubitt (1791–1863) who built this area of Poplar, about 1850.

No part of London endured more bombing during the second world war than the Isle of Dogs. Anyone who has flown over the Thames at night will recall how the river makes a splendid curve here, and how the moonlight shining on the slow oily water turns the peninsula into a perfect target. The German bombers came to know it well, and the docks and wharehouses suffered night after night. The re-building has covered many of the scars, but also many of the old romantic streets, especially in *Chinatown*, north of Millwall, where we began our tour of Poplar. Phoebe Street, with which we ended the story of Stepney, juts into *Chinatown*, and we were able to walk from here into Limehouse Causeway and across to PENNYFIELDS.[1]

My collaborator was disappointed because I had told him stories of the *Chinatown* of thirty years ago, when the pungent smell of oriental food, and the babel of Chinese, Indian and Maltese, drew us east— with the veiled promise of a fan-tan saloon to add spice to the expedition. One was too young then to realise that fan-tan was no worse than bridge.

We found *Chinatown* to be a wreck of its wicked past : in place of the poor little houses that were shattered by the bombing of September, 1940, we saw airy blocks of new flats, and the outline of new, broad streets. Beneath these, Limehouse Causeway and Penny-fields will disappear, and the *Chinatown* of Thomas Burke, and the films, will have gone up in the flames of respectability.

From Pennyfields we walked towards EAST INDIA DOCK ROAD, by way of AMOY PLACE and ORIENTAL STREET. We noticed on the map that two more streets with Chinese names lay just north of us— CANTON STREET and PEKIN STREET. We first imagined that these four names were linked with the Chinese colony in Poplar, but the Borough Librarian later told us that they have " no connection " with " China-town, so-called " ; that they are " reminiscent of the trade with China by the tea clippers from the East India Docks " ; and that Oriental Street was named " after the first American ship to bring in a cargo of tea from Hong Kong to England after the repeal of the Navigation Laws, in 1849 ".

We had come into East India Dock Road to see the beginning of the *new* East London. Opposite Oriental Street was the " Exhibition of Architecture ", organised as part of the 1951 Festival of Britain. The exhibition helped to explain the most enterprising scheme of rehousing that has been attempted in Britain since the 1939–45 war. On this land, which was so fiercely bombed, there is to be a complete town, with its own churches, schools, shops and market place. We were allowed to roam over thirty acres of the new estate, which will eventually be enlarged to about 124 acres, stretching north from East India Dock Road.

The new district is called LANSBURY, after George Lansbury (Pl. 32) (1852–1940), who " devoted his life to working for a better world

[1] The name perhaps indicates the early rental value of the land.

and a new Poplar ". The estate, planned to house almost ten thousand people in comfort and safety, is a memorial to the humanitarian who was so greatly loved in East London where he lived and worked.

Further along East India Dock Road we found another essentially British street-name—PLIMSOLL STREET, after Samuel Plimsoll (Pl. 34) (1824-98). The street is short and straight, leading into Grundy Street ; and, rightly so, it is in the heart of Poplar.

Samuel Plimsoll was a warrior with one aim. In 1850 he was destitute and forced to live in rooming-houses. During this time he often saw what were described as " coffin-ships " leaving the Thames for the open seas, overloaded and unseaworthy. When Plimsoll became Liberal Member of Parliament for Derby, in 1868, he fought for seven years to bring in a bill that would control the safety of ships, and limit the weight of their cargoes. This led to the famous scene in the Commons, in 1875, when Mr. Disraeli announced that Plimsoll's bill would be dropped. The fighter lost his temper, shook his fist in the Speaker's face and denounced the Tories as so many "villains". But Mr. Disraeli was also something of a fighter, and the scene was forgiven. In the following year the Merchant Shipping Act was passed, and the Plimsoll mark—the white sign which shows the safe loading limit of a ship—was painted on every honest hull that took to sea.

We turned back along East India Dock Road and walked down Saltwell Street, along Ming Street, and into the immense West Ferry Road that sweeps south—past Cuba, Manilla, Havannah and Malabar Streets, which we have already mentioned. West Ferry Road is almost two miles long and it runs, parallel with the river, to the southern tip of the Borough ; with West India Docks, South Dock and Millwall Dock to the east, offering very little for the name-seeker. We made this journey by car, and did not stop until we saw CHAPEL-HOUSE STREET, opening on the left, into MACQUARIE WAY and THERMOPYLAE GATE.

Chapelhouse Street suddenly plunged us from the facts of docks and commerce, back into the 14th century, when the Church chose the names for the land. It seemed incredible that here, with the utilitarian forms of marine architecture about us, once stood the manor house of Pontefract, granted in 1450 to the Abbey of St. Mary Graces by the Tower. The Chapel House was here until the 1860's when

Millwall Docks were built on the site. Macquarie Way was named after the famous sailing ship built at Blackwall in 1875, and Thermopolyae Gate—not after the pass into Thessaly, where Leonidas fought back the Persian army—but after the tea-clipper *Thermopylae*, the fastest on the seas. She was faster even than the *Cutty Sark*, also recalled in Poplar in WILLIS HOUSE, named after her captain.

The long road changes its name at the extreme south, and runs north as Manchester Road. We kept this way, passing BARQUE STREET, SCHOONER STREET and BRIG STREET, and then on, for half a mile, until we found SAMUDA STREET. Joseph D'Aguilas Samuda (1813–85) was an engineer and shipbuilder, and first treasurer of the Institute of Naval Architects. We then came to the district of Blackwall, with the deep channels connecting the docks with the river. On the right was COLD HARBOUR, a street with three sides, which needs no explanation since it is near the " chill place " of which Pepys complained, some three centuries ago.

When we arrived at Blackwall Yard—where the first *Dreadnought* was built in 1653—we realised, with the help of the map, why this *Bleak wal* became so important, long before Tudor times. There was more traffic then on the river than on the roads, but the enormous curve of the Thames, below Poplar, added some hours to the water journey. Passengers therefore landed at Blackwall and crossed the peninsula by coach—taking to the river again on the west side. Many famous mariners must have stayed at Blackwall at one time or another, but the records are scant : there is no street to remind us that John Cabot was almost certainly here—perhaps before he set out to plant Henry VII's flag on the coast of North America. But there is a RALEANA ROAD, near where Sir Walter Raleigh is believed to have had a house from which he managed his ships.

Manchester Road had given way to Prestons Road, and we passed Raleana Road on the right, as we travelled north. When we came to POPLAR HIGH STREET, which still had the subdued and wounded look of an area that has been fiercely bombed, we left our car and went in search of a public house which has a remarkable history. One hundred and fifty years ago, when sailors were tough and tipsy, Poplar High Street was the toss-pot's delight. There were twenty-nine pubs in this one street : now there are not more than a handful. Among them is the *White Horse*, notorious in the mid-18th century because of the proprietor, Mary East. She was a contemporary of

Phoebe Hessel,[1] the female soldier of Stepney, and, for many years, Mary " resolved to live as a man ". She was a good citizen and well respected, and filled " all official positions in the parish except that of Constable ". Her secret was eventually divulged by a " friend ", and Mary East had to resume her sex and give up both her tavern and her honours. She died in 1781 at the age of sixty-four, but, unlike Phoebe Hessel, she has no street named after her.

We returned to the east end of Poplar High Street and drove north, by Robin Hood Lane, into BRUNSWICK ROAD, recalling a visit to the docks by George III, and remarkable for the eight streets that open from it, to the east. Their names were all plucked from the Highlands —ATHOL, BLAIR, CULLODEN, DEE, ETTRICK, FINDHORN, GLENCOE and HIGHLAND STREETS—and bestowed in tidy alphabetical order by David McIntosh, a contractor who owned and developed the land here in the 1860's.

And thus we came to ST. LEONARD'S STREET,[2] which connects the districts of Bromley and Bow. Once more we go back more than a thousand years for the explanation of a name that appears so unromantic when we see it on the front of a bus. BROMLEY comes from the Saxon *Braembelege*, " a clearing overgrown with brambles ".[3] It will be remembered that the great parish of Stepney once covered most of East London : the exception was the little parish of Bromley St. Leonards, which grew up about a Benedictine convent, said to have been built in the reign of King Edgar, in the year 960. Here indeed we have an incongruity : parallel with Franklin, Washington and Jefferson Streets—of which we have already written—is PRIORY STREET ; and it was in this Priory, on the banks of the River Lea, which still marks most of Poplar's eastern boundary, that Chaucer's " Nonne Prioresse " was educated.

> And Frensch sche spak ful faire and fetysly
> Aftur the scole of Stratford atte Bowe
> For Frensch of Parys was to hir unknowne.

We went to the edge of the River Lea, by way of BROMLEY HIGH

[1] See pp. 90, 91.
[2] St. Leonard's Street was originally Four Mills Street. " Three acres of land in a field called ' Dune ' by the four mills " is referred to in records of the time of Richard I. This place-name still exists—with the loss of one mill—in THREE MILLS LANE and THREE MILLS BRIDGE, just east of St. Leonard Street.
[3] *The Place-Names of Middlesex*, p. 125.

STREET, and decided to end our journey near Bow Bridge (Pl. 37), which links Poplar with the district of Stratford in the Borough of West Ham.

Until the 12th century, the road from London to Colchester—by way of Aldgate, Mile End and Stratford—deviated with a considerable curve when it came to the River Lea, so that travellers could use the only bridge, at Old Ford. There is a charming story to explain why a new bridge was built, at what came to be known as Bow, in the 12th century, by order of Queen Matilda, wife of Henry I. The Queen was out hunting one day, with her bow and arrows, and when she came to the river she was almost drowned in crossing. She therefore demanded a new bridge, at a more convenient part of the river, and instructed that it be arched and shaped like the bow she was carrying.[1]

We completed our search in Poplar in the lazy way—with our map spread on the bar of THE BOMBAY GRAB, a modern tavern with an old name, some fifty yards west of Bow Bridge. A "grab", according to the dictionary, is "a large coasting-vessel, built with a prow and usually two-masted ; used in the east". The word is Anglo-Indian, dating from the end of the 17th century. The publican was delighted to tell us how this strange name came to Poplar.

Some two hundred and fifty years ago, an English ship, carrying a cargo of beer to India, was captured by a " grab "—a pirate ship—which was later seized by a British sloop, just outside Bombay. One of the sailors, who hailed from Poplar, came home and used his share of the prize money to buy an inn which he called " The Bombay Grab ".

The publican told us that the old inn was demolished, but that the name was transferred to his house, a few years ago. We like the

---

[1] Four miles from Bow Bridge, in the City, is Bow Church—the home of the Bow bells. John Stow wrote in the 16th century, " This Church in the reigne of *William Conquerour*, being the first in this Cittie builded on Arches of stone, was therefore newe *Marie* Church, of Saint *Marie de Arcubus*, or *le Bow* in West Cheaping : As Stratford Bridge being the first, builded (by *Matilde* the Queene, wife to *Henrie* the first) with Arches of Stone, was called *Stratford le Bow*, which names to the said Church and Bridge remayneth till this day."

The church was destroyed in the Great Fire of 1666, but the present building, designed by Sir Christopher Wren, is supported on the same Norman arches, and is still called St Mary le Bow.

pride with which he announced, " No other name like it in the country."

We drank a glass of beer with him, then we turned to our map. There were several streets we would have liked to visit, if there had been time, and their names reveal the diversity of Poplar's history, and interests. In the centre of the Borough, not far from Brunswick Road, which we had taken on our way north, are COBDEN STREET and BRIGHT STREET, named after the great 19th-century " Apostles of Free Trade ". At the western end of Bow ROAD are COBORN ROAD and STREET, which honour Dame Prisca Coborn, a Bow philanthropist who died in 1701, and who achieved unexpected posthumous fame some two hundred years later.

Most of the older generation alive today can remember Charles Coborn (Pl. 33) singing *The Man who broke the Bank at Monte Carlo*, and *Two Lovely Black Eyes*. The popular comedian, who was born in Mile End in 1852, was christened Colin Whitton McCallum, but he " took his stage name at random, from Coborn Road, Bow". He died quite recently, in 1945.

The last name that caught our eye on the map was BLONDIN STREET, in the north of the Borough, named after Charles Blondin (Pl. 35), the French tight-rope walker who died in Ealing in 1897. In 1862 his acrobatics had drawn huge crowds to the Crystal Palace, but his more eccentric adventures had begun three years before, in June, 1859, when he first crossed Niagara Falls. In July he crossed again, blindfolded and pushing a wheelbarrow. In August he repeated the performance, carrying a man on his back (who certainly deserved to have a street named after him). But his moment of real distinction came in September, 1860, when Albert Edward, Prince of Wales— then nineteen and on the way from Canada into the United States— paused to see Blondin perform. Blondin crossed the Falls for him twice ; first with a wheelbarrow and then on stilts. The Prince was delighted, and quite willing, when Blondin suggested wheeling the heir to the throne on to American soil, along the tight-rope. But General Bruce and the Duke of Newcastle were at hand, to represent the view of the Queen, and the enterprise was forbidden.

St. Pancras

" As many allhailes to thy person as there be haicockes in
July at Pancredge."

THOMAS NASH, the Elizabethan
dramatist, in a greeting to the
comedian, William Kemp.

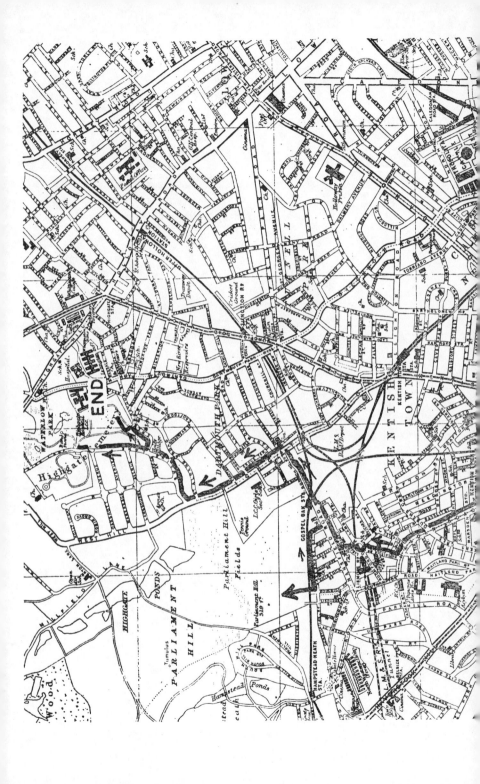

In the *Basilica di S. Pancrazio* in Rome, there is a bas-relief (Pl. 38) of a naked boy, aged about fifteen years, being slain by a soldier. The boy was named Pancratius, and he was canonised because of the miseries and death he suffered at the hands of the Emperor Diocletian, a fierce killer of Christians.

In the 7th century Pope St. Vitalian sent relics of the young saint to England, and it may be that some of them inspired the building of the ancient church of St. PANCRAS, in London. John Norden, the 16th-century cartographer, left a record of the tradition that " here, on the site of this little church in London . . . was raised the first altar to Christ in Britain, that is to say, anterior to the Saxon Invasion ". Norden added that, in his day, the church was " all alone as utterly forsaken, old and weather-beaten ", but that it yielded nothing to " Paule's in London " for antiquity.

Although St. Pancras may be the oldest Christian borough, it kept a rural look up to the early 19th century. On the site of Messrs. Heal's immense furniture stores, in Tottenham Court Road, there was Capper's Farm,[1] owned by " Two maiden ladies, sisters " who wore " riding habits and men's hats ". One of them " rode an old grey mare, and took a spiteful delight in cutting kite-strings attached to kites whenever she came across boys indulging in that pastime ". For this purpose " she provided herself with a large pair of shears ".[2] As late as September, 1801, a hare was " discovered in the fields near Kentish Town", and pursued to St. Pancras where "it swam across a pond ". It then continued its route to the turnpike " by the New Road near Battle-bridge [the present King's Cross], where a man was very near knocking it down with his hat ; and a greyhound, who happened to be there, with too much eagerness to catch it, leaped over its back and missed it. . . . It afterwards fled across the fields to Maiden Lane . . . followed by a great number of people with bull-dogs, fox-dogs, terriers, pugs, and curs in abundance." [3]

It is a far cry from Bow Bridge, in Poplar—the eastern edge of the territory covered in this book—to King's Cross, in St. Pancras,

[1] Sir Ambrose Heal informs us that the farm-house was not demolished until 1913, and that he possesses a scale model of the building as it was in his " early days ".

[2] *Marylebone and St. Pancras*, by George Clinch (1890), p. 210.

[3] *Marylebone and St. Pancras*, p. 213.

with which we begin our survey of the north-western boroughs. We are brought back to the beginning of our London journeys : to the story of Boadicea Street, in Islington.

It will be remembered that this is supposed to mark Boadicea's last battle-ground—less than half a mile away from King's Cross railway station. King's Cross bore the ancient name of *Battle Bridge* until 1830, when it was proposed to erect a memorial there by public subscription. The promoters claimed that it would honour " His Most Gracious Majesty William the Fourth, his late Majesty George the Fourth and the preceding kings of the Royal House of Brunswick ". On top of the terrible edifice was to be placed a " colossal statue of his Majesty in full Robes ". The lower part was to be " splendidly illuminated by Gas Lamps ", and the whole would form " not only an imposing ornament, but a protection to the Public from danger in crossing the six roads uniting at this spot ".

The wicked enterprise succeeded, and the memory of Boadicea's battle was reduced to a short street—BATTLE BRIDGE ROAD—which runs between the railway station and the gas-works. The monument was not a " cross ", nor did it survive very long in " honour " of the Hanoverians. It was so comical that Pugin derided it, and cab drivers laughed at it as they passed by. Fifteen years later, after being used in turn as a police station and a beer-shop, the monstrosity was pulled down " in connection with some public improvements ". But the name King's Cross remained.

We travelled there by underground and made our way through the tempest of railway station traffic to walk south, along Gray's Inn Road.[1] Two streets, opening to the left and right of Gray's Inn Road, caught our eye as we were passing. They are ST. CHAD'S STREET and PLACE, recalling a well that yielded an aperient water which was sold here during many centuries. St. Chad, to whom the well was dedicated, is referred to by the Venerable Bede. Before the saint died, in 672, he was " attended by angels ; joyful melody, as of persons sweetly singing, descended from heaven to his oratory, for half an hour, and then mounted again to heaven, presaging his decease ". As late as 1825, " an ancient female, in a black bonnet, a clean blue cotton gown and a checked apron ", sold the aperient water from St. Chad's Well for sixpence a glass ; for those in chronic need there was an annual subscription of one guinea.

[1] See chapter on Holborn, p. 31.

We wished to see MECKLENBURGH SQUARE—which opens off Gray's Inn Road, by way of Heathcote Street—because it is soon to be largely rebuilt and converted as an educational centre, for students coming from the United States and the British Commonwealth countries. This is to be paid for by Britons as a gesture of thanks for the seventy-five million food parcels received from these countries during and after the war.

The great century of Empire building and colonisation had its effect on London street-names : there is an Australian Avenue in the City, Canberra Road in Greenwich, Quebec Street in St. Marylebone, Trinidad Street in Stepney, and Toronto Road in East Ham. But there is no one area of streets to remind us that this is the shrine city of the British Commonwealth of Nations. It will be well if the change in the character of Mecklenburgh Square—of making it a centre for English-speaking scholarship—leads to a change in some of the dull names of the streets adjoining. BRUNSWICK SQUARE, a few steps away from Mecklenburgh Square, was once described as " mostly brick walls with holes in them ". The advent of thousands of students from the " new " countries might revivify this part of London, where the Brunswicks and Mecklenburghs, and the overflow from the Duke of Bedford's family names, monopolise the streets. The new world has already some exciting names we could borrow—Smuts, Sister Kenny, Lord Rutherford, Hugh Walpole, Katherine Mansfield, and Sir Harold Gillies are a few that occurred to us as we walked across the square, to the site of the Foundling Hospital. This once important hospital gave the area its only two interesting names—CORAM'S FIELDS and CORAM. STREET, and HANDEL STREET.

Captain Thomas Coram was born at Lyme, Dorset, in 1668. He was " bred to the sea, and passed the first part of his life as master of a vessel trading to the colonies ". While he lived in the vicinity of Rotherhithe, travelling to and from his business in the City, he often saw deserted infants " exposed to the inclemencies of the seasons, and through the indigence or cruelty of their parents left to casual relief or untimely death ". This excited his compassion, and led him " to project the establishment of an Hospital for the reception of exposed and deserted children : in which humane design he laboured more than seventeen years, and at last by his unwearied application obtained the royal charter. . . ." [1] Coram first opened a home, for twenty

[1] These facts about Thomas Coram were recorded by John Ireland, Hogarth's biographer. Hogarth painted a portrait of Coram (Pl. 39).

children, in Hatton Garden, where the demands of mothers to have their offspring received often led to fights in the street. Then the site now known as Coram's Fields was bought, and a home for 500 children was opened in 1747. Coram, who died four years later, was so poor after his years of kindness that he had to be supported with a pension. The Foundling Hospital continued its work through the 19th century, and was pulled down after the 1914–18 war. Coram's example inspired similar kindness in George Frederick Handel (Pl. 40), the composer, who came to England in 1710. He presented an organ to the Hospital, and on May 1st, 1750, he gave the first of many performances of the *Messiah*, which raised £10,000 for the institution. Thus, Coram Street and Handel Street in St. Pancras, north of Brunswick Square, and side by side.

We walked to Handel Street, then north into JUDD STREET, which runs parallel with TONBRIDGE STREET, for a good reason. Sir Andrew Judd, Lord Mayor, 1551–2, "erected one notable free schoole at *Tonbridge* in Kent" and was a landowner in St. Pancras. Judd Street led us to EUSTON ROAD, which forms part of "*The New Road from Paddington to Islington*", planned in 1756. The present efficient thoroughfare reminds us of a heated tennis match of words between the Dukes of Bedford and Grafton, whose estates marched nearby. The arguments regarding the new road are interesting—representing the old conservative view of the Duke of Bedford, who objected to any interference with the privacy of his house and gardens, and the practical view of the Duke of Grafton and his supporters, that "in time of public danger, by threatened invasions from foreign enemies", His Majesty's forces should be able to reach the Essex coast "without passing through the Cities of London and Westminster, or interrupting the business thereof". Horace Walpole noted the battle of the Dukes in a letter to Sir Horace Mann : "A new road through Paddington has been proposed to avoid the stones. The Duke of Bedford, who is never in town in summer, objects to the dust it will make behind Bedford House, and to some buildings proposed, though, if he were in town, he is too short-sighted to see the prospect."

The new road was made, and, a century later, the stretch within St. Pancras was given the name of the Duke of Grafton's seat, Euston Hall, in Suffolk. There was one proviso : that no buildings were to encroach within fifty feet of the road. It must have been beautiful then, with gardens before every house ; but the proviso was forgotten, and shops and buildings sprang up nearer and nearer the road, so that the plantations of trees and flowers have mostly disappeared.

Euston Road leads from the names of the Bedford family into the land of the Graftons. FITZROY SQUARE, near the western edge of St. Pancras, was named after Charles Fitzroy, 2nd Duke of Grafton, grandson of Charles II and the Duchess of Cleveland. Five streets near the square celebrate the alliance between King Charles and the lecherous and avaricious Barbara Villiers (Pl. 41), whom Evelyn described as the King's " lady of pleasure, and curse of our nation ". A long stretch of the Borough's western boundary is CLEVELAND STREET ; there are also GRAFTON WAY, FITZROY PLACE and STREET, and WARREN STREET. Warren was the maiden name of the wife of Charles Fitzroy —great-great-grandson of Charles II—who began the building of the square in 1790, with houses designed by the Adam brothers.

Although these are noble names that lie heavy on the land about Fitzroy Square, it has been the home of painters and writers from 1827, when the north side was built. Sir Charles Eastlake lived there from 1849, with the Macaulays, Lady Chantrey and Landseer coming to call. Ford Madox Brown took a house there in the 1860's, so the figures that walked this way were of a different painting breed—Burne-Jones, Rossetti and William Morris. George Bernard Shaw lived at No. 29, until he was married in 1898, so Fabians came, in place of the Victorians and Pre-Raphaelites. During the eleven years that G. B. S. lived there, he wrote his first seven plays.

Regent's Park and Primrose Hill both overlay the western boundary of St. Pancras ; but we felt that their stories belonged to St. Marylebone and Hampstead, so we turned back along Euston Road, towards two names of great antiquity. We passed the northern end of TOTTENHAM COURT ROAD, recalling the manor of *Totenhall* (*Totehele* in the *Domesday Book*), which was held by one owner after another, until 1661, when Charles II granted it to Sir Harry Wood, " in payment of a debt which that spendthrift monarch owed to that individual ". It then became the property of Isabella, Countess of Arlington, from whom it descended into the family of the Dukes of Grafton.

The other name we came on was OSSULSTON STREET, leading north from Euston Road. This is not an old street, for it was built after the main Paddington-Islington highway. But the word *Ossulstone* is both old and important, for it was the name of the Saxon " Hun-

39. CAPTAIN THOMAS CORAM, BY HOGARTH

38. THE MARTYRDOM OF SAINT PANCRAS

41. BARBARA VILLIERS, DUCHESS OF CLEVELAND, AFTER SIR PETER LELY

40. GEORGE FREDERICK HANDEL, BY SIR J. THORNHILL

dred " which included all of what are now the Metropolitan boroughs north of the Thames. Here, as elsewhere, the " Hundred " was a territorial division—with its own local authority and court of justice— enclosing one hundred families and their land. *The Place-Names of Middlesex* informed us that the first known name for Ossulstone was *Osulvestan*—" at the stone of *Oswulf* ". Some chroniclers claim that the stone—about which the " Hundred " met to demand and receive justice—was near the present Marble Arch : it was therefore near Tyburn, which was used as a place of execution, from the 12th century until 1783.[1]

At the northern end of Ossulston Street we paused, to rest and think. We stood in the shadows of modern concrete and brick, but we carried a copy of a 1732 map of London, showing St. Pancras to be almost as rural and pleasant as it must have been in Oswulf's time. Across a big portion we read the words *pasture land*, and began to sympathise less with the Duke of Grafton and his new road, and more with the old Duke of Bedford ; for the map shows how agree-able life was for a lord of the manor in the 18th century, with a bucolic view from all his windows, and the right to dispense charity instead of having it wrested from him.

We had paused in SOMERS TOWN—an area built up about 1786, on land belonging to Lord Somers. From Ossulston Street, which becomes Charrington Street to the north, we went east, along Crown-dale Road, which is interesting only because of its ancient name. It was once *Figgeslane juxta Pancraschirche* (1388)—Fig Lane by Pancras Church. We found the old church, in St. Pancras Gardens, where Percy Bysshe Shelley wooed Mary Godwin : the church dedicated to St. Pancras.

Our continuous temptation is to dwell on places because of their historical interest, and not merely because of their relationship with *existing* place- and street-names. It was not easy to ignore the St. Pancras monuments : to Daniel Clarke Esq., " master cook to Queen Elizabeth ", Samuel Cooper (1609–72), who painted Cromwell, Mary Wollstonecraft Godwin (1759–97)—mother of Shelley's Mary —who wrote *A Vindication of the Rights of Women*. But we had to move on, from these lively inscriptions on dead stones, to explore KENTISH TOWN. The name has a new ring about it, but it also goes back—to the manor held by the canons of St. Paul's, called

[1] See chapter on St. Marylebone, pp. 140–1.

" Cantelows or Kennistonne ". We walked north, along Camden Street, and into Pratt Street, to take our bearings.

It is often difficult to make the picture clear, from old names with archaic spellings, boundaries that have been as inconstant as threads in the wind, and the whims of landowners, each wishing to change a place-name to mirror his own vanity. The name *Cantelows* has not been lost. Roger de Cantilupo—a heroic name—was a canon of St. Paul's in the 1240's and he is remembered in CANTELOWES ROAD, in the extreme middle east of St. Pancras. After suffering the vicissitudes of the Reformation, the Commonwealth, then the Restoration, the manor of " Cantelows or Kennistonne " was acquired in 1670 by one John Jeffreys—no relation of Judge Jeffreys who was then beginning his infamous career, as Common Serjeant in the City of London. When John Jeffreys's grand-daughter married Charles Pratt, Earl Camden, of Bayham Abbey, on the border of Kent and Sussex, a shower of new names fell on the parish. We have CAMDEN TOWN, CAMDEN HIGH STREET, ROAD, STREET and MEWS, PRATT STREET, BAYHAM STREET and PLACE, in addition to JEFFREYS STREET, and BRECKNOCK ROAD (after Brecknock Priory, the Jeffreys seat in Wales) which forms part of the eastern boundary with Islington.

We emerged from the foliage of this Camden-Jeffreys family tree, and went by car, north-west into Camden High Street and Chalk Farm Road.[1] We had a goal—opposite Chalk Farm underground station is Belmont Street, and at the northern end of this is the MOTHER SHIPTON [2] public house. My collaborator shamelessly admitted he had never heard of Mother Shipton ; so, it being almost one o'clock, we decided to go to the tavern—to tame our hunger and make our next enquiry.

Mother Shipton, as most people know, was the great Tudor witch, from Yorkshire, whose prophecies tantalised British people for more than four hundred years—even into the late 19th century. She was said to have left a warning, that the world would end on a certain date in 1881, and, the night before, thousands of people in rural England

[1] See chapter on Hampstead, p. 129.
[2] Near the Mother Shipton is SHIPTON PLACE. We tried many ways to find out how the name came to St. Pancras ; we even consulted the solicitor to the brewers, who looked up the title deeds of the inn, on our behalf. But the results are vague. The inn was built in 1847, but the name " Mother Shipton " was not chosen until about ten years later, at a time when the prophecies of the Tudor witch were being much talked about.

spent the long fearful hours praying in the churches and fields. This threat was proved to be a fake, introduced by one of the " editors " of Mother Shipton's prophecies. As we drove towards the public house, I surprised my collaborator by recalling the story of Prince Rupert during the Great Fire of 1666—also prophesied by the Yorkshire witch. He heard of the outbreak as he was coming up the Thames in his ship, and, with apparent seriousness, said that " now Shipton's prophecy was out ". The story occurs somewhere in Pepys.

By the time we began to write this chapter on St. Pancras, we had collected some sixty books on the boroughs of London—some of them scholarly, some sentimental, some pretentious. Many of them revealed the curious parish-pump pride of the local historian—and of the local publisher who sponsored him. *The History and Traditions of St. Pancras* (68 pp.), by Thomas Coull (1861), was also published by T. & W. Coull, of 28 Upper North Place, Gray's Inn Road, and you might suppose, in reading these 68 pages, that St. Pancras was all London. Another book that we carried for this journey was *Sweet Hampstead*, by Mrs. Caroline A. White (1900). Derek Peel had made some notes from " this labour of love "—as Caroline White called it— and they served to link our morning and afternoon expeditions together. Mrs. White wrote " . . . the window near which I loved to write commanded a last fragmentary view of Gospel Oak Fields, which divided Hampstead from the parish of St. Pancras. These fields were even then (early in the sixties) in the hands of speculative builders, but a few green hedges, a group of elms, a pollard oak or two . . . remained.

" Ten years previously the hollow trunk of a very aged tree (fenced round) was still standing, and was locally said to be the remains of the original Gospel Oak, one of the many so called . . . from the use made of them by the Preaching Friars, who under their shade were wont to read the Scriptures to the people."

Having refreshed ourselves at the Mother Shipton, we returned to the car, and went north by Malden Road and Haverstock Road, in search of what remains of Caroline White's " last fragmentary view of Gospel Oak Fields ". But there was only a curve of villas called GOSPEL OAK GROVE, and GOSPEL OAK STATION.

This northern part of St. Pancras ends in woodland and park— Parliament Hill Fields, Kenwood and Hampstead Heath, all making a splendid green show on the map, where the two boroughs meet. We went along Savernake Road and then we left the car to climb— 319 feet above London. The view from the summit of Parliament Hill is the answer to those who accuse London of being a sprawling, untidy city. The distant prospect, beyond the misty bowl that lies between, varies sensitively according to the clarity of the air ; and there is no city more lovely on a late spring afternoon, dominated by the great bubble of the dome of St. Paul's—the towers of Westminster, for the ancientness of London's story—and the chimneys of Battersea, with their smoke spouts rising and mixing with the sky. From the west, where the close grey stone mass of Hammersmith touches the country edges, to the east where Poplar lies—whence the *Sarah Constant* sailed for Virginia—the Thames flows, allowing us occasional glimpses of trembling silver as it winds on—carrying the gentle whisper of its upper reaches towards the tempests of the sea.

We can offer no authentic explanation of why the mound is called PARLIAMENT HILL. The editors of *The Place-Names of Middlesex* assert that " The origin of the name is entirely obscure ". So you may let your imagination loose over the green slopes. None of the respected chroniclers we consulted even mentions Parliament Hill. Mrs. Caroline White wrote of it having borne " the more striking " name of " Traitor's Hill " when she was young. And Traitor's Hill it was for Harrison Ainsworth, when he invented the scene for the night when the Houses of Parliament were to be destroyed by Guy Fawkes. Some of the conspirators stood here, high above the city, waiting, in vain, for the sight of flames against the sky.

We ended our journey curiously—in Highgate Cemetery, in the extreme north-east of St. Pancras. There was one grave that I had always wished to see. Among my papers was a cutting I had kept, from America's *Time Magazine*. Under the heading of *Great Britain* was printed : " Perched on a hillside amid drab housing projects and crumbling Victorian relics, lies London's cluttered Highgate Cemetery. There, in a single grave, rest the remains of a onetime 19th Century German beauty, Jenny von Westphalen, her grandson Harry Longuet, her servant girl Helene Demuth and her famed husband Karl Marx."

We drove back along Savernake Road, Gordon House Road, and then north to the cemetery, by way of Highgate Road, Swain's Lane and Chester Road.

We found the grave, with a merciless tangle of weeds growing over the withered skeleton of a wreath. A new pattern of associations was suggested : the " first house in Chelsea ", in 1849, from which the Marx family were " evicted in the most brutal and ruthless fashion " —the six years in Dean Street, Soho, and the days of study in the British Museum, from nine in the morning to seven in the evening— the move to 9 Grafton Terrace, Malden Road, which we had passed after leaving the Mother Shipton—then, in 1875, the move just around the corner, into 41 Maitland Park Road, Haverstock Hill, where Marx died in 1883, while sitting in his easy chair.

Karl Marx liked his children : in the early days they could persuade him to take them to Jack Straw's Castle, in Hampstead, where they shared ginger-beer, bread and cheese. When he was older he liked to walk from Maitland Park Road, north, beyond Parliament Hill and into Kenwood, which is less than a mile from where he is buried.

We made our way there, along Highgate High Street and Hampstead Lane, into Kenwood, to begin our afternoon and evening journey through Hampstead.

CHAPTER ELEVEN

Hampstead

" Hampstead is the most delightful place for air and scenery near London. I cannot understand how the air is so good, it does not explain itself to me ; coming up out of London is like going to the top of Kirk Yetton. I have been out here all day, walking and strolling about the heath."

R. L. STEVENSON on holiday, in a
letter to a friend.

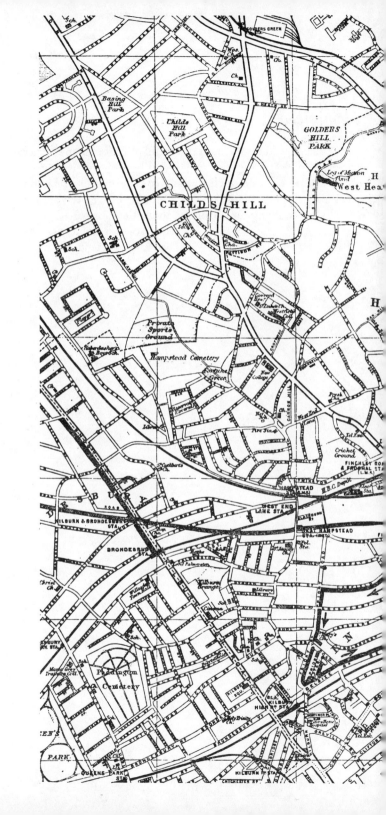

The cartographers embrace KENWOOD and Kenwood House (Pl. 42), within the Borough of St. Pancras, but their history belongs to Hampstead. Here is one more name that has kept the scholars guessing. Some claim that it comes from Reginald Kentewode, a dean of St. Paul's ; but J. H. Lloyd, in his lecture on *Caen Wood and its Associations*, published in 1892, suggests that the Conqueror gave the land to a kinsman, from *Caen* in Normandy, who planted the French name on his English estate. The old spelling survives in CAEN WOOD TOWERS, which we passed in Hampstead Lane, before we came to the broad gateway into the gardens of Kenwood House. It was near here that Shelley was once seen, notebook in hand, leaning upon the old grey gate that opened where we were walking—between voluptuous rhododendrons that suddenly parted to reveal the mansion, rebuilt by Robert Adam in the reign of George III.

Kenwood House—now a museum with an important collection of pictures—is still referred to at times as MANSFIELD HOUSE, after William Murray, the first Lord Mansfield [1] (Pl. 44), who bought the estate in 1755. The undulating park, the shining lake and majestic trees, were mostly from his plans. We stood before the simple façade of the house and looked over the beautiful landscape, that once caused Burke to say, " Oh, this is just the place for a reformer. All the beauties are beyond your reach ; you cannot destroy them." The beauties remain, undestroyed, with immense copper beeches, like great sultans, on the lawns. They were planted there by Lord Mansfield— harsh in his office as Lord Chief Justice of the King's Bench, but greatly loved in the Parish. To describe the scene of his creation we might borrow the compliment once paid to Lord Mansfield's own coun- tenance—" It was an assemblage of genius, dignity, and good nature, which none could observe without reverence and regard."

Up the slope from Kenwood House stands the eastern lodge of an ancient toll-gate, and, opposite, the famous public house, THE SPANIARDS (Pl. 43). They guard the entrance into HAMPSTEAD proper, which one approaches by way of SPANIARDS ROAD. Hampstead (*Hamestede* in the *Domesday Book*), was an ancient farm-site : and

[1] At the eastern boundary of the Borough is FLEET ROAD (recalling the source of the Fleet River, from the ponds of Hampstead and Highgate), leading into MANSFIELD ROAD, named after Lord Mansfield.

The Spaniards, so the proprietor told us, is so called because a Spaniard owned it in the 16th century. But there is a more lively story than this, in the link between The Spaniards, Lord Mansfield and Kenwood. During the Gordon Riots, in 1780, Lord Mansfield's town house in Bloomsbury was ransacked and his precious library was destroyed. The wild men then set out on the long climb to Hampstead and Lord Mansfield's country house. But the month was June, and when they reached the Heath the men were pleased to pause at The Spaniards to cool their throats. The tavern keeper was devoted to his lordship's interests, so he " affected rabble sympathies ", and encouraged them to refill their tankards. While they were refreshing their courage for the rest of the march, the landlord secretly gave information to Lord Mansfield's steward, who sent additional barrels of ale from the Kenwood cellars. In the meantime, a messenger was despatched to bring the military, who secured the drunken rioters and saved Kenwood House.

We went to The Spaniards, which had just opened, but there was no hint of drunken rioters in the small number of early guests, who were already playing darts, beside the fire-place. I allowed my collaborator to find for himself the only object that was important to our book.

Over the mantelpiece was a copy of Keats's *Ode to a Nightingale*, with the legend that the poet was drinking here with some friends on the evening in 1819, before he suddenly went alone on to the Heath, to hear the nightingale that inspired the poem.

We sent our car on, and walked across Hampstead Heath by way of Spaniards Road—with occasional great distances, like Constable land-scapes, appearing between the trees. There are two other taverns by the Heath, with stirring names : THE BULL AND BUSH, of the spanking Cockney song, and, at the southern end, JACK STRAW'S CASTLE, where Karl Marx used to sit with his children, over their cheese and ginger-beer. On public holidays these are merry drinking places for the East-End Londoners : for them this is "'Appy 'Ampstead"—one more place-name of their devising. The popular explanation of Jack Straw's Castle is that " a rude fort or mound " was thrown up here " as a defence against or by Jack Straw's or Wat Tyler's rebel army ".[1]

The inn acts as a lodge to what is still called the Village of HAMP-STEAD. In 1086 it was truly *Hamestede*—the homestead—with but

[1] *Sweet Hampstead and its Associations*, Mrs. Caroline A. White, p. 127.

five dwellings. Its height, and the distance from London, made it inaccessible : even in 1800 the inhabitants numbered only 5,000. In Tudor times, most of the women in the village were laundresses—the " suddy sisterhood ", Caroline White roguishly calls them. They took in the washing of the London nobility, who liked their petticoats to be dried in the fresh air, remote from the pollution of the city. The great drying ground was the VALE OF HEALTH, east of Jack Straw's Castle, and named after health-giving waters that flowed there. It must have been a jolly sight, on a Tudor Monday morning, when the Hampstead villagers gathered to see the clothes and fashions of their London betters, washed and laid out to dry in the Vale. There is no street-name to help us imagine this scene ; London's only Laundry Road is in Fulham.

While developing our plan of Hampstead, we realised that the streets form, roughly, five groups. In the north-centre we have *Poetry and Literature* ; south of this is the group we call the *Law* ; in the south-west we have the *Church* ; in the south-east, *Education* ; and in the extreme south, *Crime*. It is legitimate, and perhaps amusing, to take them in this order for the remainder of our journey.

The Vale of Health lies in the *Poetry and Literature* group, for we found a small cottage, with a plaque telling us that Leigh Hunt lived here in 1816. This was two years after his release from imprisonment for describing the Prince Regent, in print, as a " corpulent Adonis of fifty ". Leigh Hunt was not the first of Hampstead's great literary men, for Sir Richard Steele (Pl. 45) was living there in 1712, when he wrote to Pope, " I am in a solitude, an house between Hampstead and London ". Steele has his memorial in the Borough, in STEELE'S ROAD, running into Haverstock Hill, near the eastern boundary.

We must now group three place-names into one story : WELL WALK, with GAINSBOROUGH GARDENS opening to the east, and FLASK WALK, to which we drove, along East Heath Road.

In 1691, the mother of the infant 3rd Earl of Gainsborough presented a chalybeate spring " with six acres of land, to the use and benefit of the poor of Hampstead ". Charity proved to be a lively investment : within ten years, Hampstead's waters were recommended by " the most eminent physicians " ; and taverns, tea-rooms, dancing and gaming rooms were opened, so that visitors could take their pleasures and their cures, all in one. The Upper Flask and Lower Flask taverns increased their business by sending flasks of water each morning, to be sold in the City inns and coffee-houses, at 3*d.* a glass. But the Upper Flask was destined for nobler purposes than this.

To this tavern, in summer-time, came the members of the Kit-Kat Club—" thirty-nine distinguished noblemen and gentlemen, zealously attached to the Protestant succession of the House of Hanover ". Among them were Vanbrugh, Congreve, Addison and Steele—and Sir Godfrey Kneller, who painted the famous Kit-Kat portraits.[1]

The next "literary figure", Mrs. Barbauld, we have described in the chapter on Stoke Newington, whither she moved from Hampstead in 1802.

Hampstead has not been kind to its " literary ladies ", for neither Mrs. Barbauld, nor Joanna Baillie, who followed her, has been granted even a lane to recall their years in the Borough. Joanna Baillie must have been a great personage in Hampstead ; not only for her own numerous literary works (she wrote *De Montfort : A Tragedy*, performed at Drury Lane in 1800 by Mrs. Siddons and Kemble), but also for the society she gathered about her. There is a nice description by Crabb Robinson, of a morning in May 1812, when he met Wordsworth in Oxford Road (now Oxford Street) and walked with him to Hampstead to see Joanna Baillie.[2]

> She is small in figure, and her gait is mean and shuffling, but her manners are those of a well-bred woman. She has none of *the unpleasant airs too common to literary ladies.* Her conversation is sensible. She possesses apparently considerable information, is prompt without being forward, and has a fixed judgment of her own, without any disposition to force it upon others. Wordsworth said of her, with warmth : "If I had to present anyone to a foreigner as a model English gentlewoman, it would be Joanna Baillie."

We came back to our tracks—to Flask Walk, which leads into Willow Road, Downshire Hill and KEATS GROVE.

" I am a good deal with Dilke and Brown," Keats (Pl. 46) wrote to his brother, in 1818. " They are very kind to me . . . I don't think I could stop in Hampstead but for their neighbourhood." He had already stayed there with Leigh Hunt, in the little cottage in the Vale. " *I defy you to have lived in a smaller cottage than I have done,*" wrote Leigh Hunt. " Yet it has held Shelley and Keats and half a dozen

---

[1] KITCAT TERRACE, in Poplar, is named, not after the famous club, but in memory of the Rev. Henry James Kitcat, rector of Bow (1904–21).

[2] Lockhart's *Life* of Scott, vol II, pp. 267–8.

friends in it at once ; and they have made worlds of their own within the rooms. Keats's *Sleep and Poetry* is a description of a parlour that was mine, no larger than an old mansion's closet."

> For I am brimful of the friendliness
> That in a little cottage I have found.

In 1817 Keats was living in lodgings that are now the Well Tavern, in Well Walk. It was here that he was " a good deal " with Charles Armitage Brown and Charles Dilke, before he shared Brown's house in Wentworth Place, in 1818. Other great men lived in Hampstead : Austin Dobson, Swinburne, and, most important of all, Constable, who went there first in 1821—then in 1827 when he lived at No. 40, Well Walk. " . . . our little drawing-room ", he wrote, " commands a view unsurpassed in Europe, from Westminster Abbey to Gravesend." His paintings, and his sketch books, reveal the importance of Hampstead in developing his imagination and talent—but there is no street named after him in Hampstead ; the nearest is Constable Close in Hendon.

Romney also lived in Hampstead, in a mansion that he built on Hampstead Hill, during the closing years of separation from his wife, when he claimed to be " filled with that desire of the unsatisfied soul for a peace that the world cannot give ". But Romney is also forgotten.

Leading off Willow Road are Gardnor, Gayton, Willoughby and Worsley Streets, which might be pleasantly changed and dedicated to four of these writers and painters who turned Hampstead Village into London's Parnassus.

We drove away from Keats Grove and the Keats Memorial Museum, into Downshire Hill, which forms a crossroad with ROSSLYN HILL and THURLOW ROAD. Nearby are ELDON GROVE and LYNDHURST ROAD. We should have been a little awed had we met the four gentlemen, after whom these streets were named, for, in turn, each became Lord High Chancellor. The first, Edward, 1st Baron Thurlow (1731–1806), who is described as " vulgar, arrogant, profane and immoral ", was one of the most bigoted supporters of Lord North's American policy. Fox said of him " no man could be so wise as Thurlow looked ". The second, Alexander Wedderburn,[1] 1st Earl of Rosslyn (1733–1805), another supporter of Lord North, was

---

[1] There is also WEDDERBURN ROAD, south of Lyndhurst Road.

marked as " stiff and pompous ", and " false " in his dealings with Pitt ; but elegant and matchless at the bar, and smoothly ruthless in pursuing his ambitions. The third, John Scott, 1st Earl of Eldon (1751–1838), is accused of having been a great lawyer, but no statesman ; an enemy of reform and religious liberty, and parsimonious to boot. The last, John Singleton Copley, Baron Lyndhurst (1772–1863), the son of the portrait painter, was born in Boston, Massachusetts. He brought nobler qualities to the woolsack, with his New England blood : he did not inherit the Georgian egotism of his predecessors, and was recalled as having " never been excelled for lucidity, method and legal acumen ".

We drove away from these memorials to the *Law*—down Shepherd's Walk and Arkwright Road, then south along Finchley Road and west along Canfield Gardens, to Priory Road—the beginning of our *Church* group of streets, in the district of KILBURN. According to *The Place-Names of Middlesex*,[1] the word Kilburn—vague in meaning —goes back to *Cuneburna*, in the 12th century : it might be traced to *cyne-burna*, meaning a " royal stream ", or possibly to *cӯna-burna*, a " cows' stream ".

PRIORY ROAD, PRIORY TERRACE, ABBEY ROAD and ABBOTS PLACE are on the site of a priory founded by Henry I's wife, Queen Matilda, for three of her retired Maids of Honour. Sir Walter Scott left his own version of the legend that grew up around the Priory, in his poem *The Muckle Stain, or Bleeding Stone of Kilburn Priory*, which was not published until 1881, in *The Athenæum*.

The poem unfolds the legend of Sir Gervase de Morton the Good, his virtuous wife Dame Isabel, and his wicked brother Stephen, all of whom lived before the Priory was built. While Sir Gervase was away in the north, Stephen tried to seduce Dame Isabel, who spurned him. He swore revenge—not on her, but on his innocent brother— and he assaulted Sir Gervase on his way home, and cruelly murdered him in a quarry.

As Sir Gervase was dying, he breathed these words to his brother :

> " . . . on this stone where now I bleed
> Thyself shall breathe thy last."

The murderer returned to Dame Isabel, but she still spurned him, so he cast her into a dungeon.

[1] P. 112.

Some time later, Stephen passed Kilburn Priory, recently built from stones taken from the quarry where he had murdered his brother, and there, in the wall, he saw blood oozing from a stone—" this stone " on which his brother had prophesied that he would "breathe" his " last ". Remorse burned his heart : he confessed his sin, bequeathed his fortune to the Priory, pined away and died on the " Bleeding Stone of Kilburn Priory ". We had to shut our eyes very tight to see the typical Walter Scott romance take life again, among the respectable houses of Priory and Abbey Roads.

There was one more name in the western part of Hampstead that caught our attention on the map—SHOOT UP HILL, which is a continuation northwards of the main Kilburn High Road. My collaborator had read Scott's poem the night before, and this no doubt encouraged him to expect at least the story of a swashbuckling highwayman, to explain Shoot Up Hill. But the truth could not be duller : it is so named merely because there is a sharp rise here—a shoot-up—in the road, which follows the line of the Roman *Watling Street*, towards St. Albans.

We turned east, along Belsize Road and on to SWISS COTTAGE (named from a Swiss chalet built there in the last century). Then to ETON AVENUE, and the area of *Education*.

But we must first explain BELSIZE, named from the manor of *Belassis*—" beautifully situated "—in the 14th century. There lived Roger de Brabazon, Chief Justice to Edward III. When he died he left the estate to the Abbey of Westminster, in return for daily Masses to be said for the good of his soul and that of his friend, Edmund, Earl of Lancaster. There is no Brabazon Street in Hampstead, but there is LANCASTER GROVE (and DRIVE), leading north-west from Eton Avenue. In 1720, the mansion on the estate, and the splendid park, were opened as one more of the many pleasure gardens about London. A year later, " their royal highnesses the Prince and Princess of Wales " dined there, " attended by several persons of quality ". They were offered " the diversions of hunting, and such others as the place afforded, with which they seemed well entertained, and at their departure were liberal to the servants ".

We are told that on such occasions " the mounted company rode over the park with horns blowing, and beagles barking, the proprietor leading the hunt in person." [1] Unfortunately, the " irregu-

[1] *Sweet Hampstead and its Associations*, Mrs. Caroline A. White, p. 336.

42.   KENWOOD HOUSE

43.   THE SPANIARDS TAVERN

44. WILLIAM MURRAY, 1ST EARL OF
MANSFIELD, BY J. B. VAN LOO

45. SIR RICHARD STEELE,
BY KNELLER

46. JOHN KEATS, BY CHARLES
ARMITAGE BROWN

47. SIR EDMUNDBURY GODFREY

larities" within the mansion were such that, soon after the royal visit, the proprietor was apprehended and led to Newgate prison.

We turned to Eton Avenue—and found also ETON COLLEGE ROAD, PROVOST ROAD, FELLOWS ROAD and OPPIDANS ROAD, close together, on estates that have belonged to Eton College since 1449. Nearby are also Winchester Road, Marlborough Hill, Clifton Hill, King's College Road, Wadham Gardens and Merton Rise, all continuing the theme of *Education*.

To the east of the colony of Eton streets is CHALK FARM ROAD, running into St. Pancras. CHALK FARM is a surprising name : the soil here is clay—not chalk. The editors of *The Place-Names of Middlesex* tell us that Chalk Farm is " a corruption of an older name, *Chaldecote* ", of the mid-13th century, and give us the explanation of " cold cottages "—a descriptive place-name which we may link with Poplar's Cold Harbour. A later version of the name, *Chalcot*, survives in nearby CHALCOT ROAD, SQUARE and CRESCENT. But we did not go there : we travelled south, to PRIMROSE HILL, to end our journey on the theme of *Crime*.

Primrose Hill is a park of sixty acres, simply named from the primroses that once ornamented its slopes. The history of the Hill belies its pretty name, for it was a favourite haunt of duellists and ruffians, up to little more than one hundred years ago. The unsolved mystery of the murder of Sir Edmundbury Godfrey (Pl. 47), London's leading magistrate, in the reign of Charles II, gives the story of Primrose Hill its chief thrill. On the night of October 14, 1678, Sir Edmundbury was found in a ditch, strangled, and run through with his own sword. The crime was turned into anti-Papist propaganda—through a complication of plot and villainy that does not matter here—and the killing was finally blamed on three servants in Somerset House— the residence of the Queen. The servants were Green, Berry and Hill, and they were beheaded, some months after the crime. The startling question " Who killed Sir Edmundbury Godfrey ? " still pops up now and then in popular magazines—but the answer will never be known.

For many years after the execution of the three innocent servants, Primrose Hill was familiarly called *Greenberry Hill*, in their memory. Then the old name came back. But, for some curious reason, six hundred yards from Primrose Hill, and in the Borough of St. Marylebone, there is a short thoroughfare still named GREENBERRY STREET.

CHAPTER TWELVE

St. Marylebone

" Some Dukes at Marybone bowl time away."
LADY MARY WORTLEY.

" There will be deep play tonight at Marybone, and consequently money may be pick'd up upon the road. Meet me there, and I'll give you the hint who is worth setting."
Macheath, in The Beggar's Opera.

We fell into a miserable trap in beginning our walk in St. Marylebone. At the easternmost tip of the Borough map are HANWAY STREET and PLACE : two short thoroughfares rising, curved like the ribs of an umbrella, from Oxford Street to Tottenham Court Road, near the teeming intersection of St. Giles Circus. Nothing could seem more appropriate, for we read in a number of books that these streets were named after Jonas Hanway (1712–1786), the first Englishman to use an umbrella as part of his everyday dress.

In the 17th century there were a few umbrellas used in London coffee-houses, but only to shelter elegant customers as they stepped towards their carriages. It was not until the middle of the 18th century that Jonas Hanway defied criticism, and the climate, by *carrying* an umbrella in the City streets. Hanway was a great traveller, a trader with Russia and Persia, and author of 74 " works ". He was a man of full measure : a warm-hearted philanthropist—especially kind to chimney-sweeps—an advocate of more gentle treatment of prisoners, and important enough to have angered Dr. Johnson by making an attack on the habit of drinking tea. His bust is in Westminster Abbey, and he is one of the subjects of Austin Dobson's *Eighteenth Century Vignettes*. Over all these achievements shines his courage in being the first Englishman to " wear " an umbrella, and for this alone he deserved to have two streets named after him.

When we submitted our notes to the Borough Librarian, he replied, " The story about the connection of Jonas ' Umbrella ' Hanway with Hanway Street is a persistent legend, but it is quite erroneous. Major *John* Hanway appears in the Ratebooks as far back as 1710 and Hanway Street itself appears in the Ratebooks for 1725. Jonas Hanway, son of Thomas Hanway of Portsmouth, was a boy of thirteen at the time." The Librarian then added the doleful suggestion, " You, as authors, will welcome this chance to expose an error which has been repeated so many times."

The southern part of the Borough of St. Marylebone is enclosed within a tidy parallelogram, with Marylebone Road to the north, Oxford Street for the southern base, Edgware Road to the west, and, for the eastern boundary, an almost straight line from Hanway Street to Regent's Park. Within this parallelogram are the streets named by the great landowners, since the time of Queen Anne. To comprehend this pattern, one must have the diligence, and patience, of a silver-fish making its way through Debrett.

In 1710 the manor of Marylebone was bought by John Holles (HOLLES STREET), who married the daughter of Henry Cavendish (CAVENDISH SQUARE and PLACE, OLD and NEW CAVENDISH STREETS), 2nd Duke of Newcastle. There was no heir to the dukedom, so it was bestowed on John Holles. The Holles-Cavendish union brought other street-names : DEVONSHIRE PLACE, STREET and CLOSE, from a relative, the 1st Earl of Devonshire ; OGLE STREET and MANSFIELD STREET from family titles ; and BOLSOVER STREET and WELBECK STREET from the Cavendish estates in Derbyshire and Nottinghamshire. John Holles also failed to produce a son, and his heiress, Henrietta (HENRIETTA PLACE), was married in 1713 to Edward Harley (HARLEY STREET) who succeeded his father, in 1724, as Earl of Oxford and Mortimer (MORTIMER STREET) and Baron Harley of Wigmore Castle (WIGMORE STREET), who also had property at Wimpole in Cambridge-shire (WIMPOLE STREET).

Again there was no male heir—the only child of the marriage was Lady Margaret Cavendish Harley (MARGARET STREET), who in 1734 married William Bentinck (BENTINCK STREET), 2nd Duke of Portland and Marquess of Titchfield (PORTLAND HOUSE and PLACE, GREAT PORTLAND STREET and GREAT TITCHFIELD STREET), whose estates in Nottinghamshire gave the names to CLIPSTONE STREET and CAR-BURTON STREET. With the fourth generation came one more name, when the eldest daughter married the 2nd Viscount Weymouth and added WEYMOUTH STREET to the family album.

The streets in the western part of the parallelogram reveal an equally imposing story. Most of them took their names from William Henry Portman, of Orchard Portman in Somerset, who inherited some 270 acres of St. Marylebone in the middle of the 18th century. From him came PORTMAN SQUARE and STREET, and ORCHARD STREET. His grandmother was a Seymour (SEYMOUR STREET and PLACE), and the head of her family was the Duke of Somerset (SOMERSET STREET). The Portmans later owned Bryanston, near Blandford in Dorset, and thus we have BRYANSTON SQUARE, PLACE and STREET, BLANDFORD SQUARE and STREET, and DORSET SQUARE [1] and STREET.

There was one departure from the family rule, in the naming of BAKER STREET. In *London Past and Present*, by H. B. Wheatley and

[1] Blandford Square and Dorset Square are just north of the parallelogram.

Peter Cunningham, we were informed that Mr. Portman had a neighbour in Dorset, Sir Edward Baker, who was also an old friend, and that Baker Street was named after him. This version is repeated in *The Face of London* (p. 237), and in *The Place-Names of Middlesex* (p. 139), the latest and usually immaculate authority on street-names. Once more, the Borough Librarian saved us from following these scholars into error. He wrote, against the story of Sir Edward Baker, " An old Act of Parliament recently acquired by this library shows that *William Baker* leased a number of acres near Portman Square from William Henry Portman, for building development," and it was after him that the street was named.

Of course, it would be a popular move if the long thoroughfare could be renamed after its most famous, if mythical resident—Sherlock Holmes (Pl. 48). However, the Borough Council have compromised with SHERLOCK MEWS, opening off Paddington Street, between Baker and Chiltern Streets. (The name-sleuth must be wary here. Near Edgware Road is Watson's Mews, but it has no connection with the Conan Doyle stories.)

When we take a magnifying glass to the pattern of noble names in St. Marylebone, there are many surprises, and one more trap. We imagined that OXFORD STREET—the present canyon of department stores—was named after the husband of Henrietta Holles, the Earl of Oxford and Mortimer. But the name was here fifty years before the advent of the Holles family. This was *The Road to Oxford*.

We walked from Hanway Street, along Oxford Street, in search of a diversion, in BERNERS STREET—the third opening on the right. William Berners of Woolverstone Hall, Suffolk, owned an estate here in the mid-18th century. We were seeking two numbers in Berners Street : first, No. 13, where the Swiss painter, Henry Fuseli, was living in 1804 ; where Haydon visited him and wrote, " I fancied Fuseli himself to be a giant. I heard his footsteps, and saw a little bony hand slide round the edge of the door, followed by a little white-headed, lion-faced man in an old flannel dressing-gown tied round his waist with a piece of rope, and upon his head the bottom of Mrs. Fuseli's work-basket." Opie, Benjamin West and Copley Fielding also lived in Berners Street, and Samuel Taylor Coleridge, at No. 71.

The second house we were seeking was No. 54, the scene of the " Berners Street Hoax" perpetrated in 1809 by Theodore Hook.

His wild career included one year at Harrow, the writing of thirteen successful operas before he was twenty-one, accusations of fraud, and the wicked trick on Mrs. Tottingham who lived at No. 54. He spent six weeks in preparing for the day when " there came to her door hundreds of tradespeople bearing goods of all sizes and descriptions, from a mahogany coffin to an ounce of snuff, ordered by Hook in her name, to be delivered at the same hour ; while at the same hour, at the invitation of Mrs. Tottingham (per T. H.), came as well bishops, ministers of State, doctors in haste to cure her bodily ailments, lawyers to make her will, barbers to shave her, mantua-makers to fit her,—men, women, and children on every conceivable errand ". George Clinch's version of this story in *Marylebone and St. Pancras* [1] ends with the understandable comment, " The damage done and the confusion created were very great."

We continued along Oxford Street and turned north into Holles Street—Lord Byron was born at No. 24, in 1788—and then into Cavendish Square ; the scene of Thackeray's " Gaunt House ", the mansion of the wicked Marquis of Steyne, in *Vanity Fair*. Here also Romney lived, during the great years of his infatuation with Emma Hamilton, before he went to live in Hampstead. [2] On the northern side of Cavendish Square we came to HARLEY STREET. It is not easy for any man who has dared the luxury of ill health on a Harley Street doorstep, to think, instead, of that astonishing early 18th-century figure, Robert Harley (1661–1724), 1st Earl of Oxford in the Harley line—responsible for the treaty of Utrecht ; later disgraced and sent to the Tower ; then released into years of retirement, during which he began the great Harleian collection, now in the British Museum.

We walked half-way along Harley Street, then back again, and it was strange to realise that inside these tall houses, with their hundreds of brass name-plates—*Doctor This* and *Doctor That*—there lived Lady Nelson, the Duke of Wellington, Turner, Beechy, Ramsay, Wilkie Collins—and Gladstone, in No. 73, where his windows were broken one Sunday afternoon in 1878 by a mob that did not like his politics.

Our next move was along Wigmore Street, to Wimpole Street, which gave us two important stories of mid-Victorian literature. We found the numbers we sought—No. 67, then No. 50.

It was in 1850 that Tennyson published *In Memoriam*, written in memory of Arthur H. Hallam who had died suddenly in Vienna, in

---

[1] P. 102.   [2] See chapter on Hampstead, p. 126.

1833, at the age of twenty-two. Arthur Hallam was the son of Henry Hallam (Pl. 51), the historian, who lived at No. 67 Wimpole Street, from 1819 to 1840. HALLAM STREET, which runs parallel with Great Portland Street, in the east of the Borough, was named after him. The second address is No. 50 Wimpole Street, where Mr. Barrett and his daughter Elizabeth went to live in 1838. Seven years passed before the January morning in 1845, when a letter was delivered at No. 50 from Robert Browning, saying, " I love your verses with all my heart, Dear Miss Barrett." Four months later he called at the forbidding house, where Mr. Barrett kept his daughter almost like a prisoner. In the early hours of September 12, 1846, she left No. 50 in secret, to marry Robert Browning in the St. Marylebone Parish Church nearby.[1]

We walked along Wigmore Street and turned north by Duke Street, into MANCHESTER SQUARE. As late as 1744 this part of London was considered so remote that families living nearby " kept their coaches", and thought of themselves "as living in the country". The mansion on the north side of the Square was built by the 4th Duke of Manchester in the late 1770's, and was first called Manchester House. The Spanish Embassy occupied it in 1788 and left SPANISH PLACE, and the Catholic church of St. James, as memorials to their tenancy. But the great days of the house began with the Marquess of Hertford. " The old yellow chariot" of the Prince Regent soon included it in its wicked circuit ; and, with Lady Hertford as the chief attraction, the house became so popular with the First Gentleman of Europe that, in 1814, Londoners were buying up copies of a " scurrilous print" containing a " facetious advertisement" which announced, " Lost, between Pall Mall and Manchester Square, his Royal Highness the Prince Regent."

The three Lords Hertford who followed, acquired the pictures and *objets d'art* which we know today as the *Wallace Collection* in HERTFORD HOUSE. The 4th Marquess left this splendid and unrivalled gift to his kinsman, Sir Richard Wallace,[2] who willed that, on the

---

[1] There is a Barrett Street, between James Street and Duke Street, but this is an older name and is not associated with the Barretts of Wimpole Street.

[2] There is no street named after him in London but there is a Boulevard Richard Wallace in Neuilly. Sir Richard lived many years in Paris and he gave the city no less than 100 drinking fountains, for the wayfarer and the poor.

death of his wife, the whole collection should be given to the Nation.

We walked along MANCHESTER STREET and into ROBERT ADAM STREET, named after the greatest of the Adam brothers (Pl. 50), who built many of the fine houses in this area. (There is no street in all London to recall Wren or Nash.) Then, across Baker Street, into Portman Square. The once most celebrated house in the Square is no more : Montagu House—the home of Elizabeth Montagu, founder of " The Blue Stocking Club "—was demolished in 1941. *Chambers's Biographical Dictionary* describes her thus : " Montagu, Elizabeth, *née* Robinson (1720–1800), a blue-stocking and lion-hunter, with £10,000 a year, who entertained everyone from king to chimney-sweeps, and wrote against Voltaire an *Essay on Shakespeare*." It is a harsh estimate of an enchanting woman. " For many years her elegant home in Portman Square was opened to the world. Here the wit, rank, and talent " of the late 18th century " assembled at her receptions ; and here was the apartment covered with feathered hangings, celebrated by the poet Cowper in the lines—

> The birds put off their every hue
> To dress a room for Montague." [1]

She found time to write an informed attack on Voltaire for his abuse of Shakespeare, and every 1st of May she entertained the chimney-sweeps of London in her garden. For this kindly gesture she was given a splendid memorial.

Among Mrs. Montagu's guests at the annual parties may have been one David Porter who was described as " a sort of official chimney-sweep to the village of Marylebone ". He prospered and became a builder—then a gambler in real estate. He built on land known as Apple Village, north-east of Portman Square, and, perhaps remembering his May Day hostess, he named it MONTAGU SQUARE. Nor did he forget the warmth of Mrs. Montagu's hospitality. Ten years after her death, on the Jubilee of George III, Mr. Porter gave his workmen " a substantial entertainment " in the half-finished square. " Much conviviality and harmony prevailed around the festive board."

From Portman Square we walked west along Seymour Street to GREAT CUMBERLAND PLACE, which celebrates William Augustus, Duke of Cumberland, the " Butcher " of Culloden. Then to the whirligig

[1] *Marylebone and St. Pancras*, p. 62.

of traffic at MARBLE ARCH—an area with perhaps the most fascinating name history of any in London. The name Marble Arch is new : it came here with the monument which was removed from the front of Buckingham Palace in 1851. For the first, ancient name, we go to a plaque on the base of Hyde Park railings, opposite the Odeon Cinema. It tells us that " 69 yards north of this spot " stood the infamous three-legged gallows, known as Tyburn Tree, at which martyrs and criminals were hanged, up to the 18th century.[1] So we trace the story of the name, from *Tiburne*, in the *Domesday Book*, to *Teyborn*, and *Tyborne* ; then *Maryborne, Maribone, Mary le Bone*, and *St. Marylebone*, as it is spelled today. We begin with a brook, or bourne, that rose near Hampstead, with two tributaries : one near what is now Fitzjohn's Avenue, and the other near the site of Belsize Manor House. They flowed on as one—a double brook—*Tybourne*—*Tyburn*.

The terrible triangular gallows—" The Deadly Never Green "—were first used at the end of the 14th century for the execution of the Lollards—the followers of John Wycliffe—antagonists of the rich worldly prelates of the Church. Their martyrdom gave rise to another explanation of the name. " Tieburne ", wrote Thomas Fuller (1608–61), in his *The Worthies of England*, " some will have it so called from Tie and Burne, because the poor Lollards for whom this instrument (of cruelty to them, though of justice to malefactors) was first set up, had their necks tied to the beame, and their lower parts burnt in the fire ".

We could write for a long time, making our way through the history of *Tyburn* (Pl. 49)—the pitiless procession of violent death : The Holy Maid of Kent ; Mrs. Turner, the " inventress of yellow starch ", executed in 1615 for being implicated in the murder of Sir Thomas Overbury ; John Felton, the assassin of George Villiers, Duke of Buckingham ; Jonathan Wild, in 1725, a merry villain who " picked the parson's pocket of his corkscrew " on the scaffold—and the bodies of Cromwell, Bradshaw and Ireton, hanging from the three stilts of the gallows in 1661. The fair streams that rose on Hampstead's heights ran with some terrible blood before they were finally lost in the volume of the Thames.

[1] The site of the gallows was in the present Connaught Place, but the only street-name recalling the " Tree " is TYBURN WAY—the curved stretch of road between Marble Arch and Hyde Park.

But there is also a gentler tale, mixed in with the horror. In 1400, the parishioners of *Tyburn* were granted a licence to build a new church, dedicated to St. Mary. It was also beside the *Tyburn*— beside the bourne—so it was called *St. Mary by the bourne*—the ST. MARYLEBONE of today. Some scholars have tried to twist the origin into *St. Mary la Bonne*, but this is mere imagination.

There is one more word that has come to us from *Tyburn*, which my collaborator pointed out to me, with pleasure, as he carried his armful of maps and reference books. The first known hangman at *Tyburn* was named Derrick, and he has endured in the word now given to " a contrivance for hoisting or moving heavy weights ".

We walked north along Edgware Road, from Marble Arch, to a failure in our research. Our map showed two streets on the right, north of George Street—CATO STREET and HOMER STREET. They seemed a graceful pair, plucked from the Classics. Cato was probably Marcus Porcius Cato, soldier, and the first of Roman historians in Latin. Homer was obviously the great epic poet of Greece. Cato Street is famed for the conspiracy of 1820, rather than for the Roman from whom it takes its name. The instigator of the " Cato Street Conspiracy ", Arthur Thistlewood, was rich and educated, but he was also belligerent. After being imprisoned for threatening Lord Sidmouth, he formed the gang of some twenty-four men who met above a stable in Cato Street to plan the murder of the *entire* British Cabinet —while they were dining at Lord Harrowby's house in Grosvenor Square. But the plotters were forestalled : Bow Street officers and a detachment of Coldstream Guards stormed into Cato Street and nine of the miscreants were taken. Thistlewood escaped ; only to be caught next morning, tried, and hanged for treason.

We found Cato Street—the second of four small thoroughfares running between HARROWBY STREET (after Dudley Ryder, 1st Earl of Harrowby) and Crawford Place. Then my collaborator read me a passage from *Marylebone and St. Pancras*—" The street from whence this extravagant conspiracy is named . . . was afterwards named *Horace Street*." This is true : the residents of 1820 were so shocked by the publicity they endured that they asked for the change. But the infamy of the 19th century became the pride of the 20th century. Just before the recent war, the Borough Council persuaded the London County Council to expel Horace and restore Cato in his place—and so Cato Street came into its own again.

From Cato Street we walked to Marylebone Road, by way of Homer Street. Parallel with this is SHILLIBEER STREET, and nearby, on the south side of Marylebone Road, we found the "Yorkshire Stingo"—famous in the 18th century for its gardens and bowling-green. The old tavern has survived, and we read the story of Shillibeer in some prints and old newspaper cuttings hung on the wall of the bar. On July 4, 1829, an immense crowd gathered here, to see the first pair of London omnibuses begin their run to the Bank and back. "The fare was one shilling, or sixpence for half the journey, together with the luxury of a newspaper." Mr. George Shillibeer was the owner of these carriages and the first conductors were two sons of a British naval officer.

We continued east along Marylebone Road, and then walked north by Glentworth Street, to find a dull lane with a romantic story. A few years after Sarah Siddons (Pl. 52) retired from the stage, in 1812, she went to live at No. 27 Upper Baker Street. Such was her charm, even in retirement, that when it seemed some proposed houses would obscure the country scene she enjoyed from her windows, she made the architects of Cornwall Terrace change their plans. She appealed to the Prince Regent, and "with gracious condescension" he gave orders that her "view" was to be spared. The Borough Council named this small street SIDDONS LANE in her memory.

Our walk in St. Marylebone, up to this point, had been more or less within our southern parallelogram. The northern part of the Borough—known as ST. JOHN'S WOOD [1]—yields a different story. Few of the streets recall the celebrated men and women who lived here : there is no Landseer Grove, George Eliot Mews, or Tadema Place, although these Victorian lions had their lairs in this district ; nor is there a street to remind us that Richard Wagner stayed in Portland Terrace during his visits to London. The street-names are mostly grand—honouring families, or battles, or national heroes—having no intimate claim on St. Marylebone.

Our complaint here is the one we make in so many of the areas of dull names : that a few changes would add interest, where interest is lacking. Gibbon wrote much of *The Decline and Fall of the Roman Empire* in his house in Bentinck Street ; Sheridan wrote *The Rivals* and *The Duenna* when he was living in Orchard Street ; and—lest

---

[1] The land here was one more of the estates that belonged to the Priors of the Hospital of St. John of Jerusalem.

we seem to dwell too much on literary figures—there are great doctors who have lived in Harley Street, and cricketers who have played at Lord's, whose names could please our eye more than Oak Tree Road, Avenue Road, Park Road, Acacia Road and Violet Hill.

We summoned a taxi-cab in Marylebone Road and travelled north by one of the few streets that binds this part together with a thread of ancient history—LISSON GROVE. The Manor of *Lilestone*, mentioned in the *Domesday Book*, has a story similar to so many other venerable names that have endured the centuries. But no one would suspect this from the Grove of today, with its polite, utilitarian look.

To end our afternoon in St. Marylebone, we turned from Lisson Grove into ST. JOHN'S WOOD ROAD, which led us past LORD'S CRICKET GROUND,[1] where the Marylebone Cricket Club—the world-famous M.C.C.—has upheld the integrity of the game for more than one hundred and fifty years. Then we turned down Park Road and entered REGENT'S PARK through HANOVER GATE.[2]

The splendid stretches of the Park, with the Zoological Gardens in the north-east, cover some 460 acres : lakes, trees and gardens make it one of the most beautiful open spaces in London. When Marylebone Park, as it was originally called, assumed the Regent's name, and some of his flourish, in 1812, many lively old names were swept away. We had with us an early 19th-century map, showing " The Queen's Head and Artichoke " and " The Jew's Harp " : two inns that were demolished to make way for lawns and avenues. There were also field-names on the map—Butcher's Field, The Long Mead, Bell Field, Dupper Field, and The Nether Paddock : but these too have disappeared.

There is one new name that has come, in their place, that will never be regretted : the name of a great Londoner—Queen Mary. About the edge of the Park runs the Outer Circle, almost three miles in circumference. Within this, to the south, is the Inner Circle, enclosing QUEEN MARY'S GARDENS. Here, during the summer days, 2,500 rose bushes are in bloom, and, on warm evenings, the open-air theatre is a pleasant diversion. Queen Mary belongs to London : her interests

---

[1] The story of Thomas Lord is told in the chapter on Islington, p. 10.

[2] Almost every Royal title has been used in naming the streets in this area, which has been Crown property since Henry VIII. There are Cornwall, Sussex, Clarence, York, Hanover, Kent, Ulster, and—if we encroach on St. Pancras—Cumberland, Chester, Cambridge, Albany and St. Andrews.

and her tastes have always been urban in character ; her charities, her patronage, and her presence have been part of London life for more than eighty years. There could be no more gracious and suitable gesture than this : that a garden should bear her name—little more than two miles away from Kensington Palace, where she was born on the 26th of May, 1867.

48. SHERLOCK HOLMES'S LIVING-ROOM, 221B BAKER STREET
Recreated by Michael Weight

49. THE IDLE 'PRENTICE EXECUTED AT TYBURN, BY HOGARTH

50. ROBERT ADAM   51. HENRY HALLAM, BY G. S. NEWTO[N]

52. SARAH SIDDONS,
BY J. DOWNMAN

53. WILLIAM, 1ST EARL OF CRAVEN

54. SIR JAMES BARRIE, BY W. T. MONNINGTON

M.H.C.

55. THE GRAND UNION CANAL IN 1840

56. T. H. HUXLEY, BY HIS DAUGHTER, MARIAN COLLIER

CHAPTER THIRTEEN

Paddington

" There would be nothing to make the Canal of Venice
more poetical than that of Paddington, were it not for its
artificial adjuncts."

LORD BYRON.

With Paddington, our task of exploring the streets in the northern boroughs was almost over, and we had come to a pleasant sense of intimacy with the earth of London. As we have remarked in our introduction, each of the seventeen boroughs achieves an identity of its own, as one studies old maps, and the proud little books of parish history written by local chroniclers. Poplar has a ruddy, salt-tanned look, and its voice seems to be raised against a storm ; Hampstead has a precious, rather literary look, so different from the cheeky Cockney swagger of Bethnal Green. If this idea, of seeing the boroughs as beings, different in face and character, is reasonable, then Paddington is the orphan who did not make good until late in life ; the abandoned, backward child, left as a foundling to be brought up rather badly by the Church.

We had planned to begin our journey at Marble Arch, which links Paddington with St. Marylebone. To reach the Arch, we walked along Bayswater Road, with Kensington Gardens and Hyde Park to the south, and the district of Bayswater, within Paddington, to the north.

BAYSWATER seems an obvious name, suited to the crop of boarding-houses that flourishes here, but its history as a word is involved and surprising. An indenture of 1652, drawn up when Cromwell ordered the sale of Hyde Park, mentions " three pooles . . . two at the upper corner . . . next to a place called *Bayard's Watering*". Thus the simple explanation, of pools belonging to a farmer named Bayard. The Borough Librarian reminded us of other forms into which the name was twisted—*Beard's Watering Place* (1680), *Bear's Watering*, *Baizwater*, and even *Benardgreyn*, before it settled down as the Bayswater of today. Cunningham mentions the district as " famous of old for its springs, reservoirs, and conduits, supplying the greater part of the city of London ". As late as 1795, the houses in Bond Street were served with water by brick conduits, laid from Bayswater. The streams have long been humiliated into drains and sewers, but several of the water-names have lasted—SPRING STREET, CONDUIT PLACE and MEWS, BROOK STREET and MEWS, SMALLBROOK MEWS and UPBROOK MEWS—all near what was once the source of the early supply.

As we walked east, along Bayswater Road, we were diverted by

147

an interesting name-plate—ST. PETERSBURGH PLACE, leading into MOSCOW ROAD. The two names commemorate the visit of Tzar Nicholas I of Russia to London in 1814, after his victory over the French. With the Tzar came young Prince Leopold of Saxe-Coburg, the poor, obscure, but handsome and ambitious prince who met Princess Charlotte during the visit and married her in 1816. He was also given a street—Coburg Place. But, in 1937, this separate name was absorbed into Bayswater Road, and only the COBURG COURT HOTEL remains, in memory of this first visit.

A little further along, towards Marble Arch, we came on CRAVEN TERRACE, leading into CRAVEN HILL and ROAD, and recalling a Paddington landowner who was one of the most endearing characters of the 17th century. William, 1st Earl of Craven (Pl. 53), Colonel of the Coldstream Guards, had been one of the gallant supporters of the Queen of Bohemia [1] during her years of sorrow, and it was believed that he was secretly married to her after the death of the King. In later life, when he lived at Craven House, near the present Drury Lane, Lord Craven must have been a picturesque Londoner. He could not resist the morbid excitement of a fire, and it was said that his horse " smelt one as soon as it happened ". Pepys records a riot against houses of ill-fame, when Lord Craven rode up and down Lincoln's Inn Fields " like a madman ", giving orders to the soldiery. He was also a great gardener, and the friend of Evelyn, Ray and other naturalists. When he was too old to ride up and down " like a madman " any more, there was talk of his resigning from the command of the Coldstreams. He pleaded that " if they took away his regiment they had as good take away his life ". He remained an ardent supporter of the Stuarts, to the end, and he was with James II at St. James's when William's Dutch troops were crossing the Park to take possession of the Palace. Leigh Hunt describes the old soldier's indignation. ". . . agreeably to his chivalrous character, and to his habit of taking warlike steps to no purpose, the gallant veteran would have opposed their entrance." But King James forbade the useless protest, and old Lord Craven marched away " with sullen dignity ".

There is one small thoroughfare—BARRIE STREET—which we almost overlooked, between Craven Terrace and Gloucester Terrace. It is named after Sir James Barrie (Pl. 54), who once lived at Leinster

[1] See Bohemia Place, chapter on Hackney, p. 54.

Corner, Bayswater Road. The famous statue in Kensington Gardens, of his immortal Peter Pan, is less than six hundred yards away.

Two more names delayed us before we came to Marble Arch : WESTBOURNE STREET, leading into WESTBOURNE TERRACE[1]—a survival of 13th-century *Westeburne*, a hamlet that lay " west of the stream " ; then St. George's Burial Ground—now, to all appearances, a verdant square. Here Laurence Sterne was buried, in 1768. There is a headstone in his memory, but the only street named after him is in Hammersmith, over two miles away.

At Marble Arch we walked north-west along EDGWARE ROAD (the first stretch of the ancient *Watling Street*, that passed the village of Edgware, eight miles to the north, on its way to St. Albans), to the first turning on the left, Connaught Place—the site of the terrible gallows which we have described in our chapter on St. Marylebone. Further north are also Connaught Street and Square. The only episode of interest in the story of the square seems to have been in 1877, when the actress, Fanny Kemble, went to live at No. 15. It was from here that she wrote a letter which seems curious for the 'seventies, when domestic workers were plentiful : she was waiting " till next week " for her cook and housemaid to arrive, and she wrote that she " must tremblingly hope that they will not go away the same day ".[2]

This area seemed dull, so we went into a coffee shop near the end of Connaught Street, to plan our next move. Derek Peel had been reading a little book, *Paddington, Past and Present*, written by a diligent local resident, William Robins, in 1853. We might quote his comments on the origin of the Borough's name :

> Mr. B. H. Smart, the well-known English scholar, kindly suggested to me . . . the possibility of the word PADDINGTON being derived from *Padre ing tun, the Father's town-meadow* ; and Sir Harry Dent Goring, of Bayswater House, was so good as to suggest another derivation. . . . " A Pad is a Sussex word now in common use for Pack-Horse. . . . Now,

[1] Sarah Siddons lived in Westbourne Green, before she moved to Upper Baker Street. There is SIDDONS HOUSE, a building of flats, in Harrow Road, Paddington. Cunningham states : " Mrs. Siddons lived for many years . . . in this parish, but the *Great Western Railway* has destroyed all trace of her pretty house and grounds."

[2] *The Squares of London*, Chancellor, p. 317.

the carriers to the great City may have lodged, and had meadows for their Pack-Horses here. I humbly suggest, therefore, may not Paddington mean *the Village at the Pack-Horse Meadows* ? "

The editors of *The Place-Names of Middlesex* are more cautious : they merely list the various forms, from *Padintune* in the 10th century, to *Padintone, Padynton*, etc., through the years.

In addition to being diligent as a local historian, William Robins was fiercely angry with the Church, and most of his 200 pages are devoted to proving the perfidy of the ecclesiastical control of Paddington, since the 11th century. The details of this old argument would use up more space than we can spare, and the climax of the story must be enough. It came when the Norman conquerors, in assessing their spoils, demanded evidence that the Monks of Westminster truly owned the acres of pasture and forest that they claimed, on the west of the Tyburn river. Where were the title deeds ? Where was the proof ? The wretched monks had none, so we imagine a thrilling, if immoral scene, of them sitting up late at night, forging and illuminating the charters to prove that the land had been given them by King Edgar, in the 10th century.

The librarian to the Dean and Chapter of Westminster, in the mid-18th century, went so far as to admit that these old charters had " been proved beyond all doubt to be forgeries ".

Through hundreds of years, and the vicissitudes of the Reformation and the Commonwealth, the ghostly old fingers of the forgers did not relax their grip on Paddington, and immense tracts of land remained Church property—and do, to this day. The Bishops of London were *ipso facto* lords of the manor of Paddington from 1550, until the Ecclesiastical Commissioners pooled the resources of the Church in the 19th century.

These canonical lords of the manor of Paddington left some street-names, near the eastern boundary of the Borough. We travelled by taxi-cab along Edgware Road, to the point where it becomes MAIDA VALE,[1] which took its name from the British victory over the French at Maida, in Italy, in 1806. To the east of Maida Vale is BLOMFIELD ROAD, named after Charles James Blomfield (1786–1857), Bishop of London in 1828. He was a great classical scholar, regarded with awe

---

[1] The district here is carelessly described as Maida Vale, but the name belongs only to the street.

in his time for his editions of Æschylus, Callimachus and Euripides. North of Blomfield Road we saw RANDOLPH AVENUE, named after John Randolph, Bishop of London from 1809 to 1813.

There seemed little to interest us in the streets about Randolph Avenue, so we crossed the canal by way of Warwick Avenue, and walked south to HOWLEY PLACE, on the left. William Howley (1766–1848) followed Randolph as Bishop of London and held the see until he became Archbishop of Canterbury in 1828. We walked along Howley Place, and turned south again, down ST. MARY'S TERRACE, to find FULHAM PLACE, obviously taking its name from the London palace of the Bishops ; then, parallel, to the south, PORTEUS ROAD, named after Beilby Porteus, who became Bishop of London in 1787. It is interesting to note in his story that both his parents were born in Virginia. But the most important Bishop remembered in this vicinity is Gilbert Sheldon (1598–1677), " one of the most powerful men in England with the King ", according to Pepys. He was Chaplain to Charles I, Bishop of London in 1660, and Archbishop of Canterbury in 1663. He endowed and built the Sheldonian Theatre in Oxford, in 1669 ; but he has been given only a small street in Paddington—SHELDON STREET—north-west of the railway station.

The southern end of St. Mary's Terrace joins Harrow Road, and here, where the Town Hall and St. Mary's Church now stand, was the heart of the old-time village of Paddington. It would have been pleasant to find a *Bread and Cheese Lane* opening off these big streets that flank the church, to celebrate a curious charity that is now defunct. There was an earlier church on the site of St. Mary's, until 1791, and it was the custom to throw bread and cheese to the poor from the church steeple, every Sunday before Christmas. This rough charity was described in the *London Magazine* for December, 1737 :

> Sunday, 18th, this day, according to annual custom, bread and cheese were thrown from Paddington Steeple to the populace, agreeably to the will of two women who were relieved there with bread and cheese when they were almost starved, and Providence afterwards favouring them, they left an estate in that parish to continue the custom for ever on that day.

The grateful ladies left three parcels of land (which came to be known as the Bread and Cheese Lands), and the rents from these were to be spent on the Christmas charity. But the benefaction had to be modified in the early 19th century, because " sturdy vagabonds of London " hurried to Paddington every Sunday before Christmas " to scramble over dead men's bones " while they caught the bread and cheese as it fell from the steeple. William Robins tells us that " This custom was continued down to about 1838 ; a single slice of cheese and a penny loaf, being, at last, all that was thrown." Then the main part of the Bread and Cheese Lands were sold by the Church to the Great Western Railway, and the picturesque charity was forgotten.

From the parish church of St. Mary we drove west a short distance, until we came to the junction of BISHOP'S BRIDGE ROAD and North Wharf Road. It would help the kind reader if he looked at the map : here, within the space of one-sixteenth of a square mile, the history of Paddington is told in the street-names. Bishop's Bridge Road was the last of the ecclesiastical group, reminding us of the control of the Church, of which Harold Clunn wrote in *The Face of London*, " Those peoples who have been the most completely governed by a church are noted for making the slowest progress in all essential knowledge, and the people of Paddington furnished no exception to this rule. Although they lived at so short a distance from the two rich cathedral towns of London and Westminster, they made no greater advances in civilisation than did those who lived in the remotest village in England."

If canals and railways are signs of advance in civilisation, Paddington began its emancipation in 1801, when the Paddington Canal was opened. This progress was confirmed in 1838 with the advent of the Great Western Railway. The map shows how these enterprises affected the Borough. Between NORTH WHARF ROAD and SOUTH WHARF ROAD lies the PADDINGTON BASIN—the terminus of the canal that joins the Grand Union Canal (Pl. 55) and the Regent's Canal, thus opening Paddington's way to the Thames, and the sea. East of the Basin is Paddington Station, the railway junction that links the Borough with Bristol and all the west of England. There is PRAED STREET, named after Sir William Praed, first chairman and for many years manager of the Canal company, and SALE PLACE in memory of Richard Cowlishaw Sale, one of the Canal engineers. BRINDLEY ROAD, which runs parallel with the canal, off the Harrow Road, was named after James Brindley, another great builder of canals.

But he died in 1772, and had no hand in planning the canal in Paddington.

Lord Byron wrote, " There would be nothing to make the Canal of Venice more poetical than that of Paddington, were it not for its artificial adjuncts." It must have been a pretty scene, if we can believe the print which is reproduced as Plate 55. For many years after the Canal was opened, a passenger boat left Paddington every summer morning for a delightful excursion to Uxbridge. Breakfast was served on board, and the passengers were able to see the Surrey Hills on the way. But the insensitive demands of industry soon killed what beauty remained, and the banks of the Canal were used as a dumping ground for half the filth of London. The name " stinking Paddington " was coined, and it survived almost a century.

There is a third group of names, following the Church and the Canal—those planted in Paddington by the landowners. But we confess to a boredom in all these, and we are afraid lest we pass this mood on to our readers. So we shall hasten through this part of the Paddington story. In the extreme west of the Borough are CHEPSTOW ROAD and PLACE. Nearby are GARWAY, MONMOUTH, HEREFORD and NEWTON ROADS. They lead us to the fact that this land once belonged to William Kinnaird Jenkins, whose heart was obviously with the Herefordshire and Welsh Border. To the north is another group of streets named by an early landowner. The clue here is in GRITTLETON ROAD, which leads us to the family name of the Neilds of Grittleton, in Wiltshire. They gave Paddington a number of West Country names, in CHIPPENHAM ROAD and MEWS, FOSCOTE MEWS, SEVINGTON STREET, and CIRENCESTER STREET. And in the Harrow Road is a public house, the NEELD ARMS, with this slight modification in spelling, but also named after the Wiltshire family.

In the south-east of the Borough, near Connaught Street, are SOUTH-WICK STREET and CRESCENT. They give us the key to another group of family- and place-names. The Thistlethwaytes of Southwick Park, in Hampshire, were also landowners in Paddington, and they remembered their country estates in the names of PORTSEA PLACE, and WIDLEY and WYMERING ROADS, in the north of the Borough.

But this is dullness. The streets seem to come alive only when they are named after people, not after places or institutions. And Paddington has been especially obtuse in this. It is no stimulus to see the name GREAT WESTERN ROAD on a street corner, but it might touch our imagination if we came on a Brunel [1] or a Wyatt Street, named after the men who built the railway. Another, greater engineer, Robert Stephenson [1] (son of George Stephenson who built the " Rocket"), lived at No. 34 Gloucester Square, in Paddington, from 1847 until 1859, when he died. This was the splendid period of his invention—the years during which he built the Alexandria-Cairo railway, the Conway Bridge, the Britannia Tubular Bridge and the High Level Bridge at Newcastle. Paddington should spare a street-name for him ; and one for Rowland Hill who lived at No. 1 ORME SQUARE (named after a Bond Street printseller and Paddington land-owner), which is in the south-western corner of the Borough. Rowland Hill went to live there in 1839, a few months before his Penny Postage Bill was passed by the Commons. Here also lived John Sterling (1806-1844), founder of the Sterling Club and friend of Tennyson and Carlyle : a man of such talents and qualities that Carlyle felt compelled to write his biography.

It would be more amusing to walk along a Rowland Hill Street and think of the days of penny postage, or through a John Sterling Avenue, with memories of literary London at the beginning of the last century, than to plod along a street named after some remote corner of Herefordshire which few of us have ever seen.

But there is one group of Paddington streets that yields a little surprise. In the far north-west of the Borough, two miles along the Harrow Road, we came to the Queen's Park Estate, developed and built in the 1870's. The planners began by naming the streets running north and south, FIRST, SECOND, THIRD, FOURTH, FIFTH, and SIXTH AVENUES. Then they bent over their blue prints and hastily named the streets running east and west, A, B, C, D, etc., " for the time being ".

About this time the London County Council published their amended list of street-names, in which we found these Queen's Park streets were entered as *A Street, B Street, C Street*, etc. The owners then made a compromise and chose names that fitted comfortably into the alphabet. So we have ALPERTON STREET (named after the brick yard in Middlesex, whence the bricks were brought for the houses), BARFETT STREET, CAIRD STREET, DROOP STREET (one of the directors was named Droop), ENBROOK STREET, FARRANT STREET (named after another director), and GALTON STREET. Then, for some

[1] There are Brunel Road and Stephenson Street in Acton.

curious reason, in honour of the great scientist, *H. Street* was named HUXLEY (Pl. 56). In this way the directors of the estate made their way as far as necessary through the alphabet, and then, as a gesture to the arts, BEETHOVEN STREET and MOZART STREET were thrown in for generous measure.

CHAPTER FOURTEEN

Kensington

" My earliest recollections are connected with Kensington Palace, where I remember crawling on a yellow carpet spread out for that purpose. . . ."

QUEEN VICTORIA.

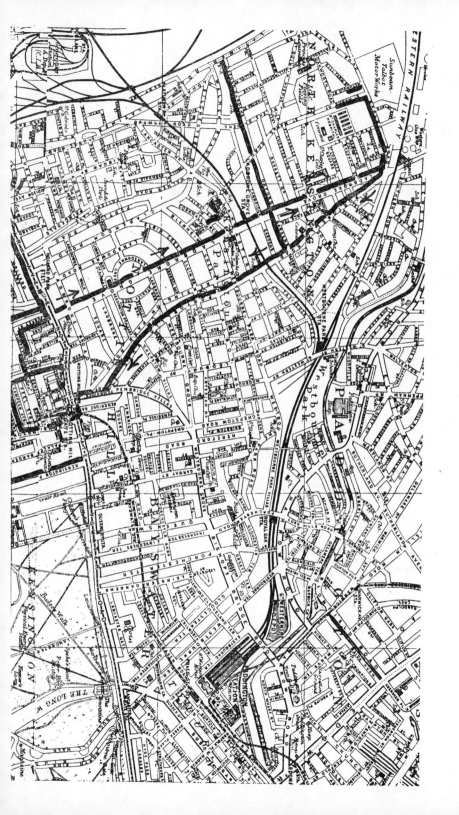

Our respect for some of the cartographers and scholars who have compiled information about old London has often been threatened while writing this book. All we can hope is that we are handing on less errors than we have inherited. The suspicions that were aroused by the incident of Bunyan's statue (see Introduction, p. xv) were often confirmed ; especially when we searched into the published records of St. Marylebone, where we might have fallen into many errors if we had not been rescued by the Borough Librarian.

My collaborator was now so sceptical, and afraid of starting new confusions of fact, that he went as far back as *Domesday Book* for his first search into the story of KENSINGTON. One afternoon in early June we went to the Public Record Office Museum in Chancery Lane, where the two ancient volumes—one bigger than the other— lie open for all to see. They must be a source of great pleasure for those who can read the archaic language, the many abbreviations and contractions, with ease. We read, on page 130B of the big volume, that, when *Domesday Book* was compiled, " Aubrey De Ver ", who came over with the Conqueror, from Ver, near Bayeux, held " Chenesit' " [1] (Kensington) of the Bishop of Constance, Chief Justiciary of England. Then followed a list of the bondsmen, serfs, ploughs, pasture for cattle, pannage for swine, and vineyards, that were spread, almost nine centuries ago, over the territory that is now crowded, genteel Kensington.

When the Bishop of Constance died, in 1093, the lands in " Chenesit' " were held directly by Aubrey de Vere, whose descendants possessed them until early in the 16th century.

We transcribed the entry in *Domesday Book*, underlining the names *Chenesit'* and *Aubrey De Ver*, and then we travelled from the Record Office to a spot south of Kensington High Street underground station. Here was the first street-name bearing witness to the Norman records. We paused in CHENISTON GARDENS, a quiet street of high-class "Bed-and-Breakfast" houses, with neglected window-boxes. Our map showed us also AUBREY WALK and ROAD, half a mile to the north, and DE VERE GARDENS, some six hundred yards to the east.

We found that the names of the streets leading from Cheniston

[1] One more name of Saxon origin.

57. HENRY RICH, 1ST EARL OF HOLLAND,
AFTER VAN DYCK

58. JOSEPH ADDISON,
BY KNELLER

59. ST. MARY ABBOTS CHURCH IN 1750

60. CAMPDEN HOUSE IN 1647, BY HOLLAR

61. KENSINGTON PALACE IN THE 18TH CENTURY

Gardens were most conveniently arranged for our purpose. The "Gardens" lead to ABINGDON VILLAS, then to ABINGDON ROAD. Aubrey de Vere's eldest son, Geoffrey, had been "cured of a sickness" by the Abbot of Abingdon, but he did not survive to inherit the title or estates. On his deathbed he persuaded his father to bestow the church and 275 acres of land on the Abbot. This land became known as Abbots Kensington, and the name survives in ST. MARY ABBOTS CHURCH (Pl. 59) at the corner of CHURCH STREET and KENSINGTON HIGH STREET.

ENTRY IN "DOMESDAY BOOK" SHOWING NAME OF "CHENESIT", THE EARLY FORM OF KENSINGTON

The De Veres ruled Kensington during four and a half centuries, ere their lands were dissipated. The third member of the family, also Aubrey, was created Earl of Oxford in 1155 by the "Empress Maud", for the part he played in her struggles against King Stephen. We followed this theme in the story by walking from Abingdon Villas into EARL'S COURT ROAD, in the district of the same name. EARL'S COURT, like BARON'S COURT in neighbouring Hammersmith, reminds us of one of the aspects of the feudal system, which allowed certain nobles to establish their own courts of justice, for the control of their tenants.

One would like to expand the story of the fourteen Earls of Oxford and their suzerainty in Kensington. A hasty reading of their records brings some romantic figures on to the stage. There was Robert, the 9th Earl, " a young man full of vivacity ", whose " youthful sallies " were so pleasing to Richard II, and whose distracting influence on the King was suddenly ended when he was gored to death by a wild boar in Holland. There was also John, the 12th Earl, who sided with the Lancastrians during the Wars of the Roses, and lost his head on Tower Hill for his trouble. The last to be associated with the lands in Kensington was the 14th Earl, known as " Little John of Campes ", simply because he was a man of " diminuitive stature " who lived at Campes Castle. When he died, without issue, the estates were divided up and the great name of Oxford vanished from Kensington, leaving only one street-name, OXFORD GARDENS, in the north-west of the Borough.

The arrangement of the streets still served us well. We walked north along Earl's Court Road, to a small street on the right, COPE PLACE. With the name Cope, we leave the costume play of knights and earls, and the dwindling spoils of conquest : we come to what seems like clever enterprise in real estate. Sir Walter Cope (d. 1614) was a favourite of King James I. He had already acquired spacious lands in this area, and in 1608 he had begun the building of what was called Cope's Castle, later the celebrated Holland House.

One imagines that the name " Cope's Castle " was a jibe at Sir Walter's riches and pretentiousness, just as John Kirby's grand house in Bethnal Green was nicknamed " Kirby's Castle " [1] when he built it a few years before. It was in 1598 that Stow wrote, " wee saw builded many faire summer-houses . . . with towers, turrets, and chimney tops, not so much for use or profits as for shew and pleasure, and bewraying the vanite of men's mindes ".

Sir Walter Cope's reign in Kensington was brief as the little street named after him. He had no male heir, so the lands, and Cope's Castle, passed to his daughter Isabella, and her husband, Henry Rich, son of the Earl of Warwick. From this step in the story we have WARWICK ROAD which runs parallel with Earl's Court Road, to the west, and WARWICK GARDENS, a shorter street, in between.

[1] See chapter on Bethnal Green, p. 76.

162

Henry Rich (Pl. 57), created Earl of Holland a year before the death of James I, became a dramatic figure during the reign of Charles I. Lord Clarendon wrote of him, in his *History of the Rebellion in England*, " The Earl of Holland was a younger son of a noble house, and a very fruitful bed. . . . He was a very handsome man, of a lovely and winning presence, and genteel conversation : by which he got so easy an admission into the court and grace of King James. . . ."

Unfortunately the Earl of Holland was also " wavering and irresolute ", and unfixed in his loyalties. At one time he sided with the Parliamentarians, but he was beheaded for his fidelity to King Charles, on March 9, 1649. " After near an hour spent, he pulled off his gown and doublet, having next him a white satin waistcoat, put on a white satin cap with silver lace, and prepared himself for the block, took his leave, and embraced, with much affection, Mr. Hodges, Mr. Bolton, his servants, and others on the scaffold, forgave the executioner, gave him money, thought to be ten pounds in gold, laid himself down on the block, and prayed awhile, then gave the sign by stretching forth his arms, upon which the executioner severed his head from his body at one blow, which was presently after put into a coffin and carried away." [1] This " once gay, beautiful, gallant Earl " gave his name to HOLLAND HOUSE, HOLLAND PARK AVENUE and HOLLAND WALK. It is mournful to think over the end of the great mansion, which reached the zenith of its fame as the meeting-place of the Whig leaders—the " Holland House Set "—early in the 19th century. It was disastrously bombed during the second world war—three centuries after the first Earl of Holland died on the scaffold.

We walked up Earl's Court Road, across Kensington High Street, to the wrought-iron gates of Holland House. We could see the neglected drive, beyond which lies the shell of the splendid mansion. Behind us, the clamouring traffic hurried between east and west ; before us was the tangle of once trim shrubs and trees. This fair corner of London seemed to be crowded with the shadows of history. One imagined Sir Walter Cope driving in to see the masons at work on the first part of the great house ; then the Earl with the " lovely and winning presence ", all glamour fallen away from him as he drove from the house for the last time, with a servant carrying " the white satin cap with silver lace ". Then Charles James Fox,

[1] *Perfect Diurnal, and Kingdome's Weekly Intelligencer*, March 9, 1649, quoted in *History and Antiquities of Kensington*, by Thomas Faulkner, p. 106.

third son of the 1st Lord Holland, the " greatest debater the world ever saw", driving quickly past ; and then the carriages of the days of the 3rd Lord Holland, bearing Scott, Sheridan, Macaulay, Lord Melbourne and Byron, towards the house, and the brilliance within. And there is a less dazzling shade : Joseph Addison (Pl. 58) as a young man arriving as tutor to the son of the Dowager Countess of Warwick ; then, as an older man, driving in once more as husband of the same Countess, and therefore as lord of the manor of Kensington. Addison died at Holland House when he was only forty-seven, in 1719.

Our readers may remember Leigh Hunt's reference, which we quoted in the chapter on Stoke Newington, to " A nobleman, eminent for his zeal in behalf of the advancement of society " who had " called a road in his neighbourhood, ADDISON ROAD ". We found it, after walking west along Kensington High Street for a few yards. So we chose this way for the next span of our journey, passing ADDISON CRESCENT on the way.

But we still depended on Holland Park for the source of our names. Addison's stepson, the young Earl of Holland, died in 1721, and the estates descended to William Edwardes, whose father had married the sister of the 3rd Earl. We had missed the place-name that celebrated this period in the history of the great house. South of Kensington High Street, half-way between Warwick Road and Earl's Court Road, lies EDWARDES SQUARE. Apart from its link with the Holland House story, this square has an interesting origin in its architecture. It is said to have been built by a Frenchman " at the time when Napoleon was massing his legions at Boulogne for his descent on these shores. So strong appears the belief of this speculator in the success of that greatest of all speculators, that he adapted the relative size of the houses and the central garden to the taste for promenading so characteristic of his countrymen, and in his magnificent imagination he saw his tenements occupied by the poorer officers of that vast army which was to be poured into this country." [1]

Otherwise, William Edwardes did not bring much grace to the street-names of Kensington. He came from Haverfordwest, in South Wales, and the Welsh names that he scattered about the land have no part in Kensington's history. Thus we have PEMBROKE SQUARE, GARDENS and ROAD (all of which we had passed as we walked from

[1] *The Squares of London*, by E. Beresford Chancellor, p. 300.

Earl's Court Road to Addison Road), and MARLOES ROAD, LONG-RIDGE ROAD, TEMPLETON PLACE, TREBOVIR ROAD, PENYWERN ROAD, PHILBEACH GARDENS, and NEVERN SQUARE, PLACE and ROAD, which lie to the south, in the district of Earl's Court.

In 1776, William Edwardes was created Baron Kensington, and one of his descendants holds the title to this day. But the family parted with Holland House, when it was bought by Henry Fox, the first Lord Holland and father of Charles James Fox. Lord Ilchester (ILCHESTER PLACE skirts the south-west corner of Holland Park) was the last owner of the house and park. His family name is Fox-Strangways, and he is descended from a brother of the 1st Lord Holland. Thus, in this network of streets, with their rows of polite houses, we have names that span almost a thousand years, beginning with Aubrey Walk and De Vere Gardens and ending with Ilchester Place. It is pleasant to note that the present Lord Ilchester adds his flourish of scholarship to this long story, for he is the author of some nine books, which include *Chronicles of Holland House* and some others recalling the long parade of famous men and women who were associated with the mansion.

At the corner of Addison Road and Holland Park Avenue we hailed a taxi-cab and travelled east, then north again, along LADBROKE GROVE,[1] named after Richard Ladbroke, son of a lord mayor of London, whose family were landowners here from the 17th to the 19th century.

We were in North Kensington, where the street-names seemed tedious and less interesting. But there were two, in this part of the Borough, that attracted us. Half-way along Ladbroke Grove, we turned into CAMELFORD ROAD, named after Lord Camelford, distinguished for " a love of frolic, and a passion for rational and scientific pursuits ", who was killed in a duel in 1804. " The quarrel, which ended so fatally ", was between Lord Camelford and a Mr. Best. The tragedy began at the Opera, where Mr. Best made some objectionable " expressions " to a favourite lady of Lord Camelford. The " favourite lady " made wicked use of her opportunity and " communicated a false statement of the transaction to his Lordship ". The next scene was Stevens' hotel, in Bond Street, where Lord Camelford came face to face with the nefarious Mr. Best and called him an " infamous scoundrel ". Then followed a challenge, and the fatal

[1] The estate now belongs to the London County Council.

duel. The "hostile meeting" was in a meadow to the west of Holland House. Unfortunately, Mr. Best was a champion with his pistols and Lord Camelford was slain. His last words to the villain were, " Best, I am a dead man ; you have killed me, but I freely forgive you." [1]

Thus died a chivalrous young nobleman, at the age of thirty, because a "favourite lady" was fool enough to repeat, and cheat enough to embroider, what had been said to her. However, Lord Camelford is not forgotten, and in addition to the street that bears his name, there is an antique Roman altar, erected by Lord Holland, upon the spot where the gallant fell.

The other street that made us curious, because of its name, is near the northern end of Ladbroke Grove, to the west. It is METHWOLD ROAD, named after William Methwold, who lived in the early 17th century. He was another of the many conscientious citizens who gave part of their fortune to help the needy. William Methwold endowed a hospital to house six poor women, but his rules for their behaviour were a trifle strict. They had to be single, aged fifty, free from vice, "and of good report". They were not to "brawl or scold" : if they did, they would lose a quarter's pension ; and if they assaulted one another, they were dismissed.[2]

Near its northern end, Ladbroke Grove meets PORTOBELLO ROAD, by which we travelled south again.

We gave up our search for the day and returned to Portobello Road next afternoon—a Saturday. This was market day for the people in the neighbourhood, so there were many ramshackle stalls in the streets. We joined the eager crowd and turned over the piles of junk —jet necklaces, bundles of old spoons, plated epergnes, and pinchbeck bangles.

It was not easy to think of Porto Bello, in Panama, and the victory of Admiral Vernon, in 1739. Nor was it easy to believe that the bargaining Londoners were walking over what was farm land, as late as the 19th century. The old meadows were part of Porto Bello Farm. The district, then, as now, was called NOTTING HILL, a name that is ancient, and vague in origin. The editors of *The Place-Names of Middlesex* state that " no certain solution is yet possible " as to the first meaning of the name, but they quote the interesting changes in

[1] Faulkner's *Kensington*, pp. 176–81.
[2] Ibid., p. 331.

its spelling, from *Knottynghull'* in the 14th century, to *Noding Hill* in 1680. The manor which was here in the 11th century was part of the estates of the De Veres, and the name survives in only one street— NOTTING HILL GATE, which passes over the site of an early turnpike gate. We must include one rather irrelevant fact from the records of Notting Hill, since names are our immediate business. In the Parish Register there is notice of the burial of a nobleman " slain at Notting wood in fight ", in 1608. He bore the valiant name of Sir Manhood Penruddock.

We walked from Portobello Road, along a stretch of Pembridge Road, to Notting Hill Gate—then east for a few yards, and down Kensington Church Street. The third turning on the right brought us into CAMPDEN STREET, which leads through to CAMPDEN HILL. Campden House (Pl. 60) was another great Kensington mansion, which was linked in name with the enchanting village of Chipping Campden, in Gloucestershire. Baptist Hickes, Viscount Campden of Campden, was a wealthy silk-merchant, and an alderman of London. He built and named the house in 1612. During two hundred and fifty years it crowned Campden Hill, but there was little continuity in its ownership to bind it into Kensington's history. In 1691, Princess Anne and her Danish husband leased the house and lived there five years. From 1823 to 1848 it was " an eminent boarding school for young ladies ". Then it was occupied by a Mr. L. T. Wooley who opened a theatre in the house for amateur theatricals. (It was here that Charles Dickens appeared in *The Lighthouse*.) Unfortunately, Mr. Wooley played hanky-panky with his insurance policies. At the moment when the house and contents were covered for £29,000, there was a fire, followed by a *cause célèbre* in the law courts. In 1866, a new house was built on the site, but it was demolished in 1900 and the existing Campden House Court took its place.

We continued down Kensington Church Street and paused at the corner of Vicarage Gardens, where a hefty building of flats, named NEWTON COURT, reminded us that Isaac Newton died in his lodgings nearby, in 1727. Then to Kensington High Street and the gardens that stretch to the east, with the peaceful façade of Kensington Palace (Pl. 61) seen at the end of a drive of elms. Until 1900, the Palace was within the boundaries of Westminster, so its history belongs outside the Royal Borough. Even so, the glittering personages who lived here have had little effect on the naming of the surrounding streets. We have KENSINGTON PALACE GARDENS, running between the High Street and Notting Hill Gate, and PALACE AVENUE. But there is no street-name to remind us that William III bought the Palace soon after his accession, in 1688, because it was far enough away from the river not to aggravate his asthma. Nor is there a Queen Anne Street, in memory of Good Queen Anne, who loved Kensington so much—in spite of the many acrimonious scenes that were staged there, with the Duchess of Marlborough. As far as names are concerned, Kensington Palace comes alive with Queen Victoria, who was born there on May 24, 1819. She afterwards recalled, " My earliest recollections are connected with Kensington Palace, where I remember crawling on a yellow carpet spread out for that purpose. . . . I was brought up very simply—never had a room to myself till I was nearly grown up. . . ."

In June, 1836, Princess Victoria sat on a sofa in the Palace, turning over a book of drawings, with Prince Albert of Saxe-Coburg beside her. She thought him " extremely handsome ", and that he possessed " every quality that could be desired " to make her " perfectly happy ".

Among those qualities were the imagination and enterprise which were to give Kensington one of its last cluster of new street-names. In 1851, after the Great Exhibition had closed, the promoters found that their profits amounted to £186,000. Prince Albert opened a map on which Kensington Gore was marked ; an area of dairy farms, market gardens and orchards, fenced with park railings, and covering about 120 acres. It might have added a touch of challenge to the Prince's plan that the immense thoroughfare which cut the area in two was named CROMWELL ROAD. The land was bought and, in place of the little farms and market gardens, there grew up the important museums and educational institutions of today ; including the Victoria and Albert Museum, the Science and Natural History Museums, the Imperial Institute, the Royal Colleges of Science, Mines, Art and Music, and the Royal School of Needlework. So we come to the end of our search in the Royal Borough, with QUEEN'S GATE, PRINCE CONSORT ROAD, and EXHIBITION ROAD, as a suitable memorial to the serious, brilliant Prince of whom Queen Victoria wrote, on the day his Exhibition was opened, " All is owing to Albert—All to him."

CHAPTER FIFTEEN

Chelsea

" Pray, are not the fine buns sold here in our town ; was it not r-r-r-r-r-r-rare Chelsea buns ? "

SWIFT's *Journal to Stella.*

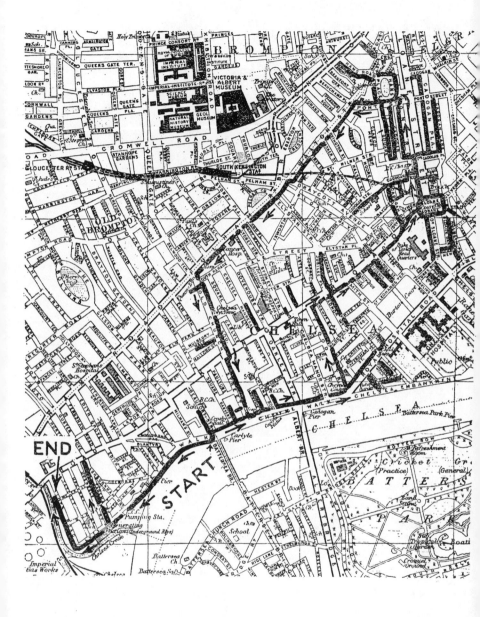

Chelsea brought us back to the banks of the Thames ; not to busy river docks like those of Poplar and Stepney, where the screech of ships' derricks is echoed in the cry of sea birds, but to the gentler stream, still patronised by land birds, and flooded at sunset by Turner's " waves of dusky gold ". Here the Thames seems to lose the memories of Runnymede, Windsor and Hampton Court, before it broadens, to assume the duties of being the Port of London.

The editors of *The Place-Names of Middlesex* describe CHELSEA as " a difficult name ", which goes back to *Celchyth*, in the late 8th century. But there are enough early references to encourage us to hope that, like the names Chiswell [1] and Chesil,[2] the word Chelsea is derived from the Saxon *Ceosol*, which describes the gravel and shingle formation of the river bank. John Norden, the 16th-century cartographer, wrote that " Cheselsey " was so called " from the nature of the place, whose strand is like the chesel . . . which the sea casteth up of sand and pebble stones. . . ." [3] Dr. John King, rector of Chelsea in 1694, described the scene pleasantly : " The soil is generally within 6 inches of the surface sand and gravell ; the Shoar along the Thames is all gravell and Pebbles wch renders it so neat and clean, that as soon as the tide is out it affords a clean walk to take Boat." [4] If Chelsea takes its name from the gravel and pebbles of its river bank, then there is added interest in the name of CHESILTON ROAD, in neighbouring Fulham, and in the name of CHESIL COURT, in Chelsea, within a short distance of the Thames.

Since the early 16th century, Chelsea has been the home of many great men, who are recalled in its street, and place-names. Among the splendid company were Sir Thomas More, Holbein, Sir John Danvers, Charles, 1st Viscount Cheyne, the 1st Duke of Beaufort, Sir Hans Sloane, Sir Robert Walpole, Dante Gabriel Rossetti, Alma-Tadema, Carlyle, and Charles Wentworth Dilke. The first of these, Sir Thomas More (Pl. 62), made Chelsea fashionable in Tudor times.

---

[1] Chiswell Street, Finsbury—see Introduction, pp. xv–xvi.

[2] There is the famous Chesil Bank in Dorset, where the shingle spreads eighteen miles along the coast.

[3] Cunningham, vol. I, p. 188.

[4] Quoted in *An Illustrated Historical Handbook to the Parish of Chelsea*, by Reginald Blunt (1900), p. 31.

We began our journey on the river bank near where he lived, from 1520 until a year before he died.

Strangers who read MORE'S GARDEN on their map, at the river end of Beaufort Street, might expect to find a flourish of green and the sweetness of flowers. They would be disappointed, for the name now belongs only to a block of flats. One hundred yards from here, Thomas More built his house, about the time that he went with King Henry VIII to the Field of the Cloth of Gold. Erasmus described the house as a " modest yet commodious mansion ". This it must have been, for Thomas More lived there with his wife and son, three married daughters and their husbands, eleven grandchildren and an adopted relative.

Henry VIII often went to what Thomas More described as his " pore howse in Chelcith ", to be " merry with him ", or to walk with him in the " fair garden . . . holding his arm about his neck ".[1] From the same house, on April 17, 1534, Thomas More walked across what is now Cheyne Walk, under arrest, and " took his boat towards Lambeth " for the last time.

Three more street- and place-names emerge from the story of the " modest yet commodious mansion ". For some three years Hans Holbein (1497–1543) lived in the house, and during this time he painted Thomas More, and his family, and many of the portrait drawings now in the Queen's collection at Windsor. HOLBEIN PLACE, MEWS and HOUSE are in the far mid-east of Chelsea, on the border of Pimlico. The second name is that of the 1st Duke of Beaufort (BEAUFORT STREET), who bought the mansion in 1681. The third is that of Sir Hans Sloane [2] (Pl. 63), who owned the house from 1736 until 1740, when it was demolished.

East of More's Garden is DANVERS STREET, named after Sir John Danvers (d. 1655), who " first taught us the way of Italian gardens ". Danvers House was set in a proud estate that spread between the river and the King's Road. Sir John was a man of incredible variety, and of such " great personal beauty " that, when he went abroad, " people would come after him in the street to admire him ". He served at the Court of Charles I, but he afterwards fought for Parliament, and he signed King Charles's death warrant in 1649. Having sided with both King and Parliament, he changed his heart once more and died

[1] Roper's *Life* of More, ed. Singer, p. 21.
[2] See p. 178, also chapter on Holborn, p. 36.

" a devout Papist ". But the English will forgive any treachery in a man who is kind to animals or fond of flowers ; so, in 1696, John Danvers's name was chosen for the street that was built near the site of his gardens.

Next to More's Garden, at the foot of Danvers Street, is the ancient Crosby Hall, built in the City of London in 1466 and moved to Chelsea in 1908. This valiant structure, described by Stow as " builded of stone and timber, verie large and beautiful ", survived the Lancastrian fire bombs in the 15th century, the Great Fire of 1666, and, on its new site, the bombing of two wars. Sir Thomas More lived in Crosby Hall before he moved to Chelsea, so it was appropriate to rebuild it near the site of his own house and garden. The ghost of the martyr seems to dominate this stretch of the river bank.

On the next corner, at the foot of OLD CHURCH STREET, we came on the shell of the celebrated Chelsea Old Church, bombed on the night of April 16/17, 1941. The chapel has been restored enough for the services to be held, and for the visitor to trace much of Chelsea's history among the cracked monuments.

We came then to LAWRENCE STREET, which recalls another Chelsea mansion, The Lawrence House, named after the prosperous and splendid family that lived there in the 16th and 17th centuries, and whose chapel and monuments have survived in the old church. There were many occupants of Lawrence House—Sir Reginald Bray, favourite of Henry VII, who fought at Bosworth Field, the Lawrences, and the widow of the Duke of Monmouth. From the grand dust of these, we come on a livelier figure, Dr. Tobias Smollett, who lived in the house from 1749 to 1765. There, he wrote *Ferdinand, Count Fathom*, which was published in 1753 ; and there, when the duns would allow, his Sunday table was spread with beef, pudding, and potatoes, port, punch and beer, for Johnson, Goldsmith or Sterne, or any other of his writing friends who liked to call.

We leap seventy years, to the story of another Scottish writer who made his home in Chelsea. " The house pleases us much," wrote Thomas Carlyle (Pl. 66), after he had seen No. 5 (now No. 24) Cheyne Row. He added that he " could shoot a gun into Smollett's old house " which was then being pulled down.

Cheyne Row, where Carlyle lived for forty-seven years, is parallel with Lawrence Street. " The street runs down to the river," he wrote. " We are called ' Cheyne Row ' proper (pronounced *Chainie*

Row) and are a genteel neighbourhood." He described the "broad highway" beside the river, "with huge shady trees", the "boats lying moored, and a smell of shipping and tar."

There is a little strip of garden at the southern end of Cheyne Row, with "shady trees". Here we passed Carlyle's statue on our way to the corner of Oakley Street, where we stopped at the Pier Hotel for a glass of sherry. My collaborator was surprised because CARLYLE SQUARE, in Chelsea, was given its name nine years *before* Carlyle's death, and I spent ten minutes trying to explain to him the splendid, if dangerous, hero-worship that was enjoyed by giants like Carlyle and Tennyson, in Victorian times. Carlyle's house, which is now owned by the National Trust, was purchased in 1895, fourteen years after his death. In reading the list of subscribers to the fund, we smiled at the item, "The German Emperor, £100."

We continued east along Cheyne Walk (Pl. 64), with the river and gardens on our right, and paused by the Rossetti memorial fountain, in front of the house where Dante Gabriel Rossetti (Pl. 65) lived from 1862 until he died. Chelsea remembers the great Pre-Raphaelite in ROSSETTI GARDEN MANSIONS and ROSSETTI STUDIOS.

Next we came to CHELSEA MANOR STREET, which runs north from the river, across the King's Road. The manor of Chelsea is believed to have belonged to the Abbey of Westminster, but the story does not concern us until we read of Henry VIII acquiring the lands, and building a house on them, which he gave to Catherine Parr as part of her marriage jointure. When the "royal ruffian" died, Catherine Parr went to live in Chelsea, with her lover-become-husband, Lord Admiral Seymour, and Princess Elizabeth, then a girl of fifteen.

There is no street to remind the passer-by of either Catherine Parr or the young Elizabeth; but, at the northern end of Old Church Street, are the QUEEN'S ELM TAVERN and QUEEN'S ELM SQUARE,[1] which present us with a pretty episode in the story of *Gloriana*. One day when she was walking this way, with Lord Burghley, a sudden storm forced them to the shelter of an elm-tree that grew on the site of the present tavern. Unlike so many graceful legends, this one is vouched for, in the parish records of 1586. (Queen Elizabeth was then fifty-three.) We are told that she made the gesture of asking that the tree should be called The Queen's Elm, in gratitude for her shelter. The name has been variously used during three and a half centuries : it was

[1] ELM PARK ROAD and GARDENS are nearby.

The Cross Tree in a survey of 1717 and, ten years later, Sir Hans Sloane wrote of *The High Elm*. But the name and the legend have survived, and later, when we called in on the Queen's Elm Tavern, we found that the proprietor's wife was very proud of the story.

Several noble families owned the manor after the death of Catherine Parr, but none of them bestowed a street-name on Chelsea until 1660, when the estate was bought by Charles, 1st Viscount Cheyne—hence CHEYNE WALK, ROW, PLACE, GARDENS and COURT.

We came to the eastern end of Cheyne Walk—to the point where Flood Street and ROYAL HOSPITAL ROAD meet and lead down to the Embankment. My collaborator suddenly reminded me of three characteristic splashes of London colour that remain merry, on the dullest day. At the foot of Oakley Street we had passed a red-painted pillar-box ; and then, by Flood Street, we saw a red omnibus, turning up from the Embankment, and two Chelsea Pensioners, in their scarlet coats. They were tough old warriors, one with a silver moustache, and they were making their way towards the Pier Hotel.

The Chelsea Pensioners had come from the ROYAL HOSPITAL and they were no doubt searching for their evening pint. Perhaps they had not read Evelyn's remark, made in January 1681, when the " hospital or infirmary for souldiers " was first planned. He said he would " needes have a library . . . since some souldiers might possibly be studious, when they were at leisure to recollect ". King Charles II laid the first stone of the beautiful Wren building in March, 1681. The only street-name depending on the Hospital, beside Royal Hospital Road, is ROYAL AVENUE, which forms a drive to the north gates, from the King's Road.

My collaborator produced an unpleasant surprise for me in regard to the history of Chelsea's Royal Hospital. I was brought up on the story that Nell Gwynne had inspired the King to this act of pity for his old and maimed " souldiers ", but, in the latest history [1] of the Hospital, the author assures us that after years of research into the relevant documents, he could not find even a hint that Nell Gwynne had any part in it.

Beyond the Hospital, and its cemetery, where there are many beautiful monuments to old warriors, are RANELAGH GARDENS, the site of the 18th-century pleasure gardens, which took their name from

[1] *The Royal Hospital, Chelsea*, Captain C. G. T. Dean, M.B.E. (Hutchinson), 1950.

the previous owner of the land, the 3rd Viscount and 1st Earl of Ranelagh (1640–1712).[1] During fifty years, the splendid Rotunda was a joy to Londoners. " Nobody goes anywhere else—everybody goes there," Horace Walpole wrote, in June, 1744. " There is a vast amphitheatre, finely gilt, painted, and illuminated ; into which everybody that loves eating, drinking, staring, or crowding is admitted for twelve pence." Boswell " felt a glow of delight " when he went there, and Dr. Johnson thought it " the finest thing " he had ever seen. But its splendour was short-lived,[2] and in 1804 the Rotunda was sold for firewood and the gardens came back into the possession of the Hospital. We found a nice note on the ways of the 18th-century " publicist " : when they wanted for patrons, the " proprietors of Ranelagh " would " send decoy-ducks among the ladies and gentle-men who were walking in the Mall, that is, persons attired in the height of fashion, who every now and then would exclaim in a very audible tone, ' What charming weather for Ranelagh. . . . ' "[3]

In the triangle between Royal Hospital Road and the Embankment there are three or four places and streets of interest. There is the PHYSIC GARDEN, given to the Apothecaries Company by Sir Hans Sloane, in 1722—DILKE STREET, named after the Victorian Radical, Sir Charles Wentworth Dilke, who was born in Chelsea in 1843 and who was its first Member of Parliament—SWAN WALK, recalling the old Swan Inn, whither Pepys went in 1666, " thinking to make merry at Chelsey ", only to find the tavern shut " for the plague "—and PARADISE WALK. This last name recalls *Paradise Row*, now absorbed into Royal Hospital Road. Many illustrious people lived here, among them John Robartes, Earl of Radnor, who entertained Charles II to supper in his house, soon after the Restoration. RADNOR WALK runs south from the King's Road, between Flood Street and Smith Street. And we must not forget Thomas Faulkner, whose early 19th-century books on west London have been so valuable to us. He kept a book shop and printing house in *Paradise Row*.

We left the riverside and walked northwards, along FLOOD STREET [4] —nothing to do with the river, but named in memory of "a charitable

---

[1] See chapter on Fulham, p. 92.

[2] The Ranelagh Club, founded at Barnes, on the south bank, in 1894, was named after Chelsea's Ranelagh.

[3] Quoted in *Highways and Byways in London*, Mrs. E. T. Cook (1902).

[4] There is also FLOOD WALK, opening from Flood Street, to the west.

63. SIR HANS SLOANE, BY S. SLAUGHTER

62. SIR THOMAS MORE, BY HOLBEIN

176]

64. CHEYNE WALK IN 1811, BY JOHN VARLEY

65. DANTE GABRIEL ROSSETTI IN 1847,
A SELF-PORTRAIT

65. THOMAS CARLYLE, BY
MILLAIS

Chelsea worthy ", Luke Thomas Flood (d. 1860), whose portrait and monument are in St. Luke's Church.

And so to the KING'S ROAD—the long thoroughfare that divides Chelsea in two. It was a mere footpath in the early 17th century, leading between pretty fields and spinneys. King Charles II realised its value and he made it into *The King's High Way from Chelsea to London* : doubly convenient for him as it led to both Hampton Court and Sandford Manor,[1] one of Nell Gwynne's houses. The important coach road remained the property of the Crown up to the time of George III ; and as late as 1731, privileged persons were given pass "tickets" of copper, engraved, "The King's Private Roads" on one side, and the crown and royal cipher on the other. King George III used the road on his journeys to Kew ; but in time, privilege had to give way, and in 1830 the King's Road became the road of the people.

We walked east towards Sloane Square, passing Radnor Walk, JUBILEE PLACE (named at the time of George III's Golden Jubilee), and WELLINGTON SQUARE, recalling the great Duke, whose body lay in state in the Hall of the Royal Hospital for seven days, before he was buried in St. Paul's Cathedral. This last place-name leads us to the story of a curious change made to a Chelsea street about a century ago. The Duke of Wellington's brother, the Hon. and Rev. Dr. Wellesley, was rector of Chelsea in the early 19th century, and the short street that leads from St. Luke's Church to the King's Road was named after him. But a violent murder brought shame on the dwellers in Wellesley Street, so the authorities changed the name to Upper Manor Street—now included in Chelsea Manor Street.

We passed Royal Avenue, then WALPOLE STREET. For more than twenty years, from 1723, Sir Robert Walpole lived in Chelsea, in a house which has since been absorbed into the Royal Hospital Infirmary. Reginald Blunt recalls, in his book on Chelsea, that from this house " England was ruled by the great Whig Minister. . . . Here Walpole received the news of George I's death, and rode post-haste to Richmond—killing two horses under him—to bring the news to the Prince of Wales."

A quarter of a mile more along the King's Road, and we came to SLOANE SQUARE, with SLOANE STREET and SLOANE GARDENS nearby. In this area, the street-names tell the closing chapter in the story of the manor of Chelsea. We recall that the manor house built by

[1] See chapter on Fulham, pp. 186, 187.

Henry VIII was bought by Charles Lord Cheyne in 1660 : in 1712, it was purchased by Sir Hans Sloane, who later increased his estate in Chelsea by purchasing Sir Thomas More's old house by the river. This celebrated physician and naturalist continued to live in Holborn where he has his most glorious memorial, in the collection of his books and manuscripts in the British Museum. He spent only the last twelve of his ninety-three years in Chelsea, where he bestowed his kindness on the people and his name on the land.

It is not easy, as one stands in Sloane Square today, with Messrs. Peter Jones's aquarium-like emporium on one side, and the new façade of The Royal Court Theatre (where George Bernard Shaw made his early successes) on the other, to realise that this orderly roundabout of traffic was once called *Great Bloody Square*, because of the bandits and burglars who skulked there.

Through the marriage of Sir Hans Sloane's daughter to the 2nd Baron Cadogan of Oakley, most of the Chelsea estates passed to the Cadogan family, who still own a big area of the Borough. From them come the names, CADOGAN PIER, SQUARE, STREET, GARDENS, LANE, GATE and PLACE, and OAKLEY STREET and GARDENS, after the estates they once owned in Buckinghamshire.

This north-east part of Chelsea is more grand than interesting. In the extreme north are the names associated with the Lowndes estates ; Lowndes Square and Street, which form the boundary with Westminster. South of these is an area once known as *Hans Town* (a compliment to Sir Hans Sloane) to which we travelled in a taxi-cab. We went north from Sloane Square by way of Sloane Street ; then west, along Cadogan Gate, and north again into PAVILION ROAD. In 1797, a Mr. Holland leased one hundred acres of the Cadogan estate—the area now bounded by Hans Place, Cadogan Square, Sloane Square and Cadogan Place. Mr. Holland mixed a talent for business with a taste for splendour. He built houses over some eighty acres, reserving for himself the remaining ground on which he built a mansion which he called *The Pavilion*. But after one hundred years the land became so valuable that the grand house was pulled down, to make room for more profitable building.

Many of the houses in this part of Chelsea are jocularly described as " Pont Street Dutch ", because of their architecture. PONT STREET itself takes its name from an old bridge across the Westbourne Stream,[1]

[1] See chapter on Paddington, p. 149.

that ran parallel with, and to the east of, what is now Sloane Street. The fact that a Mr. *Holland* built so many houses here has no link with the reproachful phrase, " Pont Street Dutch ", which refers to an architectural whim of a century later.

From Pavilion Road we drove to the western end of Pont Street and the bombed Scottish church of St. Columba. Then south-west, along Walton Street, which divides Chelsea from Kensington. The streets opening off Walton Street—Lennox Gardens and Lennox Gardens Mews, Ovington Street and Hasker Street—did not seem very interesting. With Draycott Avenue we reached the point where Walton Street becomes the FULHAM ROAD.[1] We travelled on until we came to the northern end of Old Church Street.

Our circuit was almost over. We drove south along Old Church Street (having paused at the Queen's Elm), and about half-way down we stepped out of the taxi-cab to see MULBERRY WALK and Carlyle Square. Mulberry Walk marks one of the many London areas which were planted with mulberry trees in the hope of creating a silk industry. " A sample of the satin lately made at Chelsey of English silkworms for the Princess of Wales was very rich and beautiful," wrote Ralph Thoresby, the Leeds merchant and historian, in 1720. But the silk industry failed, and only the name of Mulberry remains.

Carlyle Square,[2] on the opposite side of Old Church Street, stands on the site of what was " Mrs. Hutchins' barn ", which Thomas Faulkner mentions in describing a stag hunt in 1796 : " The animal swam across the river from Battersea and made for Lord Cremorne's grounds. Upon being driven from thence, he ran along the waterside as far as the church, and turning up Church Lane, at last took refuge in Mrs. Hutchins' barn, where he was taken alive."

We resumed our journey, crossed the King's Road, and walked back to Chelsea Old Church and the Embankment. A few yards from the foot of Old Church Street we came on a small blind street, PETYT PLACE, named after William Petyt, " a famous law-writer and antiquary " who built a Parish School here, in 1706.

[1] Originally the "highway leading to Fulham Ferry". See chapter on Fulham, p. 190.

[2] East of Carlyle Square is MANRESA ROAD, almost entirely occupied on the east side by the public library and the Chelsea Polytechnic. Manresa, in Spain, is the town where Loyola founded the Jesuit Order in 1522. Manresa House, the Jesuit College, is in Wandsworth.

So we returned to the Thames. "The evening mist clothes the riverside with poetry, as with a veil," wrote Whistler, who lived so long in Chelsea. He went on, in his written description of the scenes he painted, with phrases which helped us to make a pattern of the last names in our journey. We had enjoyed the mellow sights of old Chelsea, and the lordly spaces in the north of the Borough : we were left with the shabby west end—Whistler's " poor buildings "

THE OLD CHELSEA BUN HOUSE

which " lose themselves in the dim sky ", the " tall chimneys " that " become campanili ", and " the warehouses " that are " palaces in the night ".

We turned west along the Embankment, past Beaufort Street, to the generating stations, pumping stations and gasworks that profit so much from Whistler's " evening mist ". Here is CREMORNE ROAD, a sad, grubby street, which runs over what was once " Lord Cremorne's grounds ". Here also is TADEMA ROAD, as unlike Alma-Tadema in spirit as any road could be ; and, for the end of our journey, one of the most curious street-names in London—LOTS ROAD. My collaborator facetiously suggested that the name could not have a Biblical origin : " You cannot imagine Lot's wife bothering to turn and look back at the Imperial Gas Works." When we consulted *The Place-Names of Middlesex*, we were surprised to learn that the name is more than four hundred years old. It was *lez lotte* in 1544, when the name described the " lots " of ground which were " originally a part of the manor over which the parishioners held Lammas rights ". Thus emerge our simple present-day " allotments ".

Our journey in Chelsea was over, with one omission. On the day of our visit—June 23, 1951—Chelsea was celebrating its Festival Week, and its chief exhibit was a replica, in Sloane Square, of the *Old Chelsea Bun House*. Until it was demolished in 1839, the original Bun House was famous : there " the rank and fashion of the 18th century, from Royalty downwards, loved to dally and nibble ". On Good Fridays, as many as 50,000 people would scramble for their buns. But Chelsea has no legitimate memorial to the buns that are part of its fame. And here is the sorry end to our story. The Bun House *is* remembered, in a street-name which we found as we crossed the eastern boundary of the Borough, on our way home. An obscure little yard, big enough to hold three motor-cars—south-east of Sloane Square—bears the name BUNHOUSE PLACE. But it lies within the district of Westminster's Pimlico—not Chelsea.

CHAPTER SIXTEEN

Fulham

"Information was given that a bridge was making over the Thames, with flat-bottom boates, from Fulham to Putney, that the Lord Generall's forces might march over the river into Surry, and be ready to attend the King upon all removes."

Perfect Diurnall, November 15, 1642.

The map of Chelsea and Fulham shows a stream, dividing the boroughs to the south, before it widens and empties into the Thames. The place- and street-names printed hereabout might encourage the stranger to expect sand-banks, willows laced with sunlight, and limpid water. We read of CHELSEA CREEK, SANDS END, SANDS END LANE, and SANDFORD STREET, the last suggesting a ford across the stream—but these names are all disappointing. We entered Fulham by way of the King's Road, to see this stretch of the north bank, dedicated to gas works, timber yards and docks. From the edge of Stanley Bridge we looked through the chinks of a wooden fence : Chelsea Creek was there, but it was a stagnant ditch, with a few disheartened marguerite daisies and thistles, growing beside the green slime. As we stood on the slope which leads into the Borough—acres of pavements and houses and shops, stretching towards Hammersmith and the west—it was not easy to believe that John Florio, translator of Montaigne, lived in Fulham, and that somewhere in this conglomeration of bricks, Arthur Sullivan was inspired to write *The Lost Chord*.

SANDFORD MANOR HOUSE
From an engraving

The name SANDFORD was our first clue in Fulham. There is a story that King Charles II built Sandford Manor House for Nell Gwynne (Pl. 69), and—as we have noted in our chapter on Chelsea—

that he also made the King's Road, so that he could travel to see her. Most of Nell Gwynne's biographers cautiously dismiss the story as a "legend", but Charles James Fèret, in his *Fulham, Old and New* (1900), remarks that, at one time, "it was no unusual thing for persons to make a sort of pilgrimage to Sands End for the purpose of inspecting the supposed house of Mistress Nell".

We began our "sort of pilgrimage" at the western end of Stanley Bridge, where we found the NELL GWYNNE public house, closed for its afternoon siesta. The building is recent, but we hoped that the name might come from some old tavern, on the same site. My collaborator went into a timber merchant's office nearby and telephoned the legal department of the brewers who own the *Nell Gwynne*. Within a few minutes, the lawyer at the other end had the title deeds spread before him, and he said that there was no record of the pub, or the name, before 1864.

We walked to the end of the lane beside the *Nell Gwynne* and opened a gate into the gas works. Beyond, set in a high wall, we found another gate, with the name above it, *Sandford Manor House*. Here, menaced by all the attendant smells, was an enchanting 17th-century house,[1] set in a garden of lofty hollyhocks, delphiniums and old lilac trees. Some miscreant had covered the walls of the house with stucco, and a succession of occupants have played hanky-panky with the interior decoration, but the shape of the rooms remains unspoiled. And we saw the beautiful staircase up which, we like to believe, King Charles climbed many a time, for refreshment.

We walked on, along the King's Road, past Sandford Street,[2] and turned north into RUMBOLD ROAD. William Rumbold, born in 1613, was a devoted Cavalier. He served Charles I, was imprisoned in the Tower by Cromwell, and, at the Restoration, was "installed in the offices of Comptroller of the Great Wardrobe and Surveyor General of the Customs". He died in May, 1667, and was buried in Fulham Church.

---

[1] Joseph Addison was living at Sandford Manor House in 1708. One of his letters, written to the young Earl of Warwick (see chapter on Kensington, p. 164), describes the concert of birds which he "found in a neighbouring wood". He wrote, "I will promise to entertain you with much better music and more agreeable scenes than you ever met with at the opera."

[2] STAMFORD BRIDGE lies north of the King's Road. Stamford is a corruption of Sandford (see chapter on Hackney, pp. 52, 53).

From the northern end of Rumbold Road we turned west, along MOORE PARK ROAD, passing MAXWELL ROAD, and turning north again along WATERFORD ROAD, into Fulham Road. This area became Moore Park in the mid-19th century, when it was possessed by J. Lawrence Maxwell, of Moore Park, in County Waterford.

Then along Fulham Road, to WALHAM GREEN—a dusty parade of shops, flanking the Fulham Broadway underground station. We saw no hint of the beauty that inspired Bartholomew Rocque to write, in June, 1749,

> Hail, happy Isle, and happier Walham Green,
> Where all that's fair and beautiful are seen!

As late as 1813, this joyful description was deserved. Here, according to Faulkner,[1] was "the great fruit and kitchen garden . . . for the supply of the London market". The name, Walham Green, was *Wandangrene* in 1383, and, during five and a half centuries, it has been spelled in no less than eighty-six different ways. The 17th-century form was *Wandon Green*, and this version survives in WANDON ROAD, which we passed as we came over the bridge, from Chelsea.

From Walham Green we walked to NORTH END ROAD—*North-strete* in 1488, because it led to the hamlet of North End. It was a hot July afternoon and, for as far as we could see, the road was crowded with market stalls. We found a taxi-cab, after waiting at the corner of SHORROLDS ROAD and North End Road. (John Sherewold owned a messuage at Sands End in the time of Henry V.) We travelled slowly north, past the stalls and some dull street-names, before we came to LILLIE ROAD, which cuts almost across the Borough. This was named after Sir John Scott Lillie (1790–1868), a redoubtable old soldier who fought in every action in the Peninsular War, from Roliça to Toulouse. He also invented an early form of machine musketry, and a kind of pavement of wood and gravel He lived in Fulham until 1837, and Lillie Road was built in his time.

We travelled north for another quarter of a mile, then turned west, along STAR ROAD, named after a public house, the "Seven Stars", which still exists. We were seeking NORMAND ROAD, a name with a surprising origin. We possess a print of Normand House (Pl. 68) —a charming mid-17th-century mansion, which served many purposes, before it was demolished, after severe bomb damage, in 1949.

[1] *An Historical and Topographical Account of Fulham*, Thomas Faulkner (1813).

First it was a manor house, then a convalescent home for survivors of the 1665 plague. Early in the 19th century it was " appropriated for the reception of insane ladies ", then as a pauper school for boys. It ended, with many architectural additions and changes, as a Convent for Sisters employed in prison rescue work.

In the early 18th century, Normand House was called *Norman's End House*, and sometimes, *Nomans Land House*. The latter version leads us back to the origin of the name, in the 15th century, when, as from " time immemorial ", " little odds and ends of unused land . . . were called ' No Man's Land ', or ' Any Man's Land ', or ' Jack's Land ', as the case might be ". This part of the present Borough was referred to as " *Noemansland in ffulhamfeld* ", as early as 1492.

We left the taxi-cab and walked along some of the short streets nearby. To the south-east is MULGRAVE ROAD, recalling Mulgrave House and Little Mulgrave House at Hurlingham, named and owned by the 3rd Baron Mulgrave. But Little Mulgrave House had an older story : during the 1760's, when Sir Philip Stephens, Secretary to the Admiralty Board, lived there, Captain James Cook often visited him, when he was home from his voyages.

We drove north again, to GREYHOUND ROAD, which runs west towards the river. " The Greyhound " inn, from which the street takes its name, has been rebuilt, but there is a nice description of the early, merry tavern, in Fèret. " Its low-tiled roof was almost within touch of a pedestrian, while its tiny bar would hardly hold three people. . . . Perhaps its best-known host was Jem Burn, the celebrated pugilist." The smallness of the bar did not prevent Jem and his fighting friends from an occasional " carousal ", after one of which a " garden woman " was " found dead, face downwards, in the ditch ".

Except for this murky association, the names here are eminently respectable. In the extreme north of the Borough is a group of Breconshire names—TALGARTH, GLIDDON and TREVANION ROADS, scattered there by the ground landlord, Robert Gunter (GUNTERSTONE ROAD), and his wife Edith (EDITH ROAD and EDITH VILLAS). There are also Margravine Road and Gardens, explained in our next chapter, on Hammersmith.

There is another short street, in the north-west corner of Fulham, with a slight Hammersmith association. This is PLAYFAIR STREET, named after the first Lord Playfair (1819–1898), uncle of Sir Nigel Playfair.[1] Lord Playfair was a well-known chemist, tutor in science to Albert Edward, Prince of Wales, and Postmaster-General in 1873–4. At the end of Greyhound Road we turned south, along FULHAM PALACE ROAD. We might pause here, and try to explain the name FULHAM. We go back twelve and a half centuries, but delicately, for we are once more beset by a discord of scholars. The editors of *The Place-Names of Middlesex* (p. 101) state that the name was *Fulanham* in the year 705, and they " favour " the suggestion that *Fulla* was a personal name. Thus we have *Fulla's hamm*—the second element being a description of Fulla's land, " in a low-lying bend of the river ". Faulkner accepts a more lively explanation : he quotes Camden, the " father " of English antiquaries, who held that Fulham was derived from " the Saxon word, *Fullonham—Volucrum Domus*—the habitation of birds, or place of fowls ". Norden also agreed that Fulham was so named because it was the home of " land fowl, which usually haunt groves, and clusters of trees, whereof, in this place, it seemeth hath been plenty ".

Fulham Palace Road is a weary-looking stretch, so we paid off our taxi-cab and sought for a street that would bring us nearer the river. We chose CRABTREE LANE—the site of an early village beside the Thames, with the cottages built about a crabtree—a wild apple tree. Fulham soil must have been friendly to the wild apples, as there were once Crabtree Close, Alley, Square and Dock, and The Crabtree Tavern, all near the river. Now there are only Crabtree Lane and, on the river bank, the Crabtree Hotel.

We had come within a few yards of the river, so we turned, along Holyport Road (for which we can find no explanation), into STEVEN-AGE ROAD, which follows the curve of the Thames for more than half a mile—past Fulham football ground, and BISHOP'S PARK. Stevenage Road is a memorial to Colonel William Stevenage, " from Sandy End ", who died in Fulham in 1709.

None of the names of the streets leading from Stevenage Road seemed interesting until we came to BISHOP'S PARK ROAD and BISHOP'S AVENUE, to the north of FULHAM PALACE (Pl. 67). We walked past the lodge, into the 16th-century quadrangle—the oldest surviving part of the Palace, which has been a residence of the Bishops of London since 1141. It is curious that the long succession of prelates

[1] See chapter on Hammersmith, p. 206.

have left only two memorials in Fulham street-names.[1] FITZJAMES
AVENUE was named after Bishop Richard Fitzjames (d. 1521), who
built the existing great quadrangle of Fulham Palace, early in the
16th century ; and BISHOP KING'S ROAD, after Bishop John King
(1559–1621), " the most natural and persuasive orator of his
time ", who inspired James I to describe him as " The *King* of
Preachers ".

There was one bishop who certainly deserved an avenue, or a leafy
square, in Fulham—Edmund Grindal,[2] nominated to the bishopric in
1559. The gardens of Fulham Palace " first became remarkable " in
his time. There is a nice, if irrelevant, description in Fuller's *Worthies*
of the tamarisk tree, " first brought over by Bishop Grindal out of
Switzerland . . . and planted in his garden at Fulham . . . where
the soil being moist and fenny, well complied with the nature of this
plant, which since is removed, and thriveth well in many other
places."

We glanced into the gardens where Bishop Grindal planted the
first tamarisk, then we walked up Bishop's Avenue and turned south-
east, along the end of Fulham Palace Road. Then to the short lane
called CHURCHGATE, leading to the parish church of All Saints.
Although the fine Kentish ragstone tower of the church dates from
1440, the main body is solid late-Victorian. Many tombs from the
ancient church were carefully put into the new building, including a
beautiful monument to Katherine Hart—with her four children—who
died in 1605 ; another, of similar date, to Lady Margaret Legh, and
a splendid figure in Roman dress, of John Viscount Mordaunt, who
died in 1675. His relationship with Fulham will be explained when
we come to Peterborough Road, almost half a mile to the east. Our
chief surprise was in the churchyard of All Saints, where Theodore
Hook,[3] the hoaxer of Berners Street, was buried, in August, 1841,

---

[1] Bishop Aylmer (1521–94) is remembered in AYLMER ROAD, in Hammersmith, which formed a single parish with Fulham until 1834. He was a fearless
man : he dared to play bowls on the Sabbath, and he dared to have a tooth
drawn " to encourage Queen Elizabeth to submit to the like operation ". There
is also HENCHMAN STREET in Hammersmith, in memory of Dr. Humphrey
Henchman, who became Bishop of London in 1663. He was rewarded by
King Charles II for having helped him to escape after the battle of Worcester.

[2] The only street named after him is in Lambeth, south-east of Waterloo
Station.

[3] See chapter on St. Marylebone, pp. 136–7.

" in the presence of very few mourners, none of them known to rank or fame, including none of those who . . . had courted him in their lofty circles for his wit and fascination ".

From Churchgate we walked down Putney Bridge Approach, and turned east along RANELAGH GARDENS ; then north, by Edenhurst Avenue and Hurlingham Gardens, into RANELAGH AVENUE. The 6th Viscount Ranelagh,[1] who married the daughter of Sir Philip Stephens in 1804, succeeded to his estates in Fulham. Lord Ranelagh was " as Irish as they make them " ; he was also a suspicious old skinflint and an eccentric. He was known in Fulham as " Lord Soot ", because he once waylaid the chimney-sweep and his boy in the hall of his house and demanded to see what they carried in their sack. The chimney-sweep's boy was a match for the old peer—he emptied the sack of soot on the marble floor. Lord Ranelagh had a taste for litigation, and he died soon after the strain of horsewhipping a lawyer, in his chambers in the Temple, for having attacked his lordship's character in the Courts.

For HURLINGHAM—the name of the mansion and club nearby—we can find no satisfactory explanation. It is possible that the name arose from the field here " having been used for the ancient sport of hurling."[2] This is one more name that has been twisted into many shapes, since it was *Hurlyngholefeld*, in 1489.

We walked along HURLINGHAM ROAD, past the beautiful club grounds, to BROOMHOUSE LANE, which, like Crabtree Lane, marks the site of an early riverside village. *Broom Houses*, it was called, because yellow broom grew here in profusion.

We next came on one of the few aristocratic names in Fulham's story, in PETERBOROUGH ROAD, which runs from New King's Road to the river. The name recalls Peterborough House, a 17th-century mansion that was demolished in 1895. Peterborough House was originally the Villa Carey—owned by an heiress, Elizabeth Carey, who married John, Viscount Mordaunt of Avalon. (AVALON ROAD lies four hundred yards south-east of Walham Green.) During the Civil Wars he had been in France and Italy, but when he returned to England at the time of the Protectorate, he " determined to use his best energies to restore the exiled King ". He used his wife's home in Fulham to gather supporters about him, but his plot was discovered

[1] See chapter on Chelsea, p. 176.
[2] *Old and New London*, Thornbury and Walford, Vol. VI, p. 524.

67. FULHAM PALACE

68. NORMAND HOUSE

69. NELL GWYNNE, AFTER LELY

70. CHARLES MORDAUNT, 3RD EARL OF PETERBOROUGH, AFTER DAHL

71. VINCENT NOVELLO

and Cromwell sent him to the Tower. He was, however, acquitted, and when Cromwell died, a few months later, Lord Mordaunt again took up the King's cause. He went to Breda with Sir John Grenville, and he was with General Monk when King Charles II was rowed ashore at Dover, in May, 1660.

Lord Mordaunt then returned to his salubrious estate in Fulham, to devote himself to gardening, versifying, and one episode of impropriety. All these occupations were faithfully recorded : by Evelyn, who said that his lordship's " industry and knowledge in all hortulan elegancies requires honourable mention " ; by Pepys, who wrote of his verses, " But Lord : they are sorry things ; only a Lord made them " ; and by Andrew Marvell, who wrote of Lord Mordaunt's impeachment for ejecting one Tayleur from his apartments in Windsor Castle (of which Lord Mordaunt was Constable), and for trying to seduce Tayleur's daughter :

> Now Mordaunt may within his castle tower
> Imprison parents and the child deflower,
> Each does the other blame, and all distrust,
> But Mordaunt, *new obliged*, would sure be just.

Lord Mordaunt died at the age of forty-eight, and his eldest son, Charles, assumed his father's dare-devil role with even more remarkable vigour. (He became the 3rd Earl of Peterborough on the death of his uncle, and thus gave the new name to Peterborough House.) Charles Lord Mordaunt (Pl. 70) began with the amiable marks of both Eton and Oxford, but seven months after he matriculated at Christ Church, in 1674, he was serving with the English Mediterranean Fleet against the Barbary corsairs. In 1680 he sailed for Africa and " greatly distinguished himself at Tangier, then besieged by the Moors ". He was only twenty-two, and, momentarily satiated with war, he returned and settled on his estate in Fulham. He denied his father's love of the Stuarts and, after the accession of James II, in 1685, he obtained leave to go to Holland, where, " on his arrival at the Hague, he was one of the first of the English nobility who offered his service to the Prince of Orange ". He came with him to England, in 1688, and was made a Lord of the Bedchamber. In 1692 he fought in Flanders, and he was Commander-in-Chief of the British Forces during the War of the Spanish Succession. He landed a small force of 5,000 men in Spain, in the summer of 1705, and went through incredible adventures, which brought Barcelona and Valencia at his feet.

" The last of the knights-errant ", as Macaulay called him, died at Peterborough House in 1735.

The northern end of Peterborough Road faces a triangle of trees and lawn called PARSON'S GREEN, probably because of the parsonage that was here, until 1882. There are still some fine Georgian houses facing on to the Green, but there must have been other great houses here as far back as Tudor times. Sir Thomas Bodley (1545-1613) lived nearby, but there is no Bodley Street in Fulham, in memory of the great benefactor to Oxford. Sir Francis Child (1642-1713), Lord Mayor of London in 1698, and founder of Child's Bank, had a house here ; also Samuel Richardson, the father of the modern novel, and Mrs. Fitzherbert, morganatic wife of George, Prince of Wales.

North of Parson's Green are BEACONSFIELD WALK, named after " Dizzy ", although he had no link with Fulham ; and NOVELLO STREET, a memorial to Vincent Novello (Pl. 71) (1781-1861), the composer, friend of Leigh Hunt, and founder of the great firm of music publishers.

There was another street, PURSER'S CROSS, running between Beaconsfield Walk and Fulham Road, that made us curious. Faulkner gave us no help, but Fèret claims that it is a corruption of *Purser's Croft*, or *Field*, and he quotes an order of 1569—" Everyone having trees overhanging the highway from Wendon Green [Walham Green] to Pursere Croft shall lop the same before St. John or forfeit 12d. per perch."

After a rest in the " Duke's Head ", we caught a bus along New King's Road, and on the way we opened the map once more, wondering how many interesting street-names we had missed. We must end with one of these, which caught our eye as we travelled east—a quarter of a mile or so from Parson's Green. Here lies EEL BROOK COMMON, where some children were squeezing the last minutes of July's pleasure from the swings and roundabouts. It was simple to imagine a brook running here, parallel with Chelsea Creek, towards the river, with boys catching eels in its muddy depths—before borough councils gave them swings and roundabouts to play with. But we were wrong.

The map in Faulkner, dated 1813, shows the common as *Hell Brook*. Thus the name has changed, in less than a century and a half.

We thought that *Hell Brook* might have been an early haunt of robbers and bawds—but we were wrong again. We turned then to *The Place-Names of Middlesex*, and found that the name comes from neither eels nor hell, but from the nature of the land. There is a slight rise here, discernible even as one travels in a bus, and this rise caused the locals to name it *Hillebrook*, as far back as the 15th century.

CHAPTER SEVENTEEN

Hammersmith

" The Archbishop and myselfe went to Hammersmith to visit Sir Samuel Morland, who was entirely blind : a very mortifying sight. . . . He had newly buried £200 worth of music-books six feet under ground, being, as he said, love-songs and vanity."

EVELYN'S *Diary*, October 25, 1695.

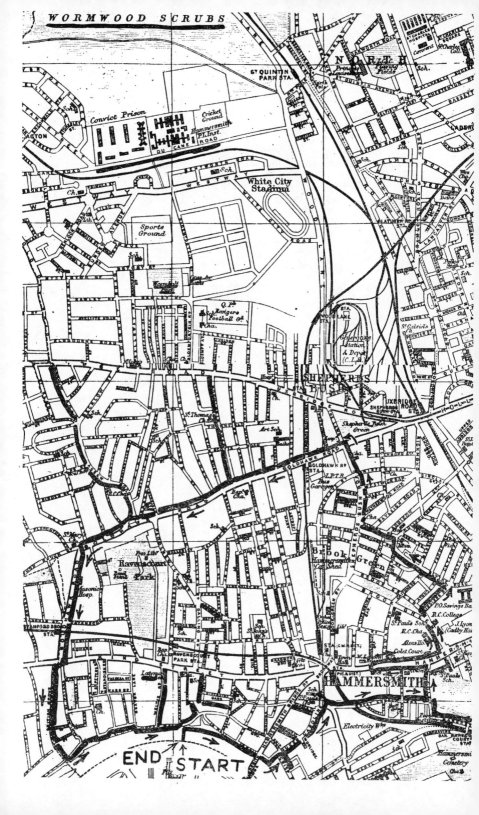

The weather was warm and gentle when we set out to explore HAMMERSMITH, so we went by river bus, carrying Faulkner's book [1] on the Borough, and some notes, to help us on our way. We had read that THAMES derives from the British *Tam-esc*, a stream, or course of waters—as in the Tame, in Staffordshire, and the Teme, in Hertfordshire. We had been less fortunate when we tried the lucky dip of scholarship for the origin of Hammersmith. Faulkner claimed that it came from *Ham*, the Anglo-Saxon word for Home, and he quoted the survival of the word in Scotland :

> I winna stay at *hame*, Lord Thomas,
> And sew my silver seam ;
> But I'll gae to the rank Highlands,
> Tho' your lands lay far frae *hame*.

The *Encyclopædia Britannica* states, " The name appears in the early forms of Hermodewode and Hamersmith ; the derivation is probably from the Anglo-Saxon, signifying the place with a haven (*hythe*)." The editors of *The Place-Names of Middlesex* claim that the name " is probably a compound of Old English *hamor*, ' hammer ' and *smyððe*, ' smithy ' ".

A river seems to wash away its own history, and, as we steamed in sight of Hammersmith Bridge, it was not easy to imagine weary Britons of two thousand years ago, coming to the water's edge for refreshment, after toiling all day on the Roman road that ran from Tyburn to Brentford and Staines [2]—within a thousand yards of the river bank. It was not easy to think of Danish marauders encamped here, in the winter of 879, on the island that is now Chiswick Eyot.

We landed at Hammersmith Pier, which leads, with a show of municipal red geraniums and lawns, to the steps and columns of the new Town Hall. Then east, along the Lower Mall, a river footpath

[1] *The History and Antiquities of the Parish of Hammersmith*, by Thomas Faulkner, 1839.

[2] When GOLDHAWK ROAD was made in 1834, out of *Gould Hawk Lane*, the remains of the great Roman causeway were found, on which the Britons had been made to work " so atrociously hard that they prayed for death as they toiled ".

" The family of Goldhawk(e) occurs frequently in 15th century Court Rolls, and we find mention of one *Goldhauek* in Chiswick near by as early as 1222."— *The Place-Names of Middlesex*, p. 110.

that reveals the separate identity of Hammersmith : pleasure boats, a rowing club, and, near the Bridge, a line of pretty little houses looking over the water to the trees and pasture of the south. After passing beneath the Bridge, we came on a shabby dock, where we turned inland, along Queen Caroline Street.

The frontispiece to Faulkner's book is an engaging print of Sir Nicholas Crispe (Pl. 72), the most picturesque benefactor in the history of the Borough. We had gone only a few yards along Queen Caroline Street when we found CRISP ROAD, on the right.

Sir Nicholas Crispe, 1598–1665, had been " bred in a thorough knowledge of business, though heir to a great estate ". He " settled the trade of Gold from Guinea, and there built the Castle of Cormantine " ; and he served Charles I, by replenishing the King's empty purse, and raising a regiment of horse, which he led against Cromwell. His devotion was such that he would wander by the river's edge, with a basket of flounders on his head, or ride between Oxford and London, dressed as a butter-woman, to spy for the King. He survived the Commonwealth and went to Breda to wait on Charles II, who embraced him as his " father's old friend " ; and he returned to rest, and to die in Hammersmith, at the age of sixty-seven.

Sir Nicholas had erected a fine bronze bust of King Charles I, on a monument of black and white marble, in what is now St. Paul's parish church. In death, as in life, his heart was with the martyred King. His body was buried at St. Mildred's Church in Bread Street, but his heart was placed in an urn below the royal bust, and refreshed with a glass of wine once each year, until, after more than a century, its became decayed. It was then added to the remains in St. Mildred's, but, in 1898, the coffin was removed to Hammersmith and buried in St. Paul's churchyard.

The name-plate at the end of QUEEN CAROLINE STREET reminded us that King George IV's unhappy consort moved to Brandenburgh House, Hammersmith, in June, 1820, before her trial. When, in November, the House of Lords rejected the bill to dissolve her marriage, the tradesmen of Hammersmith were so delighted that they illuminated their buildings and made merry, with bonfires, before her house. Nine days later, when she took the sacrament in Hammersmith Church, her way to the door was " laid with matting " and the local officials attended her, carrying white wands.

But more history than this fell into the rubble when the mansion was destroyed in 1821. The original house (it was not given the name of Brandenburgh until the late 18th century) was built by Sir Nicholas Crispe, early in the reign of Charles I. General Fairfax used it as his headquarters during the Civil War, when Cromwell's men were stationed at Hammersmith. Sir Nicholas later returned and lived there until he died.

The house then passed among many owners, until Lord Melcombe bought it in the reign of George III. He had begun life as George Bubb, the son of a Dorset apothecary, and his story provides an argument against the sins of ambition and pride. George Bubb changed his name to Dodington and succumbed to his "reigning passion", which was "to be well at Court". He achieved office, and a peerage ; and when he died in 1762, his heir enumerated his benefactor's virtues at the foot of a lofty column, east of Brandenburgh House, claiming that his lordship was "admired and beloved by all that knew him". For a few years the land about the column was known as *Monument Field*, and the noble memorial survived there until 1788, when it was taken to Lord Aylesbury's park in Wiltshire, and re-erected to commemorate George III's recovery from madness. So George Bubb's monument was scattered and the name of *Monument Field* was rubbed off the map.

The only tribute to Lord Melcombe that we found is in the dedication of one of James Thomson's *Seasons* : "O Dodington ! attend my rural song. . . ." Thomson's association with the Borough ended sadly. Eight years after his verses, "Rule, Britannia", were first sung on a London stage, he became heated one day while walking through Hammersmith. He took a river boat, and soon died—most unsuitably for the author of our ringing anthem of the sea—from a chill caught on the Thames.

Queen Caroline Street and Crisp Road are at the south-east corner of the Borough, near where Brandenburgh House once stood, " by the waterside". Just across the boundary, in Fulham, are MAR-GRAVINE ROAD and GARDENS, named after the wife of the next owner of Brandenburgh House—the Margrave of Brandenburgh-Anspach and Bayreuth, who bought the property in the early 1790's. He shared the Hammersmith mansion with Lady Craven, whom he married when Lord Craven died. This remarkable lady was served by thirty servants, she rode her choice from a stud of sixty horses, and enlivened the house with every extravagance of entertainment. Before we left Queen Caroline Street, we observed WORLIDGE STREET, leading into Hammersmith Bridge Road. To the north-east, in Hammersmith Road, Messrs. Lee and Kennedy had their famous mid-18th-century nurseries, to which they imported the first China rose ; also trees from America and the Cape. The gardens surrounded a thatched house, for storing and selling burgundy made from grapes grown on the spot. But before this, the house had been the home of Thomas Worlidge (1700–66), the famous engraver. Perhaps the best known of his prints is of Rembrandt's *The Hundred Guilders*.

We then came to SUSSEX PLACE, named after George III's sixth son. In May, 1825, he laid the foundation stone of a magnificent " Bridge of Suspension "[1] which crossed the Thames at Hammersmith. But his nicest association with the Borough is through his Smoking Box that stood beside the river. This surprisingly liberal gentleman, who favoured the abolition of slavery and the emancipation of Catholics, Dissenters and Jews, used to sit here " in the summer season ", with his pipe. Faulkner wrote ". . . the back of this cottage is pleasantly shaded by fresh luxuriant foliage, and here His Royal Highness retires to smoke the social tube, and to enjoy the prospect of the winding stream. The scene, to a contemplative mind, must be delightful."

Sussex Place forms the lower part of the triangle in which stands the parish church of St. Paul, which was consecrated as a Chapel of Ease by Archbishop Laud in 1631. In 1834, it became the parish church of Hammersmith, and in 1882 it was rebuilt. The memorials which have survived gave us many keys to names of streets in other parts of the Borough.

On the north-east side of the churchyard is the Weltje tomb, in which rest the members of a remarkable family. On top, we read the name of Christopher Weltje, who was appointed Clerk of the Duke of York's Kitchen in 1788. On one side there are touching lines in memory of his daughter Elizabeth, " cut off at the early age of 15 " by the smallpox.

> In beauty's bloom, adorned with every grace,
> Here a meek virgin consecrates the place. . . .

[1] The bridge was removed in 1887 and the existing suspension bridge was built in its place.

On another side of the tomb is the name of Louis Weltje (Pl. 73), favourite of the Prince Regent, who was chief cook and purveyor in the Pavilion at Brighton. He was a man of such "taste and discernment" that he was sent to sales in Paris, where he bought many of the splendid pieces of French furniture now in the Royal collections, at Windsor and in Buckingham Palace.

The Weltjes became great figures in Hammersmith, after they gave up serving the two princes : Louis was particularly well-liked for his rich hospitality, which was a miniature copy of the luxury of his royal master. He also has a road named in his honour—WELTJE ROAD, half a mile along the river bank from Hammersmith Bridge, and leading into King Street.

Other good citizens, associated with St. Paul's and remembered in street-names, are the Reverend T. S. Atwood, and Anthony Askew, M.D. ATWOOD ROAD is lost in a network of streets between Hammersmith Broadway and Goldhawk Road. Thomas Stephen Atwood, who was "perpetual Curate" of the church for thirty-eight years, gave Queen Caroline the sacrament after her trial, in 1820.

ASKEW ROAD is an important main thoroughfare running north and south between Uxbridge Road and Goldhawk Road. Anthony Askew's wife was buried in the church, beneath "an elegant marble tablet, surmounted with an urn and foliage ". Askew, born in 1722, was a classical scholar, a physician at St. Bartholomew's and Christ's Hospitals, and registrar of the College of Physicians. Faulkner was a forthright judge of his fellow-men, and he said of Askew : "This gentleman was very conspicuous among the *literati* of the last generation, and was possessed of considerable classical erudition, but he is better known in the present day as a victim to the disorder lately arranged in the catalogue of human woes, under the name of *Bibliomania*."

We sat in the church for a little time, and bemoaned the construction of long, modern thoroughfares which have done away with many charming old street-names. Similarly, little streets and lanes are no longer made, which might immortalise great men, or perpetuate pleasant episodes in history. There should be a street in Hammersmith to remind us of Sir Samuel Morland (1625–95), an attractive old eccentric who lies buried in the church. He built a pump and well in front of his house, near the river bank, for the passers-by, and hoped that none who came after him would "adventure to incur

God's displeasure by denying a cup of cold water, provided at another's cost and not their own, to either neighbour, stranger, passenger, or poor thirsty beggar ". But the borough fathers eventually tempted God's displeasure by removing the pump. Sir Samuel invented many things, from water engines and pumps, to the speaking-trumpet. This latter novelty he announced in his " Description of the Tubasten-torophonica, an instrument of excellent use, as well by sea as by land ". He became blind and, in this state, he made a last protest against vanities, by burying £200 worth of music, mostly love-songs, in his garden. His descendant, George Morland the painter (1763–1804), was married in Hammersmith church, so there is added reason why the name should appear at the end of one of the streets.

It would be some pleasure also to find a Billington Place, in memory of Mrs. Billington, a late 18th-century singer who lived in Hammersmith. Her talents made her a star at Covent Garden and brought her fame in Italy. Her hearing was so acute that she could hear " not only the insects in the hedges, but also the smallest flies in a room. . . ."

When we left the church, the shadow of the oak tree in the church-yard had lengthened and we were still only on the fringe of the Borough. So we moved on, across Queen Caroline Street again, across the end of Fulham Palace Road and into GREAT CHURCH LANE, which leads to COLET GARDENS. Here, with recreation grounds covering some ten acres, is St. Paul's School. But the names of both John Colet, and the school he founded, in 1509, belong to the City. It was not until 1883 that the school was moved to Hammersmith from its ancient site, beside St. Paul's Cathedral.

We left Colet Gardens and walked west along Hammersmith Road, to find the LATYMER FOUNDATION SCHOOL, opposite the West London Hospital. Unlike St. Paul's, this school, which was founded in the early 17th century—in 1625—truly belongs to Hammersmith.

It is incredible, in reading books about early London, to note how many of the 17th and 18th century business men were inspired by a sense of civic consciousness ; how they deemed it their duty to pour back some of their fortune, among the destitute. In Faulkner, we read a list of forty-two citizens who, between 1594 and 1833, left sums of money to help the poor of Hammersmith. The most imaginative of these was Edward Latymer, described as a " citizen and feltmonger ". He was born " at Ipswich, in the reign of Mary ", and when he moved to London, he prospered. There is no proof that he ever lived in Hammersmith, but, two years before he died, he made a will in which he instructed his executors as follows :

> To elect and choose eight boys, inhabitants of Hammersmith, within the age of twelve, and above the age of seven years, and to provide for every boy a doublet, and a pair of breeches of frieze or leather, one shirt, one pair of stockings, and a pair of shoes, to be made and delivered on the first of November ; and also to provide yearly, against Ascension-day, a doublet and pair of breeches of coarse canvas, lined, and to deliver them to the boys, and also a shirt, and a pair of stockings, and a pair of shoes, and that on the left sleeve of every poor boy's doublet, a cross of red cloth should be fastened and worn ; and that the feoffees should cause the boys to be put to some petty school, to learn to read English, till they attain the age of thirteen, and to instruct them in some part of God's true religion. . .

The Latymer Foundation School has survived all the educational changes of three and a quarter centuries, and it is still a lively influence in training the young of Hammersmith. In 1894, LATYMER UPPER SCHOOL was opened, in King Street, by Weltje Road ; so the name of this imaginative old 17th-century benefactor is doubly certain of being remembered.

We avoided Hammersmith Broadway, where five roads pour their traffic into the central bedlam, and, crossing Hammersmith Road, we made our way back, into BROOK GREEN—through which a tributary once flowed into the Thames. We had walked only a few yards when we came to GIRDLERS ROAD, on the right. The Girdlers Company, founded by Henry VI in 1449, were willed considerable properties in this district : the street no doubt was named because of this. We passed then into BLYTHE ROAD, which twists and turns, for some distance, towards Shepherd's Bush. We tried to find a famous Blythe, in the reference books, who might have been associated with Hammersmith, but we discovered, surprisingly, that the name is a corruption of *Blind*, and that in John Rocque's survey of 1741-5, the Blythe Road of today is a lane ending " blindly " in the fields.[1]

As we walked towards Shepherd's Bush Road, we passed within a stone's throw of IRVING ROAD, named after the great Victorian actor who lived in Brook Green. (" He acted wonderfully " and he was "very gentlemanlike " wrote the Queen, after seeing him in *The Bells*.) But the actor most closely associated with Hammersmith was Sir

[1] *The Place-Names of Middlesex*, p. 110.

Nigel Playfair (1874–1934),[1] whose production of *The Beggar's Opera* ran at the Lyric Theatre for 1,467 performances. NIGEL PLAYFAIR AVENUE, and ROAD, both close to the new Town Hall, are the Borough's tribute to this actor manager who created a world record with his revival.

From the northern end of Blythe Road we walked towards Shepherd's Bush Green ; and on the left we passed CROMWELL GROVE, which we immediately associated with Oliver Cromwell. We now suspect, but cannot prove, that the street was named after James Cromwell, a brewer and also, apparently, a keeper of hogs,[2] who died in 1816. Warwick Draper records in his study of Hammersmith that James Cromwell " commenced in a small way by taking out the beer himself on a barrow, and left a fortune of £40,000, dying, at the age of 75, from a seizure which attacked him on horseback near Tottenham Court Road ".

James Cromwell must have been a rare old character. " His hog-feeders and other men sat at the table with him in their working dress ; if a friend happened to dine with him, his men were made company for them, and he did not deviate from his daily plan, although he had company, of helping his men first."

By coincidence, Cromwell Grove happens to be near the site of Miles Syndercombe's plot against Oliver Cromwell, in 1657. He had hired a house near Shepherd's Bush Green from which to carry out his plan. Having failed with his " guns made on purpose, to carry ten or twelve bullets at a time ", Syndercombe was sent to the Tower, where he cheated his judges by dying in his sleep. His dead body was placed on a hurdle and dragged through the streets to Tower Hill, where it was publicly executed—as Cromwell's own body was to suffer when it was dragged from Holborn to Tyburn, four years later.

Shepherd's Bush Green, with its merry-go-round of vehicles, was described in 1839 as a " pleasant village ". But its history has been exciting, from the day that Miles Syndercombe arrived there, to the day in 1845, when the villagers were surprised as they looked up and saw " Mr. and Mrs. Green " descending upon them, in a balloon that had gone astray from Vauxhall Gardens.

[1] See chapter on Fulham, pp. 189–90.

[2] HAMPSHIRE HOG LANE, and the HAMPSHIRE HOG public house in King Street, may be further memorials to James Cromwell.

The northern stretches of the Borough did not seem to offer much adventure, so we skimped our plans and walked towards the west, along Goldhawk Road. But there are some names in the north which should be noted ; among them, WORMWOOD SCRUBS, probably from the old-English *wyrma holt*, a snake-infested holt or wood [1]—a pitiably suitable name for the prison that stands there. WORMHOLT PARK has the same origin. There is also DU CANE ROAD, in front of the prison, and obviously named after Sir Edward Frederick Du Cane (1830–1903), who " held several high appointments in connection with convict discipline ".

The evening was upon us, so we kept to the main road, noting GODOLPHIN ROAD on the way, about half a mile west of Shepherd's Bush Green. Sir William Godolphin (1634–96), the "learned gentleman" with whom Evelyn went to see "the rhinoceros, or unicorn, being the first . . . ever brought to England", gave his ringing Cornish name to both the road, and to Godolphin School in Hammersmith.

Our curiosity for the day was almost spent, so we made our way back to the river bank, by British Grove, which brought us to the water's edge, opposite Chiswick Eyot. Then along the Upper Mall, past Weltje Road, and so back to Hammersmith Pier. Our map gave us one, last promising street-name with which to end our journey. But the map was a trifle old, and we were disappointed. The name was *Marryat Street*—but the town-planners had been at work, to add new confusion to the cartographers, and *Marryat Street* had disappeared. So we lessened our grief by making our way to King Street and drinking beer with the host of the " Hampshire Hog ", who showed proper respect for the history of his pub, and what he described as " this ancient stretch of the River ".

There are great rebuilding schemes for this part of Hammersmith, which will engulf still more of the little old streets and their names. So we had to imagine *Marryat Street*—named after Captain Marryat, R.N. (Pl. 74), who retired to Hammersmith, after he had witnessed some fifty engagements, to write his novels—*Mr. Midshipman Easy*, *Masterman Ready*, and *The Children of the New Forest*. His street will lie buried beneath a new arterial road, or a concrete colossus of flats. One can only hope that the boys of the Latymer Schools will besiege the mayor in his parlour and threaten to scalp him if he does not build a street of some sort, to inherit Captain Marryat's name.

[1] *The Place-Names of Middlesex*, p. 110.

When we looked over our books and notes, in the evening, we came on a fact that seems to tie all the threads of the story of Hammersmith together. When Captain Marryat retired from the Navy, he became an equerry to the Duke of Sussex : so we imagine him, on a summer evening now and then, joining the Duke in his Smoking Box beside the river. It cannot be thought that he presumed to smoke a " social tube " on these occasions, but the etiquette required would not prevent him from sharing " the prospect of the winding stream ", and a glimpse of the trees and fields on the Surrey side.

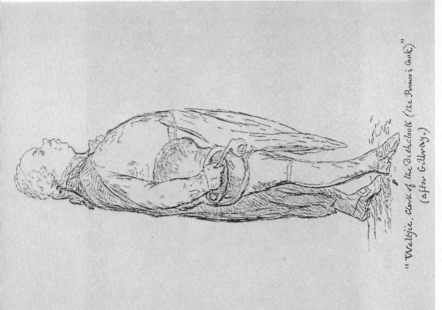

"Weltje, Clerk of the Batholouth (the Prince's Cook)"
(after Gillray.)

73.   LOUIS WELTJE, AFTER GILLRAY

72.   SIR NICHOLAS CRISPE

74. CAPTAIN MARRYAT, BY JOHN SIMPSON

75. THE THAMES AT HAMMERSMITH

BOOKS OF REFERENCE
AND
INDEX

BOOKS OF REFERENCE

The authors wish to acknowledge their debt to the following authorities.

The Place-Names of Middlesex, by J. E. B. Gower, Allen Mawer and F. M. Stenton, Cambridge University Press (1942).

A Survey of London, by John Stow. Edited by Charles Lethbridge Kingsford, M.A., Oxford (1908). Text of 1603.

The Face of London, by Harold Clunn, Simpkin (1932).

The History of the Squares of London, by E. Beresford Chancellor (1907).

A Dictionary of London, by Henry A. Harben, Herbert Jenkins (1918).

London's Markets, by W. J. Passingham, Sampson Low (1935).

A Handbook for London, by Peter Cunningham, John Murray (1849).

Old and New London, by Thornbury and Walford (1883-5).

The Town, by Leigh Hunt (1848).

Highways and Byways in London, by Mrs. E. T. Cook (1902).

The History and Antiquities of Stoke Newington, by William Robinson (1820).

Glimpses of Ancient Hackney, by F. R. C. S. (1893).

History and Antiquities of Shoreditch, by Henry Ellis (1798).

Old Bethnal Green, by George F. Vale (1934).

History of East London, by Sir Hubert Llewellyn Smith, Macmillan (1939).

The History and Traditions of St. Pancras, by Thomas Coull (1861).

Marylebone and St. Pancras, by George Clinch (1890).

Sweet Hampstead and its Associations, by Mrs. Caroline A. White (1900).

Paddington, Past and Present, by William Robins (1853).

History and Antiquities of Kensington, by Thomas Faulkner (1820).

An Illustrated Historical Handbook to the Parish of Chelsea, by Reginald Blunt (1900).

Fulham, Old and New, by Charles James Fèret (1900).

An Historical and Topographical Account of Fulham, by Thomas Faulkner (1813).

The History and Antiquities of the Parish of Hammersmith, by Thomas Faulkner (1839).

INDEX

Abbey Road, 127–8
Abbots Place, 127
Abernethy, Dr., 11
Abingdon, Abbot of, 161 ; Villas and Road, 161
Abney, Sir Thomas, 44 ; Park Cemetery, 44
Adam, Robert, 122, 139
Addison, Joseph, 41, 164, footnote 187 ; Road, 41, 164 ; Crescent, 164
Adshead, Harold, 23
Albemarle, Earl of, 36
Albert, Prince (Prince Consort), 168
Alie Street, footnote 83
All Saints Church (Fulham), 191
Alma-Tadema, Sir Lawrence, 171
Alperton Street, 154
Amazon Street, 90
Amherst of Hackney, Barons, 53 ; Captain John, 53
Amhurst Road, Park and Terrace, 53
Amoy Place, 99
André, Major John, 54 ; Street, 53
Angel, The, 8
Anne, Queen, 33, 167–8
Apothecaries Company, 176
Approach Road, 72
Arnold, Sir Arthur, 75 ; Circus, 75
Arnold, Benedict, 54
Artillery Ground, The, 18
Askew, Anthony, 203 ; Road, 203
Athol Street, 102
Atwood, Rev. T. S., 203 ; Road, 203
Aubert, Colonel, 5 ; Park, 5
Aubrey Walk and Road, 160
Australian Avenue, 110
Avalon Road, 192
Aylmer, Bishop, footnote 191 ; Road, footnote 191

Bagford, John, 5 ; Street, 5
Baillie, Joanna, 125
Baker, Sir Edward, 136
Baker, William, 136 ; Street, 135–6
Balch, John, 86
Balfe, Michael William, 6 ; Street, 6
Ball, John, 6
Balls Pond Road, 6
Balmes Road, 58 ; *House*, 58, 67
Barbauld, Anna Letitia, 46–7, 125 ; Road, 46
Barebone, Dr. Nicholas, 34
Barebones, Praise-God, footnote 34
Barfett Street, 154
Barham, Richard, 28
Barn Street, 44
Barnard's Inn, 32
Barnsbury Street, xvi, 4
Baroness Road, 74
Baron's Court, 161
Barque Street, 101
Barrett, Elizabeth, 138
Barrie, Sir James, 41, 148 ; Street, 148
Bartholomew Fair, xii
Barton, Bernard, 9
Bath Street, 17
Batten, Lady, 76
Battle Bridge, 109
Battle Bridge Road, 109
Bayham Abbey, 114 ; Street and Place, 114
Bayswater, 147 ; Road, 147–8
Beaconsfield, Benjamin Disraeli, Earl of, 100 ; Walk, 194
Beaufort, 1st Duke of, 171–2, Street, 172
Bedford, Dukes of, 35–6, 111 ; *House*, 36
Beethoven Street, 155
Belinus Magnus, King, xiii

COMMON READER EDITIONS

As booksellers since 1986, we have been stocking the pages of our monthly catalogue, A COMMON READER, with "Books for Readers with Imagination." Now as publishers, the same motto guides our work. Simply put, the titles we issue as COMMON READER EDITIONS are volumes of uncommon merit which we have enjoyed, and which we think other imaginative readers will enjoy as well. While our selections are as personal as the act of reading itself, what's common to our enterprise is the sense of shared experience a good book brings to solitary readers. We invite you to sample the wide range of COMMON READER EDITIONS, and welcome your comments.

www.commonreader.com

A COMMON READER'S LONDON LIBRARY

Without the City Wall is the third volume in A COMMON READER'S LONDON LIBRARY. It is our hope that the books we choose for this series will, like this one, rank among the best ever written about London, and be of enduring interest to all those who are fascinated by the city and its storied history. The editors invite suggestions from readers for other out-of-print titles to be considered for inclusion in the LIBRARY.

ALSO IN A COMMON READER'S LONDON LIBRARY:

Nairn's London

England's Hour